SOCIAL PEDAGOGY IN EDUCATION

This book, written by educators with a wealth of expertise across all age phases, provides an accessible, informative and thought-provoking exploration of how practitioners might place the human-centred values of social pedagogy at the heart of their own education and care practice to enrich and transform the learning experience.

A clear overview of why and how the underpinning principles of social pedagogy can benefit both the learner and the educator is provided, and answers to current educational challenges are offered. Chapters in the book cover topics including:

- supporting children with special educational needs and disabilities
- working with marginalised families and communities
- tackling bias in higher education
- alternative approaches to education leadership
- establishing relationships within an online environment

This book concludes by considering the value of social pedagogical approaches beyond the realm of education, in wider work with children and families. It discusses how this approach can build communities, offer hope and provide opportunities for all. Supplying a fresh and highly relevant perspective to help face the challenges in education today, this book will be key reading for policymakers, teachers and students in the field of education studies and beyond.

Carla Solvason, **Nicola Stobbs** and **Geoffrey Elliott** are all based at the University of Worcester. They have always had an interest in more human-centred approaches to education, illustrated by Carla and Geoffrey publishing *Ethics in Education* in 2023. Just prior to this, Nicola had embedded a social pedagogical approach within the BA Early Childhood in Society course that she led, and they established a Social Pedagogy Research Group at the university. This group has grown from strength to strength, and their seminal publication, *A human approach to restructuring the education system: why schools in England need social pedagogy*, published in the *International Journal of Social Pedagogy*, has been read by thousands of people keen to see educational change.

The Routledge Education Studies Series

Series Editor: Stephen Ward, Bath Spa University, UK

The Routledge Education Studies Series aims to support advanced level study on Education Studies and related degrees by offering in-depth introductions from which students can begin to extend their research and writing in years 2 and 3 of their course. Titles in the series cover a range of classic and up-and-coming topics, developing understanding of key issues through detailed discussion and consideration of conflicting ideas and supporting evidence. With an emphasis on developing critical thinking, allowing students to think for themselves and beyond their own experiences, the titles in the series offer historical, global and comparative perspectives on core issues in education.

Pedagogies for the Future
A critical reimagining of education
Gary Beauchamp, Dylan Adams and Kevin Smith

Understanding Education Studies
Critical Issues and New Directions
Edited by Mark Pulsford, Rebecca Morris and Ross Purves

Leadership and Management for Education Studies
Introducing Key Concepts of Theory and Practice
Edited by Catherine A. Simon ad Deborah Outhwaite

New Studies in the History of Education
Connecting the Past to the Present in an Evolving Discipline
Edited by Nicholas Joseph

Understanding the Further Education Sector
History, Challenges, and Achievements
Jim Crawley

Critical Histories in Care and Education
Understanding the Connections Between the English Care and Education Systems from the Nineteenth Century to the Present Day
Kate Brooks

Learner Voices, Perspectives, and Positionings
Providing Agency to Empower Learning
Edited by Simon Taylor and Seán Bracken

Social Pedagogy in Education
Re-establishing Relationships and Enriching Learner Experience
Edited by Carla Solvason, Nicola Stobbs and Geoffrey Elliott

For more information about this series, please visit: www.routledge.com/The-Routledge-Education-Studies-Series/book-series/RESS

SOCIAL PEDAGOGY IN EDUCATION

RE-ESTABLISHING RELATIONSHIPS AND ENRICHING LEARNER EXPERIENCE

Edited by Carla Solvason, Nicola Stobbs and Geoffrey Elliott

LONDON AND NEW YORK

Designed cover image: Getty Images

First edition published 2026
by Routledge
4 Park Square, Milton Park, Abingdon, Oxon, OX14 4RN

and by Routledge
605 Third Avenue, New York, NY 10158

Routledge is an imprint of the Taylor & Francis Group, an informa business

© 2026 selection and editorial matter, Carla Solvason, Nicola Stobbs and Geoffrey Elliott; individual chapters, the contributors

The right of Carla Solvason, Nicola Stobbs and Geoffrey Elliott to be identified as the authors of the editorial material, and of the authors for their individual chapters, has been asserted in accordance with sections 77 and 78 of the Copyright, Designs and Patents Act 1988.

All rights reserved. No part of this book may be reprinted or reproduced or utilised in any form or by any electronic, mechanical, or other means, now known or hereafter invented, including photocopying and recording, or in any information storage or retrieval system, without permission in writing from the publishers.

Trademark notice: Product or corporate names may be trademarks or registered trademarks, and are used only for identification and explanation without intent to infringe.

British Library Cataloguing-in-Publication Data
A catalogue record for this book is available from the British Library

ISBN: 978-1-032-87556-9 (hbk)
ISBN: 978-1-032-87555-2 (pbk)
ISBN: 978-1-003-53327-6 (ebk)

DOI: 10.4324/9781003533276

Typeset in News Gothic Std
by Newgen Publishing UK

Contents

List of Contributors   vii

1. The case for social pedagogy in education   1
   NICOLA STOBBS

2. What does it mean to be a social pedagogue?   11
   JACQUELINE HINE AND AMANDA SHEEHY

3. Creating a nurturing environment in early childhood education and care, with a focus upon relationships, awe and wonder   21
   JOHANNA CLIFFE

4. Adopting social pedagogical values to support children with SEND   32
   SUE BAYLIS

5. The potential of art to break down barriers and draw together   41
   KAYTIE HOLDSTOCK

6. Harmony and connection: integrating social pedagogy with music education   52
   KATE HOWEN

7. Taking a social pedagogical approach to including Gypsy, Roma and Traveller communities in a setting   62
   STACEY HODGKINS

8. Creativity and the common third: approaches in education   72
   NICOLA WATSON AND ROSEMARIE HILL

9. Managing emotions and maintaining wellbeing as an empathic social pedagogue   82
   ANGELA HODGKINS AND SUZANNE ALLIES

10. Why college-based higher education needs social pedagogy   95
    OLIVIA STOREY AND GEOFFREY ELLIOTT

11 A social pedagogical approach to tackling social-class bias in higher education RAQUEL LABELLA JARA	107
12 Building relationships within blended learning SAMANTHA SUTTON-TSANG	118
13 A head, heart and hands approach to collaborative mentoring YVONNE CASHMORE AND MARGARET TILDESLEY	130
14 Leadership: not a role but a way of being SHAUN MCINERNEY AND EMMA LAURENCE	140
15 Accepting relationships and emotions in research CARLA SOLVASON	155
16 The next chapter STUART GALLAGHER	165
Index	*171*

Contributors

Suzanne Allies is a psychotherapist with a private practice, having been a teacher, senior university lecturer, author, and mental health trainer. She is passionate about reducing mental health stigma and using trauma-informed approaches to create proactive, preventative mental health solutions. She has designed the CORE PSHE mental health and wellbeing curriculum that is currently being piloted in Worcestershire primary schools.

Sue Baylis has dedicated over 30 years to working with children and their families within various statutory and private organisations. Sue specialised in working with young children being assessed for, or diagnosed with ASD and during this period completed an MA in Special and Inclusive Education, researching innovative methods to support communication and reflection with nonverbal children. In 2006, Sue joined the University of Worcester as a senior lecturer in the Institute of Education and is a member of the Social Pedagogy Research Group at the University. Sue contributes to the community as a governor at a school for children with special educational needs.

Yvonne Cashmore leads PGCE Business with Economics and PGCE Business at the University of Worcester. She coordinates Regional Training Hubs and works as Quality Coordinator and Academic Integrity Tutor. She has extensive teaching experience in Sussex and Worcestershire and has held various senior roles. With 20 years in examining, writing and training for national qualifications, she is now an external examiner for PGCE. Yvonne trains mentors on PGCE course developments and has a research interest in mentoring and coaching.

Johanna Cliffe has worked in education for over 20 years. Initially, she worked within grassroots practice in the early years sector before moving into higher education. Throughout her career, Johanna's professional approach has been deeply rooted in fostering and nurturing strong relationships; making connections; and forging positive partnerships with children, families and students: often those facing vulnerabilities and socio-economic challenges. Johanna has long been interested in post-humanist and social pedagogic approaches, as well as drawing heavily on Deleuzo-Guattarian concepts such as the rhizome, assemblages and nomad, within her practice, research and published work.

Geoffrey Elliott is Professor of Post-Compulsory Education at the University of Worcester, having taught in comprehensive schools, further, adult and higher education. He edits the international peer-reviewed journal *Research in Post-Compulsory Education*, and his current research interest is exploring diversity across all phases of education. He is a volunteer for Schoolreaders, mainly working with local primary schools.

Stuart Gallagher leads two courses at the University of Worcester: Education Studies BA (Hons) and Leading Culture Change in Safeguarding (PG Cert). Previously, he led the undergraduate module Utopian Childhoods and Child-Centred Advocacy, which was based on principles of social pedagogy and Ruth Levitas's Utopia as Method. His background includes working with school-excluded children and young people as an informal educator and, later, as an Education Welfare Officer in Bristol and Cambridge, UK. He is interested in corporate parenting and coaching safeguarding leaders across a range of sectors, including health, education and sport.

Rosemarie Hill worked as a primary school teacher for 15 years before moving into higher education. Now working as a teacher educator, Rosemarie's research interests include primary history and creativity.

Jacqueline Hine worked as a primary school teacher in the UK and the Middle East specialising in pastoral care, geography and science leadership. Upon returning to the UK, she spent some time as a STEM officer for STEM Learning, supporting primary and secondary schools with STEM enrichment activities. Jacquie currently works at the University of Worcester in Initial Teacher Education leading Primary Geography. Jacquie has research interests in Social Justice, Professional Identities, and Geography amongst many others.

Angela Hodgkins' professional background is in the early years, having worked with young children in a wide range of settings for over 20 years. After this, she moved into teaching in further education, then into higher education, where she is now a senior lecturer and course leader. Angela's interests are in empathy, compassion and reflective practice. In 2024, she completed a PhD which examined empathy in early years practice.

Stacey Hodgkins comes from Romany gypsy heritage and has worked in early years and education for over 20 years. Passionate about working with marginalised groups throughout this time, she has now moved into advocating for Gypsy, Roma and Traveller communities within the University of Worcester and external organisations. Over the past two years, she has also contributed to publications and been involved in research projects and a training package for social workers and other professionals working with Gypsy, Roma and Traveller communities with an introduction to using social pedagogy in practice.

Kaytie Holdstock worked as a primary school teacher for 20 years where arts-based learning has been her passion. During her time in primary education, Kaytie worked as an art advisor working with many schools to raise the profile of art and design by advocating for the limitless benefits this subject contributes to children's holistic development. Kaytie now works in higher education, empowering future teachers to deliver high-quality art whilst contributing to the knowledge base of this area through research and publications.

Kate Howen is Senior Lecturer at the University of Worcester, specialising in Primary Music Education. Before moving into higher education, she gained a varied experience across Early Years, KS1 and KS2, as a Teaching Assistant, SENCo Assistant, Physical Therapy, Speech and Language, and 1:1 support assistant. Her dedication to fostering creativity, accessibility and holistic development in education has been a consistent focus throughout her career. Now, as a senior lecturer, Kate draws on her years of classroom experience to support and inspire future educators. Through her work, she continues to champion the importance of creativity, inclusion and social pedagogy in education.

Raquel Labella Jara is a Doctor of Education candidate at the University of Bristol's School of Education and a member of the Bristol Doctoral College. Her research focuses on social class perception as a potential cause of exclusion in English new universities. Raquel has worked in higher education for over 20 years, both in England and the United States, and is a member of the Social Pedagogy Research Group at the University of Worcester.

Emma Laurence is currently a lecturer in the Department for Children and Families at the University of Worcester and Course Leader of the BA (Hons) Early Childhood. She has recently completed a PhD looking at how collaborative leadership development programmes can provide a unique source of support for educators. Emma had experience in a range of EY settings and primary schools before moving into higher education. Social pedagogy is a key area of focus for Emma who is currently a trustee of the Social Pedagogy Professional Association and a member of the Social Pedagogy Research Group at the University of Worcester.

Shaun McInerney taught and led schools in the UK and India for over 25 years and was founding Principal of a successful and innovative Studio School in Liverpool. Now working with the School Effectiveness Team at the University of Worcester, he coaches leaders, delivering leadership development that supports them to unlock potential and respond to the needs of young people in a rapidly changing world. Alongside international colleagues, he co-created the Togetherness Practice – a framework to support changemakers evolve capacities and create conditions for a more equitable and sustainable world. He is a trustee of the Impact Trust and vice chair of governors at his local primary school in Worcestershire, England.

Amanda Sheehy is an educator, communicator and researcher and an Associate Lecturer in the Department of Children and Families at the University of Worcester. She has been a primary school teacher since 2006 and continues to teach part time at a primary school. As a result of her PhD research into promoting gender equality in schools, Amanda has developed workshops which she has delivered in primary schools. She continues to conduct educational research focusing on social pedagogy and promoting equality in primary education.

Carla Solvason worked as a primary school teacher in areas of deprivation for 15 years, followed by a short sojourn with the children's communication charity, I CAN, before moving into higher education where she has remained for almost 20 years. Carla has long been interested in ethical (and caring) research and has published widely in this area. Carla started the Social Pedagogy Research Group at the University of Worcester two years ago (at the behest of her colleagues, all authors in this book), and its strong values base has seen it grow from strength to strength ever since.

Nicola Stobbs was Senior Lecturer and Course Leader for the BA (Hons) Early Childhood in Society at the University of Worcester and introduced a social pedagogical approach to this course. Subsequently, the course was endorsed by the Social Pedagogy Professional Association. She has undertaken considerable research with groups experiencing adversity and marginalisation, for example, kinship children and carers, children and families in areas of deprivation and Roma, Gypsy Travellers inequalities. Nicola is the chair of Play Worcester, a charity committed to ensuring children have opportunities to play outside more often in their communities.

Olivia Storey began her career in youth work and family support before qualifying as a teacher and entering the field of education 18 years ago. Prior to joining the education department at the University of Worcester, Olivia taught in Further Education Colleges for over 13 years, including 10 years in College-Based Higher Education. She is now researching the intersection between FE and HE. Olivia values her membership in the Social Pedagogy Research Group, where her involvement and relationships within this community of practice continue to inform her knowledge, beliefs and practices.

Samantha Sutton-Tsang is Senior Lecturer and Course Leader for the FdA Early Years Flexible and Distributed Learning pathway at the University of Worcester. With extensive experience in early childhood education, Samantha is dedicated to fostering innovative teaching practices and supporting professional development. Her work emphasises the integration of technology in education and the promotion of high-quality early years practice through research.

Margaret (Maggie) Tildesley is Senior Lecturer in Primary Education and Education & Inclusion at the University of Worcester. As Mentor Lead for the Primary Phase, she supports teachers to mentor trainees in schools and alternative provision. Maggie has taught children in the Early Years Foundation Stage (EYFS) to Upper Key Stage 2 (UKS2) across London and taught in West Africa and South India. Throughout her career, she mentored early career teachers (ECTs). Additionally, Maggie worked in Arts Education for organisations such as Shakespeare's Globe Theatre and Guildhall School of Music & Drama. She is passionate about creativity and social justice in education.

Nicola Watson taught in the early years, primary and higher education sectors for over 20 years, most recently at the University of Worcester. Prior to this, she was a lawyer and mediator. Nicola has written extensively on supporting the development of creativity as a means of resolving conflicts and nurturing compassion and care for the human and the more-than-human world.

1 The case for social pedagogy in education

Nicola Stobbs

Introduction

As I write this in early 2025, Donald Trump, a twice-impeached convicted felon, has been sworn into office for the second time as the President of the United States. He promises an administration that will withdraw from climate treaties, engage in the mass deportation of illegal immigrants, including children and cancel 'woke' diversity programmes. He has also pardoned over 1,500 of his convicted supporters for their part in the storming of the Capitol building in 2021 (BBC News, 2025). To many (me included), Trump's behaviour seems shocking; how, I wonder, could the American people be so blind to this man's failings? And yet the American people, including some of my own genuinely delightful friends and relatives, voted Trump convincingly into office. This logic-defying phenomenon is being repeated across the world as charismatic, convention-defying leaders grow in confidence and popularity. What can those of us with a social conscience do, beyond hoping that things will work out in the end? Beyond hoping that sanity will, eventually, prevail.

Disruptors wanted!

Populist leaders are disruptors, and if people are turning to them because they feel betrayed by the current modus operandi, then we, too, must become disruptors offering a better, values-based alternative. A vision founded on longevity, on building all people and communities up, not, as we so often see, based upon offering easy solutions where the vulnerable are made scapegoats.

It is time for educators (in the broadest sense) to acknowledge the power that is in their hands as they contribute to the raising of a nation's children, nurturing our future leaders. All of us in human-facing professions, whereby our advice and opinions influence the decisions of others, need to become agents for positive change in a world that appears to have lost its way. In a world that is so entrenched in selfishness and greed that people no longer see it, consciously choosing to show kindness and care rather than respond with anger is to be a disruptor. To listen to understand, not to speak, and to help others to feel empowered to make changes in their own lives is to be a disruptor. And we must learn about others before we can educate them. In order to educate others to make wise decisions, we must first understand what motivated them to make choices that may not have been in their best interests. Let us use Brexit, the UK's withdrawal from the European Union in 2016, as an example. Many voted for Brexit because they felt a loss of control and security and were struggling economically, despite working long hours (Dorey, 2022). These people were collateral damage of consumer-oriented economic policies combined with shrinking life chances that

DOI: 10.4324/9781003533276-1

enabled the rich to become richer and the poor to become poorer (Bauman, 2011), damaging the self-worth of those who had been managing until this point and threatening their children's futures. When someone is sinking, they will grasp for anything that might keep them afloat. When people feel threatened, they are more likely to embrace anti-establishment sentiments and populism (Abadi et al., 2024). We need to provide a more positive alternative.

The pandemic offered a time for reflection, and there was a hope that we would emerge from it ready to 'imagine another (better) world' (Cameron and Moss, 2020, p. xvi). However, in Britain, a legacy of failures that had been pushed into the long grass for many years, such as the disasters of Hillsborough, Grenfell, the Post Office, Windrush and Infected Blood scandals, amongst other everyday injustices, were revealed, leaving many citizens feeling like 'little people', disregarded by the state and powerful institutions (Vaughan, 2024). Sadly, the pandemic did not bring any positive change to political strategy. But we cannot accept a return to 'business as usual' because our systems were already failing so many. If we are to transform our society into one where people feel noticed, safe and valued, then we need radical change. We need disruptors offering a philosophy that seeks to make people invested in their communities again. A values system that offers hope, respect and empowerment. Step up, social pedagogy.

As Shaun McInerney and Emma Laurence state in their chapter, policy is a blunt instrument. While there is still a need for policy and legislation to tackle injustice and social inequalities, it is people who enact positive change in their communities. Harnessing the power of education in its broadest sense is the logical route to improvements, yet education has been neglected by governments for over a decade (Education Committee Report, 2021). With the 'belief that you can decisively influence social circumstances through education' (Hämäläinen, 2003, p. 71), social pedagogy offers a hopeful, outward-facing driver of policy and practicable change. It is flexible and built upon a strong foundational value, something that cannot be designed into policy and legislation. It is not a toolkit or a process to be followed, but herein lies its power: it is an approach that thrives in the 'it depends' messy mix of local problem solving and solutions.

A new vision bringing together social pedagogy and education

We live in an exciting time where digital and creative skills, the ability to articulate ideas and problem solve will take you far (Sharland and Slesser, 2024) and these should be at the heart of teaching, inspiring children and young people, yet our education systems are firmly entrenched in transmission approaches to education and compliance (Department for Education, 2024). Children are part of (and a product of) their community, so why shouldn't their education involve visiting local art galleries and studios, getting involved in community theatre and dance productions, using public libraries and eating healthy food in local restaurants? Rather than social-capital-building activities, for example enabling young people to talk to inspiring local entrepreneurs or craftspeople who can mentor, advise and work with them on innovative opportunities, our education system suggests that there is a single route to success, and that is through going to university, a luxury out of the reach of many.

John Bird, founder and editor of *The Big Issue* magazine, asked what prevents middle- and upper-class individuals from knifing people, concluding that 'prevent' was the key word (Bird, 2024, p. 17). He suggested that parents and teachers create conditions that stop more privileged children from taking violent paths through 'prevention devices', the social devices of ballet lessons, good food, warm beds and holidays. Bird argues, 'prevention is the greatest tool in the toolkit of bringing up children so that they don't end up knifing each other or perfect strangers' (Bird, 2024, p. 17). He calls for a societal change in approach to prevent poverty that goes beyond 'holding the poor's hand' – offering free school meals will stop starvation but will not prevent the starvation of the 'mind and spirit' (Bird, 2024, p. 17). Instead, Bird (2024, p. 17) stresses, to offer a genuine alternative to a life of poverty and crime, the poor need an education that 'enables them to climb on the shoulders of others', and to lead themselves and their communities out of inherited poverty through social prevention mechanisms. Perhaps social pedagogy, education in the broadest sense (Petrie et al., 2009), can enable this.

The fightback

A fightback is possible, and in this text, we propose that social pedagogy is the vehicle for this. It is a discipline that is complex, multi-faceted and diverse, while also being remarkably simple because it values people, not structures. Although social pedagogy is well established in other countries, it is still in its infancy in the UK. Writing in 2013, Pat Petrie (2013, p. 10) explained:

> In the UK we still need to develop our own authentic social pedagogy, not one that attempts to import practice and theory from societies which have their own traditions, histories and concerns.

In the chapters that follow, we outline our vision of an authentic social pedagogy for education and care today. It is aimed at those who work in the human professions, both practitioners and future practitioners, and especially social disruptors. We do not claim to have all the answers; it is not perfect, and the views expressed here will, no doubt, continue to develop as we continue to live experiences and reflect. Each chapter is a snapshot of how the authors, many of whom work in higher education, have found a place for social pedagogy in their theory and practice.

Approach to practice

As might be expected for those working in public-facing roles, the emphasis on relationships resonates with every author. For some, this is situated in their teaching, others start from this perspective, seeing the potential of relationship-based practice to impact positively on the world by creating change agents. Some of the authors that are included in this text found that social pedagogy encapsulated their existing theoretical framework for practice, and there was resonance between those theories that they already valued and the aims of social pedagogy. Some of those theories and approaches are mentioned in the chapters that follow, including: slow pedagogy (Clark, 2023); Reggio Emelia; affective pedagogy (Hickey-Moody, 2012, p. 79); emotional intelligence (Mayer and Salovey, 1997); unconditional positive regard (Rogers, 1959); professional love (Page, 2018); systems theory (Maclean and Harrison, 2015); Breath of Life Theory (Blackstock, 2011, 2019); critical pedagogy; (Freire, 1970 [2017]); scaffolding (Bruner, 1960); and the Zone of Proximal Development (Vygotsky, 1978) and caritas. Communities of practice (Wenger, 1998) is also mentioned by several authors. You may have already come across many of these concepts yourself.

In her 2013 (p. 10) paper, *Social Pedagogy in the UK: Gaining a firm foothold?* Pat Petrie noted:

> ...there is certainly a desire to improve pedagogic practice, but we are still light on theory. Policy, theory and practice should be in a dynamic relationship, each informed and shaped by the others, in the context of this particular society and all its diversity: only this parallel development will permit social pedagogy to gain a firm foothold in the UK.

We hope that this book will play a part in enabling social pedagogy to gain a firm foothold in the UK, as it offers insights into how it can improve pedagogical practice and discusses some of the theories that the authors have found it aligns with. It is part of our fightback armoury of better ideas, offering hope for transformation of broken systems. We present it as a provocation for discussion on how to enact inclusive values that invoke feelings of belonging and pride in our families, community and culture.

The contents

Let us now turn to the authors and their chapters.

In Chapter 2, Jacqueline Hine and Amanda Sheehy address the question of what a social pedagogue is, analysing interviews with professionals who consider themselves social pedagogues. An overriding theme noted by them is the importance of relationships and advocating for children and young people, seeing the world from their perspective and providing positive experiences for them. This includes sometimes being willing to 'swim against the tide' of behaviour management policies, examining personal actions and motivations. Positive relationships with young people, families and colleagues were recognised as a tentative theory for why some practitioners stay in their roles despite workload challenges, providing joy-filled moments in what can sometimes be an exhausting profession. Within social pedagogy, these relationships become central to all practice.

Johanna Cliffe takes a similar perspective in Chapter 3, discussing the importance of relational pedagogy when working with our youngest children. Taking a broad and holistic perspective of education and its purpose, Johanna theorises that children learn from adults in a way that is similar to an apprentice learning from their mentor. Going far beyond curriculum knowledge, this includes identity formation, the ability to give and receive love, and learners understanding their place in caring for the world. Hope for responding to the challenges of the Anthropocene is found as practitioners model how to care for the planet alongside their little apprentices. Reference is made to slow pedagogy and features of the Reggio Emelia approach are also recognised as consistent with this wider view of the purpose of education. In these approaches, individual paths to learning are celebrated and encouraged, through a rhizomatic approach which offers time and flexibility for awe and wonder to be a part of the education experience.

In Chapter 4, Sue Baylis, similarly, focusses on the relational aspect of social pedagogy, re-imagining this as a 'magic key' to unlock the potential of people with special educational needs and disabilities (SEND). The chapter invites us to take a social pedagogical perspective when reflecting on our view of disability. Based on the assumption that everyone has potential to contribute to society if we find ways of including them (Thempra, nd), social pedagogy categorically rejects the premise that people with SEND are inferior to neurotypically developing individuals (Zaks, 2023). Instead, Sue aligns a social pedagogical approach with the social model of disability, emphasising social inclusion, individual rights and wellbeing (Rothuizen and Harbo, 2017). When holding a human rights perspective of SEND, practitioners must take time to understand how children and young people with SEND communicate, and how their identity is shaped by their different life worlds (Eichsteller and Holthoff, 2011), rather than only seeing their disability. Sue advocates that genuine relationships with children and young people who have specific needs are key to unlocking the magic within them, in both a micro and a macro context.

For Kaytie Holdstock, author of Chapter 5, the potential for art as a force for good takes it out of settings and into the community, using it as a tool for connection and bridge-building. The social pedagogue may not be an art teacher but can still utilise art to bring communities together. By guiding participants to develop empathy and a sense of shared heritage through art activities, the social pedagogue can re-engage people with their immediate world. Kaytie explores the potential of art as a tool for social justice and the alleviation of societal inequalities, offering a platform for expression for those who may struggle with more traditional forms of communication. This chapter explores how, when utilised by a skilled social pedagogue, art can also be a democratising force, through which skills and knowledge are shared bi-directionally, transcending boundaries. Community art projects initiated by social pedagogues can offer opportunities for reflection on identity and belonging, fostering curiosity and openness about the identity of others. For Kaytie, social pedagogy aligns with the principles of 'affective pedagogy' (Hickey-Moody, 2012, p. 79), with both perspectives considering education a relational practice.

In Chapter 6, Kate Howen explores music education in its wider sense, and its alignment with social pedagogy principles whereby individuals are understood within their cultural context. She advocates for the use of music as a source of wellbeing, bringing people together, transcending culture, gender, class, race and religion. Kate argues that stereotypical, enculturated views of what music is, or should be, should be challenged. For Kate, it is the relationship-based practice aspect of social pedagogy that resonates, particularly the association with life-long learning and music. The chapter also explores a democratic perspective of music, where everyone can contribute, not only those who are deemed musical because they can play an instrument. Kate sees music as a uniting force that can, and should, be utilised for societal good.

Stacey Hodgkins, who identifies as Gypsy, Roma, Traveller (GRT), shares her unique understanding of issues facing this marginalised community in Chapter 7. She proposes that adopting a social pedagogy perspective can enable practitioners to more effectively support GRT's inclusion and engagement with public services through building positive relationships, with the holistic Head, Heart, Hands approach suggested as particularly useful. Stacey invites readers to use their Heads to reflect on any subconscious bias they may harbour towards GRT communities, then lay that prejudice aside. GRT families are likely to experience anxiety and fear about engaging with professional services, and approaching them with empathy can help establish trusting relationships (Heart). On a practical level (Hands), Stacey explains how practitioners can devise support plans that take individual interests and circumstances into account. The author stresses, however, that engagement must be bi-directional, and while practitioners should appreciate and accommodate the family's unique culture and aspirations, the family must also appreciate and accommodate the culture and aspirations of the school in a reciprocal relationship of mutual respect.

For Nicola Watson and Rosemary Hill, the authors of Chapter 8, creativity is positioned as the soul of social pedagogy. They hold similar viewpoints to those outlined in Chapter 4, recognising the potential of art for bridge-building and community strengthening, seeing creativity as a democratic phenomenon. As in Chapter 5, Nicola and Rosie consider that the role of the social pedagogue is to provide a platform for the marginalised to express their voice through creativity, which can increase wellbeing and feelings of empowerment.

Rejecting creativity as outcome-focussed and instead valuing the process is aligned with the principles of the Diamond Model. The authors discuss the disposition of imagination, outlining the many positive aspects that result when it is applied. Curiosity is another disposition associated with creativity and is central to the social pedagogy concept of *Bildung*, defined as a 'holistic, humanistic concept of education' (Cleary, 2019, p. 1) and seen as necessary in a meaningful life. The authors contend that social pedagogical practice is, in itself, creative, as it advances lateral and independent thought regarding educational solutions to societal problems.

Nicola and Rosie also outline the potential of the Common Third as an enactment of democratic education, when practitioners learn and are curious alongside the children they work with. The authors suggest that social pedagogy is 'post-inclusive', because diversity is not only accepted but is essential for creativity to flourish. This, they propose, offers the potential to increase our understanding of what it means to be human, enhancing both our own lives and the lives of others.

For Angela Hodgkins and Suzanne Allies, the authors of Chapter 9, social pedagogy encapsulates concepts that underpin relationship-based practice, including emotional intelligence (Mayer and Salovey, 1997), unconditional positive regard (Rogers, 1959), professional love (Page, 2018) and systems theory (Maclean and Harrison, 2015). This, they suggest, is demonstrated through the Diamond Model of learning in social pedagogy and applied authentically in practice through practitioners who adhere to their *Haltung*. Angela and Suzanne take a similar stance to Johanna Cliffe in Chapter 3, whereby practitioners start by forming trusting relationships. The social pedagogue then weaves networks of interconnection that provide the other with the social and emotional scaffolding needed to navigate the challenges of life, increasing resilience and feelings of empowerment. The authors align this to the concept of the relational universe.

In Chapter 10, Geoffrey Elliott and Olivia Storey, likewise, draw on concepts that have underpinned their practice and recognise how these are reflected in the socially engaged principles of social pedagogy. Central to this is *Haltung*, to which they draw comparisons with the Breath of Life Theory (Blackstock, 2011, 2019). For the authors, the enactment of these concepts offers a solution to the challenges facing the college-based higher education (CBHE) sector. They contend that there is a collective *Haltung* at the heart of CBHE because CBHE considers the unique life world of non-traditional students and seeks opportunities for all, in opposition to the creation of winners and losers embedded within marketisation policies. Similarly, in CBHE, non-traditional students are given the opportunity to access degree-level education in accessible ways, aligned to the social justice aspect of social pedagogy. One of the authors shares how approaching their teaching in CBHE by drawing on the social pedagogy concepts of the Common Third and the three Ps enabled her to navigate demands on her mental health and wellbeing.

Samantha Sutton-Tsang continues the theme of alternative, inclusive delivery methods of higher education as a social justice issue in Chapter 11. Samantha draws upon reflections from students who have engaged in blended learning and outlines some of the advantages and challenges of this for non-traditional students. Central to her discussion is how relationships can be nurtured when there is little opportunity for face-to-face meetings. The chapter explores how the Diamond Model can guide those delivering blended learning to enable students to feel valued and confident, illustrating how each aspect of the model is interrelated and dependent on the other. Samantha reminds readers that these aspects must also be applied to the tutor if they are to support their own wellbeing. The concept of caritas is introduced, and Samantha poses a question that is also considered in the previous and following chapters; how to show loving kindness towards students without taking away the growth that comes from autonomous academic struggle, building the muscle of scholarship, critical thinking and analysis. This is recognised as a balance that must be made by social pedagogues in every context of their professions.

Continuing the theme of social justice through higher education in Chapter 12, Raquel Labella-Jara argues that a negative side-effect of the Widening Participation agenda may be that working-class students' university experience is diminished by lecturers who perpetuate the assumption that these students lack aspiration. Pressurised to score highly in student evaluations, lecturers may adopt a 'dumbed down' pedagogy, altering their teaching and assessment tasks to try and ensure that working-class students achieve high grades and are 'satisfied customers', rather than pushing them to higher-level critical thinking.

Raquel outlines four aims of higher education, divided into those that promote personal and societal advancement ('soft purposes') and those that contribute to the economic growth of the country ('hard purposes'), all of which, she asserts, are equally valid. Unconscious bias in higher education pedagogy, however, may lead to the assumption that working-class students favour an education that results in a vocational outcome (hard purposes), focussing on practical skills rather than critical and independent thinking. The concept of *Haltung* can be utilised to reflect on any unconscious bias towards working-class students. Raquel suggests that we must consider how our views have been influenced by societal attitudes towards working-class students, ensuring that these biases are challenged in practice and in expectations, thus preventing the curtailment of progression possibilities for some individuals.

For Yvonne Cashmore and Margaret Tildesley, the authors of Chapter 13, social pedagogy draws together theories that align with their pedagogical beliefs and values. The Head, Heart, Hands model holds particular resonance for them as they facilitate collaborative mentoring. The authors hold a democratic view of education, underpinned by Pestalozzi's belief that the practitioner's role is to bring out the humanity within the person, rather than filling them with knowledge (Brühlmeier, 2010, p. 18). Similarly, they are influenced by the concept of pedagogical love (Määttä and Uusiautti, 2013), highlighting the interdependence of recognition and acceptance that fuels learning and creates a more 'humane world'.

The works of Freire (1970 [2017]) also resonate with Yvonne and Margaret, particularly critical pedagogy and social justice in education, whereby oppressive hierarchical structures are challenged and democratic relationships prevail. Bruner's concept of scaffolding and Vygotsky's Zone of Proximal Development model also feature, based on a commitment to respecting all learners as individuals. The authors emphasise that in collaborative mentoring, the mentor is considered a leader, but not an authority (Gazibara, 2013, p. 80), a subtle difference that does not induce behaviour founded on fear. The Common Third is suggested as a tool for bringing mentor and mentee together, improving the practice of both as they reflect, set targets and act based on new insights gained from the process. The authors highlight that it is through shared action that transformation occurs, both individually, institutionally and in wider society.

In Chapter 14, Shaun McInerney and Emma Laurence focus on the challenge of how to lead practice, create conditions for human flourishing and enact positive change. This is examined from the perspective of individual, community and society. Shaun and Emma outline why social pedagogy in education is necessary now. They argue that the narrow, performance-driven agendas focussing on instrumental knowledge and assessment have hindered a more holistic approach, one that includes wellbeing and growth, for example. They discuss the pressing issues of today, climate change, artificial intelligence (AI), diminishing resources and social and economic disruption, suggesting that we must channel education to build community cohesion through authentic relationships.

Shaun and Emma explore how a leader's *Haltung* will drive them to consider the root causes of social problems and seek long-term solutions rather than just dealing with the symptoms. The authors concur with Yvonne Cashmore and Margaret Tildesley (Chapter 13), whereby leadership is not reliant on authority invested in individuals because of their position in an organisation. For them, social pedagogical leadership is fluid, emerging in the interactions between individuals where decisions regarding human flourishing are made. Everyone in an organisation is responsible for perpetuating an ethos of psychological safety and trust so that all individuals feel empowered to be bold. As social pedagogical practice is developed, a new educational paradigm can evolve.

In Chapter 15, Carla Solvason investigates the connection between education and social research, aligning these with social pedagogy's purpose to positively influence individuals and society. She posits that without social research, education quickly becomes irrelevant; you cannot provide an answer to current issues by using a museum of ideas belonging to previous generations. Carla draws on Pestalozzi's Head, Heart, Hands model, stating that while the Head and Hands aspects are readily recognised as central to research, the Heart is often seen as less so, yet social research always involves decisions of the heart to which there are no definitive answers. Carla argues that attempting to conceal how the researcher's emotions, experiences, and perspectives inevitably influence the research, and the researched, is futile, and that by recognising these aspects, the authenticity of the work is strengthened.

The chapter details Mührel's 2008 concept of two pillars of *Haltung* – *comprehending and regarding* (cited by Charfe and Gardner, 2020). When we *comprehend* someone, we try to imagine their life world and show empathy; controversial in research terms because it brings emotions to the foreground. The *regarding* pillar of *Haltung* relates to the way humans seek connection with others. This can result in 'dis-regarding' the unfamiliar and consequently reducing the other person. This is important to be aware of, not just in research but in all of our dealings with others, so that we do not reconfigure information to fit our own understandings.

In another echo of social pedagogical values, Carla states that researchers should not only 'do good' research, but 'bring about good' (Bloor, 2010). This, however, requires reflection on what 'bringing about good' is, as everyone is influenced by their own experience and beliefs regarding what a good outcome would be. However, holding those we research with in unconditional positive regard, we should always aim to make a positive difference to their lives and that of society.

Finally, in Chapter 16, Stuart Gallagher considers what is next for social pedagogy in education in the UK.

We hope that you enjoy the chapters. We have placed them in a tentative logical order of flow, but they do not need to be read in chronological order – please do go straight to those chapters that most pique your curiosity. The chapters highlight how broad social pedagogy can be but also how each author has found a central characteristic, one of hope for the future. Social pedagogy 'comprises the idea that education takes place primarily for the society or community rather than for the development of individual personalities' (Hämäläinen, 2012, p. 99, citing Salo, 1952) and in doing so rejects the 'each man for themself' mindset which plagues western societies. This book is based upon the belief that 'education can create inclusive communities, which will in turn foster inclusive individuals' (Stobbs et al., 2023, p. 3). And, as educators, we hold the responsibility for this. How we raise the child is how we shape our future (Popkewitz, 2008).

References

Abadi, D., van Prooijenb, J. W., Krouwele, A. and Fischer, A. H. (2024) Anti-establishment sentiments: Realistic and symbolic threat appraisals predict populist attitudes and conspiracy mentality. *Cognition and Emotion*, 38(8): pp. 1246–1260. https://doi.org/10.1080/02699931.2024.2360584

Bauman, Z. (2011) *Collateral damage: Social inequalities in a global age*. Cambridge: Polity Books.

BBC News (2025) Six Trump executive orders to watch. Available at: www.bbc.co.uk/news/articles/cqld6wnv1rgo (Accessed 28 January 2025).

Bird, J. (2024) Poverty prevention needs an updated, knife-free toolbox. *The Big Issue*, 1640, 04-10 November 2024: pp. 17.

Blackstock, C. (2011) The emergence of the breath of life theory. *Journal of Social Work Values and Ethics*, 8(1): pp. 1–16.

Blackstock, C. (2019) Revisiting the breath of life theory. *British Journal of Social Work*, 49(4): pp. 854–859.

Bloor, M. (2010) The researcher's obligation to bring about Good. *Qualitative Social Work*, 9(1): pp. 17–20. https://doi.org/10.1177/1473325009355616

Brühlmeier, A. and World, P. (2010) *Head, heart and hand: Education in the spirit of Pestalozzi*. Cambridge: Sophia Books in association with Pestalozzi World.

Bruner, J. S. (1960) *The process of education*. Cambridge, MA: Harvard University Press.

Cameron, C. and Moss, P. (2020) *Transforming early childhood in England towards a democratic education*. London: UCL Press.

Charfe, L. and Gardner, A. (2020) 'Does my Haltung look big in this?': The use of social pedagogical theory for the development of ethical and value-led practice. *International Journal of Social Pedagogy*, 9(1): 11. https://doi.org/10.14324/111.444.ijsp.2020.v9.x.011

Clark, A. (2023) *Slow knowledge and the unhurried child: Time for flow pedagogy in early childhood education*. Abingdon: Routledge.

Cleary, B. (2019) Reinterpreting bildung in social pedagogy. *International Journal of Social Pedagogy*, 8(1): pp. 3. https://doi.org/10.14324/111.444.ijsp.2019.v8.1.003

Department for Education, DfE (2024). *Behaviour in schools. Advice for headteachers and school staff*. Crown Copyright. Available from: https://assets.publishing.service.gov.uk/media/65ce3721e1bdec001a3221fe/Behaviour_in_schools_-_advice_for_headteachers_and_school_staff_Feb_2024.pdf (Accessed 29 January 2025).

Dorey, P. (2022) Explaining Brexit: The 5 A's – Anomie, alienation, austerity, authoritarianism and atavism. *French Journal of British Studies*, XXVII-2 | 2022 Electronic version URL: https://journals.openedition.org/rfcb/9060 (Accessed 28 January 2025).

Education Committee Report (2021) The forgotten: How White working-class pupils have been let down, and how to change it. *UK Parliament*. Available at: https://publications.parliament.uk/pa/cm5802/cmselect/cmeduc/85/8502.htm (Accessed 28 January 2025).

Eichstellar, G. and Holthoff, S. (2011) Conceptual foundations of social pedagogy: A transnational perspective from Germany. In C. Cameron and P. Moss (Eds) *Social pedagogy and working with children and young people*. London: Jessica Kingsley, pp. 33–52.

Freire, P. (2017) *Pedagogy of the oppressed*. Penguin Classics; 13th edition (first published 1970, 1993). Harmondsworth: Penguin Random House.

Gazibara, S. (2013) 'Head, heart and hands learning' – A challenge for contemporary education. *The Journal of Education, Culture, and Society*, 4(1): pp. 71–82.

Hämäläinen, J. (2003) The concept of social pedagogy in the field of social work. *Journal of Social Work*, 3(1): pp. 69–80.

Hämäläinen, J. (2012) Social pedagogy in Finland. *Kriminologija i socijalna integracija*, 20(1): pp. 1–132.

Hickey-Moody, A. (2012) Affect as method, feelings, aesthetics and affective pedagogy. In R. Coleman and J. Ringrose (Eds) *Deleuze and research methodologies*. Edinburgh: Edinburgh University Press, pp. 79–95.

Määttä, K. and Uusiautti, S. (2013) Pedagogical Love and good teacherhood. In K. Määttä and S. Uusiautti (Eds) *Many faces of love*. Rotterdam: Sense Publishers, pp. 93–101.

Maclean, S. and Harrison, R. (2015) Systems Theory and Family Therapy: Beyond Structure and Process. *Journal of Family Therapy*, 37(4), pp. 445–462.

Mayer, J. D. and Salovey, P. (1997) What is emotional intelligence? In P. Salovey and D.J. Sluyter (Eds) *Emotional development and emotional intelligence: Educational implications*. New York: Basic Books, pp. 3–34.

Page, J. (2018) Characterising the principles of Professional Love in early childhood care and education. *International Journal of Early Years Education*, 26(2), pp. 125–141.

Petrie, P. (2013) Social pedagogy in the UK: Gaining a firm foothold? *Education Policy Analysis Archives*, 21(37): pp. 1–16. https://doi.org/10.14507/epaa.v21n37.2013

Petrie, P., Boddy, J., Cameron, C., Heptinstall, E., McQuail, S., Simon, A. and Wigfall, V. (2009) *Pedagogy – A holistic, personal approach to work with children and young people, across services*. Briefing Paper. London: Thomas Coram Research Unit, Institute of Education, UCL, UK.

Popkewitz, T. (2008) *Cosmopolitanism and the age of school reform science, education, and making society by making the child*. New York: Routledge.

Rogers, C. (1959) A client-centred/person-centred approach to therapy. In H. Kirschenbaum and V. Henderson (Eds) *The Carl Rogers reader*. London: Constable, pp. 135–152.

Rothuizen, J. J. and Harbo, L. J. (2017) Social pedagogy: An approach without fixed recipes. *Internation Journal of Social Pedagogy*, 6(1): pp. 6–28.

Sharland, L. and Slesser, C. (2024) The workforce of tomorrow needs creative thinking now. BERA blog. Available at: www.bera.ac.uk/blog/the-workforce-of-tomorrow-needs-creative-thinking-now (Accessed 28 January 2025).

Stobbs, N., Solvason, C., Gallagher, S. and Baylis, S. (2023) A human approach to restructuring the education system: Why schools in England need social pedagogy. *International Journal of Social Pedagogy*, 12(1): p. 8. https://doi.org/10.14324/111.444.ijsp.2023.v12.x.008.

Vaughan, J. (2024) *From Hillsborough to the Post Office Scandal*. Online Blog: Labour Hub. Available at: https://labourhub.org.uk/2024/01/14/from-hillsborough-to-the-post-office-scandal/ (Accessed 28 January 2025).

Vygotsky, L. S. (1978) *Mind in society*. Cambridge, MA: Harvard University Press.

Wenger, E. (1998) *Communities of practice: Learning, meaning, and identity*. Cambridge: Cambridge University Press.

Zaks, Z. (2023) Changing the medical model of disability to the normalization model of disability: Clarifying the past to create a new future direction. *Journal of Disability and Society*, 39(12): pp. 3233–3260. https://doi-org.apollo.worc.ac.uk/10.1080/09687599.2023.2255926

2 What does it mean to be a social pedagogue?

Jacqueline Hine and Amanda Sheehy

Introduction

A key component of social pedagogy is a commitment to building positive relationships and nurturing individuals. Many practitioners value these ideals, yet some are driven to take this further, adopting the title **social pedagogue**. What inspires them to do this? And what might encourage others to do the same? This chapter aims to help both experienced and trainee educators and carers better understand social pedagogy and explores some of the benefits and challenges that they might anticipate if they choose to identify as such. To aid understanding of these elements, primary qualitative data in the form of semi-structured interviews was collected from three experienced social pedagogues (SPs) currently working within a higher education setting. Our interviewees will be referred to collectively as SPs, and individually by the gender-neutral pseudonyms Hollis, Greer and Emerson, in order to maintain their anonymity. The SPs have varied professional backgrounds, including experience in law, family mediation, family support work, social work and counselling, before becoming lecturers in higher education. All three SPs have taught in a range of settings, including higher education, further education, primary schools and early years settings, and so are able to bring a richness of experience to the discussion.

As authors who are relatively new to social pedagogy, we wanted to deepen our own understanding of the rationale for using social pedagogy in a range of educational settings. We considered that the information might also be of value to readers such as experienced professionals or those training in the spheres of education or social care. As a result of talking to the SPs, our understanding of how deeply social pedagogy is intertwined with personal identity has grown. The conversations that we had helped us to better understand why social pedagogy is such an important discipline, and one that should be more widely discussed in education and care settings. We hope that our reflection upon those conversations might impact upon you likewise.

> **Reflection point**
>
> What values do you hold dear in your professional and personal life? Where do these coincide? Do you feel any conflict between these two versions of yourself?

12 Social Pedagogy in Education

How do social pedagogues define social pedagogy?

Eichsteller and Holthoff's (2011) 'Diamond Model' (see Figure 2.1) is one of the most powerful concepts in social pedagogy and consists of five key elements. Positive experiences are central to the other four elements, as these experiences are recognised as leading to and emanating from empowerment, wellbeing and happiness, positive relationships and holistic learning. This model helps identify key principles of social pedagogy; however, as a concept, it is notoriously tricky and nuanced and defies a single definition. It takes a little effort, time and experience to start conceptualising what social pedagogy actually means, but it is worth bearing in mind the words of Theodore Roosevelt (1910) who said that 'Nothing in the world is worth having or doing unless it means effort'. One of the purposes of this chapter is to examine multiple definitions of social pedagogy, and to explore how it is understood by those who call themselves SPs. Below, responses from the SPs form the basis of some helpful descriptions which can serve as starting points. For ease their actual words are easily identifiable in italics.

All of the SPs had clear ideas about social pedagogy. Although they held *similar* values to one another, each showed flexibility to allow for different interpretations or ways of working, as long as these still embraced empathy, empowerment and positive experiences. Their ideas about social pedagogy were aligned, but allowed for individual difference. This is what Emerson referred to as an individual "*life-world orientation*", recognising that not only children and young people (CYP), but practitioners will have differing perspectives on how they approach their role, dependent on their life experiences and values. Noticing the individual and taking an individualised approach to education was at the centre of all three of the SPs' responses. In line with the Diamond Model, the SPs were also unanimous about the need for practitioners to provide positive experiences. They

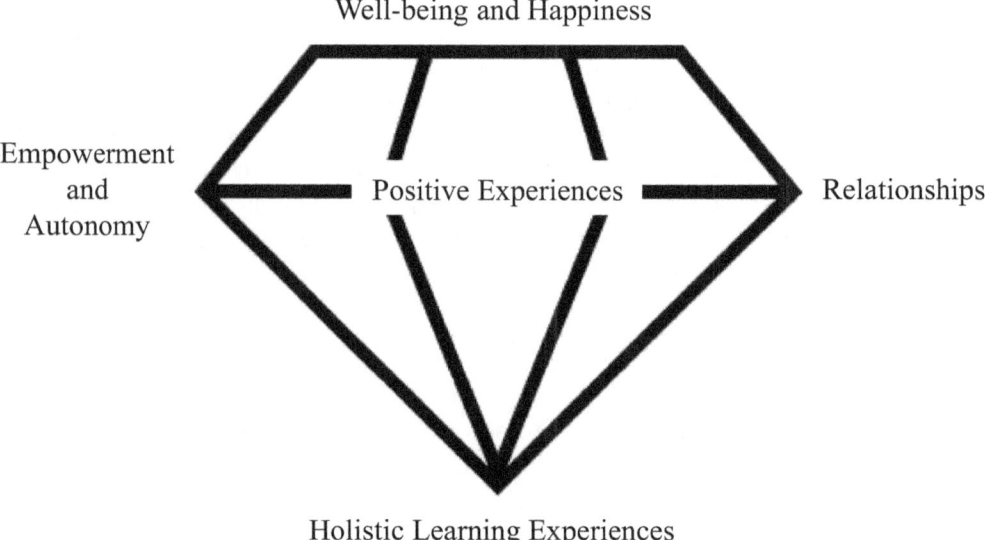

Figure 2.1 Based upon "The Diamond Model" by Eichsteller and Holthoff (2011).

took a holistic perspective on education and sought to enhance wellbeing and happiness beyond delivering a curriculum. They spoke of the need to prioritise making connections and building positive relationships, offering opportunities to experience autonomy and empowerment before any meaningful learning and development could take place.

The value of positive relationships was seen by all three SPs as more than just good practice in order to manage behaviour, but as a moral and ethical imperative. Emerson summed this up by drawing on Monro (2011, p. 72), saying *"It's about having the courage to do the right thing, not just do things right"*. These SPs stressed that for practitioners to truly empower CYP, they need to advocate for them, respect them as individuals, connect with their community and nurture positive relationships. It is far more than just trying to teach. Essentially, these SPs confirmed that social pedagogy assumes a commitment to examining your interactions with CYP, parents, colleagues and members of the wider community, asking whose best interests you are acting in, and being brutally honest about the answer.

A strong rationale for social pedagogy

Relationships and resultant joy

A dominant theme that came out of the conversations held with the SPs was the way the underpinning values of social pedagogy helped them build rewarding relationships with pupils, carers, communities and colleagues. These enriching relationships grew as a result of consciously prioritising the learner's wellbeing and positive experiences. Relationships were a particular source of joy for the SPs. This was demonstrated by Greer, who talked about a positive approach to relationships becoming increasingly reciprocal as they modelled social pedagogical values to those about them. They cited this as being a significant reason why they had remained in education for over 20 years – four times the length of career of the average primary school teacher (DfE, 2023).

Although considering the small number of interviews in this chapter it would be too big a leap to say that practitioners who prioritise relationships stay in the education profession longer, there is evidence of this. For example, Kelchtermans (2017) suggests that those who invest in the relationships they have with pupils and those within their spheres of influence (a phrase coined by Bronfenbrenner and Morris, 1998), tend to be able to find more joy in an otherwise challenging profession. It is reasonable to assume that it would be the same for all caring professions. Emerson shared how through prioritising relationships, and sharing this approach, they created a micro-culture of compassion and care in their own setting. As a result, CYP gained a deeper understanding of the value of empathy and supporting each other, carers were more willing to talk through issues that were troubling them and colleagues became more willing to discuss and seek advice about workplace climate.

Of course, this approach is not without challenges, and not all practitioners in a setting will choose to prioritise relationships. Emerson was frank in sharing how this might create tensions in the setting that cannot be overcome. They described the greatest barrier as uncritical *"group think"* where ideas about alternative pedagogies were dismissed in favour of a uniform *"consistent"* approach. This, Emerson shared, was particularly disheartening, as they, likewise, subscribed to the importance of consistent interactions, but also believed that this should not come before recognising and responding to the lived experiences and life-world orientations of CYP.

> **Reflection point**
>
> Reflect upon a time when you have felt that your preferred practice was in conflict with the policy of your setting or the practice of your colleagues. Did you feel able to act in the best interests of those within your care? How might you feel more empowered to do so?

The SPs' experiences suggest that their personal values may not always align with those of their colleagues. Hollis found it highly empowering to find a setting with similar core values to their own, and to find colleagues with the will to adopt a CYP-focussed approach and the flexibility to respect individual difference. Working alongside like-minded colleagues also brought satisfaction to Greer who described the mutual joy that relationships rooted in the principles of social pedagogy could deliver, saying: *"You get a lot back, don't you? You gain a lot from those relationships too, so it's mutual"*. Greer's statement exemplifies the potential for joy that can be found in the meaningful relationships developed as a result of the pedagogues' effort to build deep connections. Although research into the links between social pedagogy, joy and longevity in a chosen career does not yet exist, it seems reasonable to suggest that an individual is more likely to stay in a profession in which they are able to find joy.

Authenticity

Nias (1989, p. 201), specifically addressing primary school teachers, describes authenticity as feeling:

> Relaxed, whole, natural in the exercise of one's job, and that these states in turn rely upon a sense of being in control (of oneself, one's pupils and their learning, one's environment, one's destiny) which enables one's relationship with children to be responsible and loving.

This, of course, could apply to any education or care environment. The description links cohesively to the key themes of social pedagogy as illustrated in the Diamond Model (Figure 2.1) and hints at the significance of authenticity when trying to build positive relationships. All three of the SPs mentioned authenticity. Greer explained how social pedagogy legitimised their decision to educate in a way that made them feel a professional version of themselves in the setting and enabled them to avoid the dissonance of having a separate personal and professional identity. Hollis echoed this, reflecting upon how they could *"be themselves"* in the classroom, thus avoiding some of the internal tensions that might arise from having a separate *"teacher persona"*. All the SPs echoed this idea and went so far as to suggest that social pedagogy had always been their *modus operandi*, but it was helpful now to have a name for how they conducted themselves in their professional life. The label of 'social pedagogy' lent further authenticity and legitimacy to their practice, particularly when their pedagogical values, such as time spent prioritising relationships, seemed to conflict with the knowledge-driven curriculum found in some of the settings they had experienced.

> **Reflection point**
>
> Consider whether behaviour changes in different settings. Do any elements of your professional performance feel inauthentic? How do you feel about this?

Emerson described authenticity as remarkably freeing, allowing them to prioritise pupils' personal needs over expected academic standards. They noted, with irony, that when they did this, pupils tended to meet or exceed standards set for them as a by-product of the resultant positive experiences and holistic approach to teaching. The idea of being authentic and allowing CYPs to know a little of your personal identity remains a contested topic. Hollis identified how developing a sincere relationship that might be viewed as *"professional or pedagogical love"* (Page, 2018) still had professionals in the education and care sectors divided. Hollis was right to have reservations about this. Clarke, Michell and Ellis (2016), for example, identify that authenticity, or bringing your 'whole self' to work, can be misinterpreted as a lack of professionalism, or a blurring of professional standards. However, there are clear advantages to such an approach, as Emerson explained:

> I also would talk to parents a lot about what [social pedagogy] was and why I was doing it, and because they trusted me, and because their children were happy, and because their children just understood, somehow, that it was just a better way.

Hollis recommended having clear boundaries between practitioner and mentee, sensitively asserting yourself with the CYP in order to retain the sense of a safe and professional space. The strength of that relationship is important; as Kreber (2013) notes, stakeholders can easily detect inauthenticity and with that trust can be lost. Nias (1989) describes how the feeling of being authentic, genuine, in harmony with those you support and your setting can be powerful, empowering even. And for our SPs, behaving authentically – appropriately sharing your true self – was deemed remarkably liberating, although there was a caveat. Emerson did recognise that authenticity without compromise, and without thought for others, just like any other extreme, had the potential to be damaging.

Empowerment and advocacy

Despite the apparently joyful and rewarding benefits of identifying as a SP which have been expressed above, the UK is not yet a country that openly embraces social pedagogy in educational settings. One potential barrier may be that empowering service-users can be at odds with the smooth running of an organisation. Empowerment and advocacy, two of the core principles of social pedagogy, are celebrated by some, but avoided by others who are fearful of the consequences of encouraging stakeholders to question the authority of those making decisions for them. Empowerment gives CYP agency, and, as a result, might question your 'authority' as professional practitioner. For some this is unthinkable, something to avoid at all costs. Framing such behaviour in a more positive light, Kuczynski *et al.* (2018) suggest that these challenges to authority should be seen as a sign of agency and social competence and should not be dismissed as 'disobedience' or disrespect. Such 'challenges to authority' provide opportunities for practitioners to recognise the value in listening to CYP and carers, thereby creating more flexible and reasoned approaches to education and care.

Greer found that when flexibility, empowerment and advocacy were at the heart of practice, most settings in which they had worked were willing to embrace their suggestions about supporting CYP. They felt that identifying as a social pedagogue gave them a vocabulary and legitimate principles to explain why they had chosen to respond to others in the way they had, thus empowering themselves in the process. However, Hollis outlined that the additional emotional work that empowering and advocating for learners demanded could be physically and emotionally exhausting. They noted the need to always be nimble, flexible and watchful so that each interaction could be tailored to the learner. But Hollis was also quick to point out that the exhaustion was worth it. They could see how being a "*chalk and talk*" kind of practitioner might be easier, but they could not imagine missing out on the relationships and satisfaction of seeing a learner's needs being met and watching them flourish. The demands inherent in the approach, perhaps, help us understand why social pedagogy has not yet been widely embraced, despite the apparent benefits to learners.

> **Reflection point**
>
> In a setting you have known, what might be the barriers to advocating for CYP agency? How might these be overcome?

All three SPs talked about being able to see CYP, and their carers, as individuals with whom they would help to develop their tools of agency – their aim being that learners and families could advocate for *their own* needs. SPs saw this as having a more *sustainable* impact on the lives of those they are supporting. As a result, there seems to be an exchange that takes place within a social pedagogical approach. Although greater emotional input is needed from the practitioner at the start of relationships, longer term, greater independence and empowerment of the CYP is the result. These SPs shared evidence of greater initial investment reaping rewards that are not only improved, but which also have greater longevity. In this way there is a 'pay-off' for the initial emotional investment. Only time, and further research, would be able to provide a clear answer to whether this is the case, although we can already see glimpses of the possibilities in projects such as the pilot carried by Berridge *et al.* for the Department for Education in 2011.

Acceptance and community

Identification as a social pedagogue had a marked impact on how the SPs that we spoke with felt valued and part of their settings' community. Hollis and Greer had an interesting parallel with one another as they recognised that being part of that community was not about everyone thinking the same or having the same values about education and care. Instead, they felt it was more that it provided space for people to work in ways that best fit them and the people they were supporting, whilst being based upon some fundamental priorities, such as relationships, holistic education and creating and building upon positive experiences for the CYP. Emerson noted how empowering it was when social pedagogy inadvertently became a way of thinking within a team of colleagues, whether they identified as a social pedagogue or not, due to fundamental shared values.

When developing a curriculum that is based upon an understanding of the CYP's needs and community, the SPs noted that the shared values of social pedagogy became centralised. Emerson shared how conversations about education and development priorities became more learner-centred and felt more exciting; staff members could disagree, but there was a shared desire to make purposeful and constructive decisions. This reinforces the concept that the space social pedagogy affords practitioners is empowering, it helps to make room for different approaches and values, whilst helping colleagues agree on foundational principles, based upon those set out in the Diamond Model in Figure 2.1. This also demonstrates that social pedagogy gives the opportunity to develop a like-minded community amongst practitioners, something Day et al. (2005) recognise as essential to the retention and satisfaction level of professionals.

Greer noted that applying such values in varied settings evoked very different experiences. For example, they had, in the past, faced strong opposition when they focussed on the values of social pedagogy when discussing CYPs' needs and the curriculum. Greer recalled that some settings they worked with were wary of a lack of focus on academic development and resistant to the SP approach, considering the time given to developing its wellbeing-focussed priorities as time wasted. This was disappointing to Greer, who considered this a lost opportunity to enhance CYP's experiences and fulfil basic needs, before turning the focus to what their colleagues considered more 'purposeful' learning. Greer's wish to help settings understand the benefits that focusing on a more holistic, integrated approach could offer was captured in this comment:

> I wish we could get into that [setting] and talk to them about social pedagogy and about relationships and get them to think how that would be, you know, received by the majority of children there.

Greer contended that by helping practitioners to conceptualise the key principles of social pedagogy, CYPs would likely have more positive educational experiences and be more positively predisposed to learn. Likewise, research such as that carried out by Solvason, Webb and Sutton-Tsang in 2021, provides strong evidence that by prioritising issues of physical and psychological welfare first, academic results will follow.

Settings' fears regarding focusing upon social pedagogical values because of a perception that it would neglect the 'proper' academic focus was echoed by Emerson. They noted that *"arbitrary rules"* such as uniform restrictions and *"top down"* approaches to behaviour seemed to destroy any sense of community between practitioners, carers and CYP, focusing only upon normative measures of attainment. Social pedagogy can be a challenging concept for some settings as it requires a balance between keeping pupils safe, flattening hierarchy and allowing CYPs a voice and more autonomous approaches to their own learning. This is still quite a controversial way of thinking about education in particular, particularly in the wake of 'no excuses' schools that have risen in popular education thinking since 1994 (Lack, 2009). These schools, regard a child's domestic context, however challenging, as irrelevant to their educational performance. They also directly oppose social pedagogy's cultural perspective that recognises that an individual's choices will have been influenced by their upbringing and the challenges, or opportunities, that it presented. These 'no excuses' schools offer the reward of academic attainment as the singular pathway to pupils' success. Although their attainment data is impressive, Horn (2010) explains how this comes at the cost of high expulsion and exclusion rates for many of these schools' most vulnerable pupils, thus excluding those children most in need of care.

Social pedagogy offers an alternative conception of success, where the goal is for CYP, professionals and carers to share positive experiences, create trusting relationships, build community cohesion and work towards social justice, as well as academic success. Identification, acceptance and community building are imperative to SPs if they are to enact change.

> **Reflection point**
>
> As you find out more about the values underpinning social pedagogy, do you consider yourself a social pedagogue? What benefits might this label bring? Can you identify any colleagues who you believe to share these values?

Conclusion

Each of the SPs interviewed viewed the principles of social pedagogy (empowerment, wellbeing and happiness, relationships and positive experiences) as core to their professional values. They explained that they had felt that they were a social pedagogue long before they knew of the term and identified as such. Because of this, when they learned of social pedagogy, they felt a sort of 'epiphany' and validation that the priority that they placed on the values *they* felt were important to education had been recognised as legitimate and purposeful practice. Essentially, they described a sense of wholeness and authenticity from their occupation, similar to that previously described by Nias (1989). Whilst this feeling cannot be generalised as an aim for all practitioners, the SPs interviewed regarded it in positive terms and as an achievement that social pedagogy had helped them attain, leading to a higher sense of satisfaction in their professional roles.

These discussions suggest that deep personal and professional fulfilment can be gained by identifying as a social pedagogue. Before doing so, however, it is important to gain an understanding of social pedagogy and decide whether your values align with it. In addition to the benefits described above, as authors we have found other benefits through interacting with like-minded individuals. One benefit is the sense of community to be found with other SPs – built upon an acceptance of the language used to legitimise a practice that puts CYPs' needs at the heart of conversations, the language of social change and the language of authenticity.

Like the SPs in this chapter, you may discover that enacting the values of a social pedagogue is less of a choice and more of a necessity, as they speak to who you are. As you learn more about the approach and its core principles, you may begin to feel that you now have a label to define how you want to work. However, be prepared for the challenges you may face from others, including: a lack of understanding of social pedagogy; a fear that focusing on its key principles may distract from academic attainment; and even direct opposition if your setting's values do not align with yours. Please be encouraged to be brave, to learn more and start connecting with other SPs with whom you can build a network of support, as the rewards of this approach far outweigh the challenges.

Summary of key points

- Many professionals may be unknowingly acting out the values of social pedagogy without awareness of the term.
- Adopting the label *social pedagogue* (SP) enables some practitioners to feel empowered or validated.
- Identifying and prioritising their own professional values allowed the SPs to feel more authentic in their professional lives.
- SPs advocate for CYP and champion their holistic development.
- A social pedagogical approach can challenge traditional hierarchies and be difficult for some.
- Making strong relationships central to your professional life can bring increased joy and satisfaction.
- SPs feel stronger through being part of a like-minded community.

Recommended reading

Moss, P. and Petrie, P. (2019) Education and social pedagogy: What relationship? *London Review of Education*, 17(3), pp. 393–405. https://doi.org/10.18546/LRE.17.3.13

Storo, J. (2013) *Practical Social Pedagogy, Theories Values and Tools for Working with Children and Young People*. Bristol: The Policy Press.

References

Berridge, D., Biehal, N., Lutman, E., Henry, L. and Palomares, M. (2011) *Raising the Bar? Evaluation of the Social Pedagogy Pilot Programme in Residential Children's Homes. Research Report DFE-RR148*. https://assets.publishing.service.gov.uk/media/5a7561fced915d6faf2b28f2/DFE-RR148.pdf (Accessed 7 November 2024).

Bronfenbrenner, U. and Morris, P. A. (1998) The Bioecological Model of Human Development. In R. M. Lerner (Ed.) *Handbook of Child Psychology*. Hoboken, NJ: Wiley and Sons, pp.793–825

Clarke, M., Michell, M. and Ellis, N. J. (2016) Dialectics of development: Teacher identity formation in the interplay of ideal ego and ego ideal. *Teaching Education*, 28(2), pp. 115–130. https://doi.org/10.1080/10476210.2016.1211631

Day, C., Elliot, B. and Kington, A. (2005) Reform, standards and teacher identity: Challenges of sustaining commitment. *Teaching and Teacher Education*, 21(5), pp. 563–577. https://doi.org/10.1016/j.tate.2005.03.001

DfE (2023) School Workforce Census, Online https://explore-education-statistics.service.gov.uk/find-statistics/school-workforce-in-england/2023 (accessed 27.5.25)

Eichsteller, G. and Holthoff, S. (2011) Conceptual Foundations of Social Pedagogy: A Transnational Perspective from Germany. In C. Cameron and P. Moss (Eds) *Social Pedagogy and Working with Children*. London: Jessica Kingsley Publishers, pp. 35–52.

Horn, J. (2010) Corporatism, KIPP, and Cultural Eugenics. In P. E. Kovacs (Ed.) *The Gates Foundation and the Future of US Public Schools*. Oxford: Taylor & Francis Group, pp. 79–103.

Kelchtermans, G. (2017) 'Should I stay or should I go?': Unpacking teacher attrition/retention as an educational issue. *Teachers and Teaching*, 23(8), pp. 961–977. https://doi.org/10.1080/13540602.2017.1379793

Kreber, C. (2013) *Authenticity in and Through Teaching in Higher Education: The Transformative Potential of the Scholarship of Teaching*. Abingdon: Routledge.

Kuczynski, L., Pitman, R. and Twigger, K. (2018) Flirting with resistance: Children's expressions of autonomy during middle childhood. *International Journal of Qualitative Studies on Health and Well-being*, 13(1), pp. 1564519-11. https://doi.org/10.1080/17482631.2018.1564519

Lack, B. (2009) No excuses: A critique of the knowledge is power programme (KIPP) within charter schools in the USA. *Journal for Critical Education Policy Study*, 7(2), pp. 126–153.

Monro, E. (2011) *The Munro Review of Child Protection: Interim Report: The Child's Journey*. https://assets.publishing.service.gov.uk/government/uploads/system/uploads/attachment_data/file/624946/DFE-00010-2011.pdf (Accessed 21 January 2025).

Nias, J. (1989) *Primary Teachers Talking: A Study of Teaching as Work*. Abingdon: Routledge.

Page, J. (2018) Characterising the principles of Professional Love in early childhood care and education. *International Journal of Early Years Education*, 26(2), pp. 125–141, https://doi.org/10.1080/09669760.2018.1459508

Roosevelt, T. (1910) *American Ideals in Education* [Speech]. https://obamawhitehouse.archives.gov/blog/2011/12/06/archiveS-president-teddy-roosevelts-new-nationalism-speech (Accessed 4 November).

Solvason, C., Webb, R. and Sutton-Tsang, S. (2021) What is left…? The implications of losing maintained nursery schools for vulnerable children and families in England. *Children and Society*, 35(1), pp. 75–89.

3 Creating a nurturing environment in early childhood education and care, with a focus upon relationships, awe and wonder

Johanna Cliffe

Introduction: the importance and power of relationships

Focusing on relationships and connections is arguably the most important aspect of ECEC, or, one might argue, education as a whole. When relationships are the cornerstone of ECEC practice it supports our youngest children to feel seen, heard and accepted. And in doing so it provides the blueprint for how children should see, hear and accept themselves, others and the world around them. It sows the seeds for nurturing on every level, while additionally supporting young children's innate curiosity, awe and wonder for life and everything in it (Clark, 2023). However, even more than that, relationship and connection-focused pedagogy facilitates ethical encounters that serve, *each and every time*, as teachable moments for children in actively caring for, and learning how to take responsibility for, themselves, other people and the planet.

Noddings (2013) notes this kind of relational pedagogy functions like a caring apprenticeship, where children observe and practise, building on their sociability and social competences via their experiences. Through this they learn how to function as the *cared for* and *the one caring*. Noddings (2013, p. 122) notes that 'training for receptivity involves sharing and reflecting aloud. It involves the kind of close contact that makes personal history valuable…a relationship is required'. Without these shared foundations with familiar people in active relationships to support more positive life affirming connections, there may not be a point from which children can reflect back on and draw forward and apply in the present. Alternatively, the experience that may exist might be one of deficit and lack, uncaring and isolating, with no competent model to emulate stronger and more positive reference points for future endeavours and encounters.

> **Reflection point**
>
> Reflect on the concept of caring apprenticeships. What do you feel they may add to ECEC provision? Do you feel you are supported in your practice? Why?

Rosa (2020) discusses in detail that babies are born to connect from the moment they take their first breath; that, in fact, from the moment of conception they are already part of a complex relational web. He goes on to suggest the orientation, design and functionality of every part of the body, including our senses, is entirely geared towards mediating the relational world. Essentially, he concludes, humans are geared to be sociable and to interact. This is somewhat reminiscent of the thoughts expressed by Trevarthen (2005) and Narvaez (2014) who argued that a biological drive to connect is not merely about an individual's quest for knowledge, but that it also encompasses a drive to share experiences with others. This suggests that survival requires more than just curiosity about the world, or getting deficiency needs met, but that relationships, building a life with meaning and purpose and sharing this with significant others, is also intrinsic to our wellbeing. Trevarthen (2005) and Narvaez (2014) argue that this is exemplified in the concept of companionship attachment. This concept builds on Bowlby's (1988) notions of secure attachment, by considering the wider implications of a rich sense of belonging, within family, community and culture, through relational encounters that include human and more-than-human relationships.

Children do not develop in a vacuum and families do not function in isolation; human beings are constantly in relationship with something or someone. Bronfenbrenner's (1974) bioecological theory unpins the spheres of influence that make up the entirety of a child's (and family's) collaborative and relational worlds. The bioecological model depicts clearly how children *impact* and are *impacted by* the micro aspects of immediate experiences, through to the direct and indirect sociocultural implications of wider community and life, to finally the macro and chrono constraints of policy, society, time, place and space. Essentially, this serves as a reminder that all individuals are the sum of their parts and of the relationships and connections that are afforded *to* and *with* them by their experiences and environments around them. Thoughts, feelings, learning, development and behaviour are all shaped by the complexities of life and by the relational encounters that individuals 'affect' and the ones they are 'affected' by. Therefore, accepting that relationships and connections are fundamental to who and what we are and what we do as individuals and collectively, as a society, makes coherent sense. (Re)imagining ECEC education through a social pedagogic lens, honours present-child, living in the moment, with their interests and needs paramount (Hayes and Filipović, 2018). The power and richness of 'in the moment' interactions affords early childhood practitioners (ECPs) opportunities to explore with children how to be in relationships and eventually leads to how to effectively live within communities.

> **Reflection point**
>
> Consider you own bioecological model, how have you been shaped by your own experiences? What can you learn from this about the children and families in your care?

Within ECEC there is a tacit understanding of the power of relational pedagogy which is tenaciously upheld by ECPs at grassroots level. Yet, despite this, and the growing evidence of the crucial role relationships and connections play in children's learning, development and social and emotional wellbeing, it is not prioritised at policy level. Moss and Cameron (2020) and Cliffe and Solvason (2023) argue persuasively that ECEC educative policy and dominant sector discourse, actively marginalise, or largely ignore the importance of connections, relationships and social pedagogy.

As ECEC becomes increasingly homogenised, the pressures of more neoliberal priorities are brought to bear in curricula provision. Future-focused, outcomes-driven practice directs the focus of ECEC practice away from relational focused pedagogy, towards a more academic and cognitive skills-based pedagogy, prioritising intellectual capacities over social competences. Robert-Holmes

(2020, p. 235) describes this version of ECEC as merely a 'school readiness factory' which has the very real potential to lose sight of the complex and relational child, in favour of neoliberal and outcomes-driven top-down 'schoolification' (Moss and Cameron, 2020). This polarised tension within ECEC demonstrates a lack of understanding for how fundamental the underpinning values of social pedagogy are to supporting and facilitating all other areas of children's learning and development.

However, while it could be argued that social pedagogy is a more socially just resistance to future-focused and outcomes-driven policies and practices, this is not all that it is, and not all that it should be. Martin (2007, cited in Taylor and Giugni, 2012) suggests that deeper considerations of relational pedagogy include far more than just the relationships engendered with other people; it focuses also on those that are created with that which is more-than-human. From the common world perspectives, relationship barriers between environments and species are more flexible and encompass 'people, plants, animals, waterways, climate, land and skies' (p. 116). In his recent work, Mcphie (2019) argues that mental health and wellbeing have an ecological aspect; essentially mental health (even physical health) and environmental health are inextricably linked. He goes on to state that there is an unhelpful division, a bifurcation, promoted between humans, nature and environments, even within anthropocentric perspectives, which may be adversely impacting on health and wellbeing. We are nature and, according to Mcphie (2019, p. 28), 'humans and other-than-humans have the same ontological status', therefore, the health of both is mutually intertwined.

By ensuring that children have a deeper awareness of their connection to nature we are cultivating the health and future of both. When considered in conjunction with Noddings' (2013) notions of caring apprenticeships, acknowledging wider notions of connections and relationships in ECEC that span all relational encounters, would provide the blueprint needed to facilitate future caring adults with the capability and capacity to take responsibility for others in all its forms, including themselves the planet and everything in it.

Why it matters now

Cliffe and Solvason (2023) discuss how, despite living in a world that is potentially more connected than ever before due to technological advancements, there is a worrying decline in sociability and social competence, a decline which was further compounded by lockdowns and the social isolation that arose from COVID-19. Even before the pandemic, Narvaez (2014) noted that from a phylogenetic perspective (that considers human diversification and relational evolution) humanity, as a whole, appeared *off track*. She goes on to argue that, despite being hard-wired to seek out reciprocal relational encounters, human beings are increasingly less socially and emotionally competent, with mental health concerns and depression in young people increasing as a result. While the wellbeing picture is less clear within the field of ECEC (Cliffe and Solvason, 2023), the importance of social and relational pedagogic approaches to ECEC appear obvious to anyone with any experience in the field. Yet, as previously stated they are often marginalised or overlooked.

Moore (1993, p. 28) points out that the inability to adjust to life and the challenges that living in relational worlds brings may be the result of not 'attending to the soul'. Moore implies that 'soul' is not necessarily a religious concept but one that aligns more closely with the 'spirit of family' (p. 28). He argues that without listening to, valuing and honouring our innermost needs and the innermost needs of others, we cannot effectively care for the soul. While it is not clear from Moore whether the spirit of family relates only to relational encounters between humans, he does argue for a deeper spiritual awareness that represents a connection with something 'bigger than ourselves'. If we accept the notions of Mcphie (2019) regarding our status as inherently part of nature, and the lifeworld view articulated by Martin (2007, cited in Taylor and Giugni, 2012), it is more than conceivable that attending to the soul through the spirit of family might incorporate an interconnection with all life and the Earth. Therefore, without understanding and prioritising the importance of connections and relationships with all life, it becomes impossible for the needs of self, community and planet to be met. With the deterioration of social competencies, the spiralling concerns regarding mental health and wellbeing and the consumptionist approach to the planet and her resources, humans, as well as the planet, are in decline. A (re)focusing on relationships, of 'caring for the soul' through a wider view of the spirit of family, alongside Noddings' (2013) understanding of caring apprenticeships, may provide the only hope within our current challenges.

> **Reflection point**
>
> Consider how you might facilitate children and their families in your professional contexts to 'care for the soul'. What might this look like?

However, relationships do not come without conflict: this is an integral aspect of living collaboratively and in relationship with self, others and the world. Noddings' (2013) notion of caring apprenticeships demonstrates how new and unexpected events, both present and future, can be navigated, and that includes the acceptance that on occasion life requires the possibility of us having to live in conflict or discomfort. Our media and social media demonstrate the propensity for more judgement and less tolerance within our cultures. Moore (1993, p. 29) observes that inadequate attention to the soul has resulted in individuals being less able to view life experiences with 'critical discernment' leading to a 'blind faith' that permeates beliefs, values and actions. Unchecked, we witness this leading to acceptance of socially unjust behaviours in a whole host of relational (and political) arenas without thought or question; a reality that exacerbates social injustice, discriminatory and silencing practices of self or others. Therefore, a greater capacity for acceptance, respect and tolerance needs to be considered when educating young children if we are to have any hope for a more respectful and nurturing society.

While sustainability and the implications of global warming are contentiously debated politically and globally, the urgency to act for mutual survival for all is becoming more pressing (Intergovernmental Panel on Climate Change, 2018). The implications of the era of Anthropocene are gaining more traction in research, and emerging alongside the notion of eco-cultural literacy within ECEC (Ritchie, 2017). While this encourages an approach to education that facilitates young children's empathy for the planet and more-than-human kin, as identified by Ritchie (2017), and in the analysis of current research presented by Bjerknes, Wilhelmsen and Foyn-Bruun (2023), Mcphie (2019) argues that the Anthropocene supports an unhealthy and unhelpful division between humans and nature. Mcphie (2019) suggests that despite *being* nature, humans are subjected to a continued psychological disconnection from nature at micro and macro levels and from human-centric approaches to the world. This will inevitably cause a potential rupture that destabilises the self and has implications for what it is to be human. He continues that the damage being inflicted on the planet (ecocide), will lead to a corresponding self-sabotaging implication for every individual's mental health and wellbeing (Mcphie, 2019). With both planetary survival and human flourishing at risk, there is no longer the option of inaction: a sobering thought. It is not overreaching to assume that without adequate nurturing of relationships in ECEC, relationships that bridge human and more-than-human caring connections and encounters, the future on every level looks uncertain.

Considering the in-between

When considering relationships and connections, it is important to focus more on what may be occurring in the spaces in-between, the points of connection between an individual and something or someone else. DeleuzioGuattarian philosophy can support ECPs in this by drawing on concepts and principles that facilitate this process. Deleuze and Guattari (1987) refer to the concepts and/or figurations of rhizomes, assemblage and nomad as conceptual frameworks to consider not only the importance of relational encounters, but also the very nature of exactly what 'goes on' within the in-between spaces of relational connections. Essentially, they maintain that life is made up of a series of constantly (re)evolving encounters that are generated by assemblages combining and converging together. Assemblages emerge from the collation of elements, often a range of heterogeneous and disparate elements, that make up the complexity of our lives and experiences. These elements come together, or territorialise, briefly before dispersing – (de)territorialising and (re)forming – (re)territorialising as something new in a continuously changing cycle.

Each individual might be considered their own assemblage as well being considered part of the assemblages that make up each relational encounter. A rhizomatic lens considers the implications of these encounters and connections, in a way that respects many layers of meaning inside assemblages and in the way they interact and converge. A rhizomatic approach focusses on how something works, what else might be occurring, engaging with and employing the conjunction 'and…and…and' (Deleuze and Guattari, 1987) for multiplicity of meaning. By applying the Deleuze and Guattarian (1987) concept of the nomad, this affords ECPs with the freedom to follow the many pathways and directions that learning may take, in a bid to seek out new meanings, new territories and new lines of flight that often occur in or as a result of the in-between spaces.

Research presented by Sellers (2013) and Cliffe and Solvason (2023) suggests that children are inherently and by nature more rhizomatic and nomadic than adults, and this influences their approach to their interactions, learning, development and meaning making. They are constantly seeking out new experiences and weaving effortlessly between different fragments and encounters within their lives. As such, children are constantly creating diverse connections and traversing blurred relational boundaries in ways that (de/re)territorialise the world around them. Sellers (2013) noted that when traversing and (de/re)territorialising these shared spaces, children's connections may, on occasion, appear random and without sense or meaning to adult interpretations. However, when focus is placed on the nature of what is occurring in between their interactions a wonderfully rich and complex web of interaction unveils. Therefore, from a Deleuzio and Guattarian (1987) perspective, relational encounters provide opportunities for ECPs to find greater understanding for the way in which children relate and make sense of their world. Without a focus and awareness of the children's emerging connections, precious moments of awe, wonder and complexity may be missed or truncated, and the child then left feeling unheard, unseen or unknown. The importance of this is articulated more clearly when considered alongside understandings of the purpose of education.

> **Reflection point**
>
> Reflect on what you feel the purpose of education is. How might this influence your own professional practice?

Biesta (2012, p. 95) suggested that education was primarily about focusing on the relationship 'between child and world', where neither child nor world is of ultimate importance. Instead, the focus of quality education becomes synonymous with the quality of the encounters in the *space between the two*. Hayes and Filipović (2018, p. 225) articulate this well when they state 'it is the process of travelling the pathways rather than the destination' that should carry more weight within learning and education. This emphasises that the way that ECPs and children enjoy shared spaces, and their time with each other, rather than outcomes and end points, are not only cornerstones of ECEC but fundamentally *the purpose of* education. Therefore, in order to provide a rich nurturing environment in ECEC, the nature of connections, in-between spaces and co-created and negotiated meaning has to have a prominent role within provision. This links directly with the social pedagogical Diamond Model (Eichsteller and Holthoff, 2011) explored in the previous two chapters.

Again, echoing Eichsteller and Holthoff's (2011) Diamond Model, a US study by Ródriguez-Carrillo, Mérida-Serrano and González-Alfaya (2020) identified that for children aged four to six years, the key factor in their engagement was happiness. Children noted what made them happy was adults taking the time to get to know them, considering their interests, following their lead in play and listening and valuing their contributions and ideas within meaning-making processes. Essentially, the children valued the relationally responsive approach within learning encounters. The children were able to articulate that this supported their self-esteem and confidence in generating and exploring their own ideas, gaining a sense of agency and autonomy within their learning and development. Although they do not refer to it as such, it could be argued that Rodríguez-Carrillo *et al.* (2020) were adopting a social pedagogical approach to practice, placing the emphasis upon following the child's lead and collaborating and (re)negotiating sense and meaning in more purposeful ways.

The implications of this are clear and significant. While the current propensity within ECEC is to overly focus on academic activities that measure learning is occurring, a social pedagogical approach supports not only the looked-for outcomes and learning, but, more importantly, wellbeing and happiness. This relational approach is key to the Diamond Model (Eichsteller and Holthoff, 2011, see Chapter 2 for an illustration of this) which considers the interconnectedness of health and wellbeing, empowerment, relationships and holistic learning. Through a social pedagogical lens, ECPs acknowledge the fundamental premise that all children (indeed, all individuals) have within them all that they need to shine and thrive. In order to nurture this rich potential and facilitate experiences that promote long-lasting positive outcomes and long-term wellbeing, ECPs need to consider encounters more holistically, with an eye to the benefits now (for example happiness) but also for developing a lasting blueprint for long-term sustainable individual and collective wellbeing.

The notion that social pedagogy promotes happiness and wellbeing resonates with Csíkszentmihályi's (2014) notions of flow. Flow is where individuals immerse themselves in experiences that are the right level of interest and challenge, which creates a state of optimum happiness that is vital for wellbeing. Csíkszentmihályi (2014, p. 72) draws on the work of Aristotle when stating happiness as 'the virtuous work of the soul', a thought that lends itself to Moore's (1993) notion of environments that care for the soul and the spirit of family. Social pedagogical concepts such as flow, and the Diamond Model, demonstrate the profound impact of happiness and wellbeing, and the importance of engaging with activities that promote these experiences, for children's present and future learning and development.

Similarly, Clark (2023) considers the power and purpose of what she terms 'slow pedagogy' and the concept of the 'unhurried child'. Clark observes that it is vital that ECPs take the time to be 'in the moment' in their relationships with children, working as co-creators at the pace that is right for each individual encounter if rich learning is to occur. Clark states that individually and collectively society is moving ever faster and demanding increasingly more in a bid to continue to maintain position and power, both individually and collectively, in the globalised world. Rosa (2020) notes that the drive to compete in this way is interwoven with notions of social capital and an almost insatiable need to increase what we have at every level. This is being born out in ECEC, as, indeed, in education as a whole, in the fixation on ever-changing learning, development and outcome goals. The results of success today becoming merely the benchmarks to improve on tomorrow, in a constant striving for better, for the next goal, rather than being mindful of the richness of the now. Clark (2023, p. 5) articulates this clearly when stating 'not only do we find a desire to put as much world as possible into the child or student. We also find a desire to do this as quickly and cheaply as possible'. This not only diminishes the potential and possibility within each encounter, but leads ECPs towards didactic teaching strategies and dogmatic approaches to the child's development (Deleuze, 1994).

The moments of awe and wonder that might inspire children's curiosity and their creative and innovative thinking, can be lost in a bid to fulfil learning objectives and teach for tests or assessments. Clark (2023) offers 'slow pedagogy' as a way to (re)focus on relationships and connections and to work towards what Robert-Holmes (2020, p. 245) refers to as a 'rich child, rich ECP' vision for ECEC. This is a vision where both child and ECP express themselves in a hundred different languages and are mutually active and honoured as co-creators of knowledge, always in relation to, and with, each other and their environment. This understanding is one that many will recognise within the philosophy of Malaguzzi and the founding principles underpinning Reggio Emilia. In an acknowledgement of a pedagogy of listening and relationships, Rinaldi (2006, p. 113) stated that 'children are the most avid seekers of meaning and significance', and it is through this relational creativity that children are curious, inspired by and make sense of their word.

From a rhizomatic perspective, there is an openness within these approaches to ECEC, to consider many different pathways or changes of direction that might emerge within the learning process, as new connections within the assemblage are considered and a process of (de/re)territorialising or 'and…and…and' occurs (Deleuze and Guattari,1987). Drawing on a rhizomatic philosophy and applying the concept of the nomad, ECPs can nomadically follow the child's lead with more fluidity and an acceptance of taking whatever time (fast or slow) is appropriate for the moment. This allows children to experience learning as a *child* rather than as *an adult in waiting*, promoting a 'timelessness' within the learning process that allows both parties to 'wallow' in experiences (Clark, 2023), to be in 'flow' (Csíkszentmihályi, 2014) for optimum happiness and wellbeing. Learning that follows these ideals opens up the potential for new, for difference and possibility to emerge, promoting space for happiness and a sense of 'unity and interconnectedness' (Clark, 2023, p. 30). Clark's (2023, p. 30) notions on ECEC practice stem strongly from a connection and relationship focus, which is epitomised in a simple but powerful question 'what would learning look like if the relationships were visible?'

The role of curiosity, awe and wonder

There is an acknowledgement in ECEC of children's biological drive to explore their world, to draw sense and meaning form their experiences, which is often seen as the fundamental premise of learning and, therefore, education. However, this is primarily driven by Piagetian and Vygotskian notions of constructivist pedagogy which is promoted almost entirely through cognitive development and sustained shared thinking, or metacognitive approaches to practice. L'Ecuyer (2014) suggests that from more recent neurobiological understandings there is an acceptance that the traditional approach to supporting children developing knowledge and sense and meaning in education may, in fact, be stifling the development of wonder. While curiosity aligns strongly with notions of inquisitiveness, developing cognitive awareness and knowledge, it is wonder that supports a deeper ability to draw *meaning* from experiences.

L'Ecuyer (2014), Schinkel (2019) and Bjerknes *et al.* (2023) all argue that curiosity drives inquisitiveness to find out and increase knowledge; it facilitates the process of breaking things down into component parts to deepen understanding. In this way it supports the normative approach to learning and education, the striving for even more knowledge, which eventually leads to more social capital. Rosa (2020) and Clark (2023) suggest that the escalation of the need for knowledge is indicative of the accelerated nature of the current climate. However, Bjerknes *et al.* (2023) argue that academic achievement can inhibit wonder, as children shift their own focus from the enjoyment of their initial intrigue and explorations, to responding to the outcomes-driven external motivations of future-focused curricula. Curiosity, therefore, may unintentionally begin the search for a right answer, a definite end point, rather than exploring new, innovative and uncharted territories.

Wonder, and ultimately awe, enable deeper contemplation, with the former considering the search for meaning, and the latter accepting that some experiences can and should retain a sense of mystery outside of ourselves. L'Ecuyer (2014) considers that it is wonder that drives us to question and explore something again and again, making even the familiar appear strange. Schinkel (2019, p. 307) adeptly articulates the power and importance of this in the following:

> Wonder essentially entails an openness to the world, and this makes it educationally important, since to open up the world — allowing us to perceive more, understand more, appreciate more, and act and move about in it more competently — is (arguably) what education is ultimately about.

Wonder respects the whole child in a rather Pestalozzian approach of head, heart and hands (cited in Sellers and Imig, 2021), allowing children to engage with emotional aspects of learning that can be overlooked in more traditional approaches to cognitive development, but which do play a significant role in developing new knowledge (Cliffe and Solvason, 2023). Wonder is more than just the ability to find answers to questions: it provides opportunity for both children and ECPs to explore otherness, diversity and difference in the world around them (L'Ecuyer, 2014; Schinkel, 2019; Bjerknes *et al.*, 2023). In this way wonder and awe acknowledge and accept that answers may not always be possible and are almost never the complete story. They require us being open to the ways in which children wonder *at* and wonder *about* or wonder *how*, echoes the slow pedagogic approach described previously by Clark (2023), with the ability to wallow in experiences to their fullest possibility and potential. This inspires innovative and creative thinking, where thinking that has never been thought before is nurtured.

From a Deluezio and Guattarian (1987) perspective, supporting children to continue their wondering journeys, to critically explore what else might exist, how it might work, and…and… and in everyday situations, facilitates children's development of wonder and allows space for awe. A rhizomatic approach acknowledges that there are multiple pathways to sense and meaning, that each engagement engenders lines of flight within the rhizome with no ends or beginnings, just multiple entries and exits and points of intensity that generate a pause, a moment to stop and contemplate more deeply. Such an approach accepts that something can be pondered just for the sake of pondering, and this too is a rich learning experience.

> **Reflection point**
>
> Do you make time for wonder in your own life? What does this look and feel like? What impact does it have on you?

Rhizomes not only provide more fluid and flexible approaches to the process of learning and development, they also naturally facilitate wonder in ways that acknowledge how different assemblages function independently and together. The concept of assemblages lends itself to experiences of wonder as the self is often decentred, but not discounted, in the implications of the encounter (Deleuze and Guattari, 1987). Wonder focuses on the process of deep contemplation, supporting the desire to look and look again, rather than merely seeking the answers which, when found, encourage the seeker to move on. In assemblages everything has both equal value and importance, therefore, the focus shifts to reflect on what occurs *within* the connections and in-between spaces.

Concluding thoughts

Allowing time for children to fully wonder for its own sake stops children from feeling the need to dismiss the breadth of potentiality and instead direct their energies towards a definite, recognised, end point. It allows children to dig deeper and explore difference and diversity, to make different versions of sense, to (de/re)territorialise new terrains that have been, as yet, unseen. Nomadically following children on these journeys to sense and meaning avoids more fixed positions in relation to ECEC curricula and opens up learning to possibilities for new and different. In this way awe and wonder provide opportunities for ECPs and children to consider the as yet unthought, the different, the remarkable, in a way that is empowering for both.

Essentially, when considered through an awareness of multiplicity, curiosity, awe and wonder need to be allowed to function together to inspire children (and ECPs) to consider the world differently. An ability to grapple with difference, to be able to contemplate problems and issues deeply, and to decentre human-centric approaches that support more consumptionist, neoliberal priorities, will enable both our children now, and their future selves, to successfully navigate the challenges of the Anthropocene.

This chapter has argued for the (re)positioning of connections, relationships wonder and awe within ECEC. In line with the social pedagogical concepts of the Diamond Model and Flow, this (re)positioning could enable a more rich and nurturing environment for young children which not only facilitates their learning, but is also crucial in supporting their physical, mental and emotional wellbeing. While this does offer resistance to the current prevalence for academically driven practice, the benefits of a social pedagogic approach is so much more than this. Reconceptualising ECEC in this way can provide a strong foundation from which children can confidently and competently fulfil their biological and social drives to explore their worlds and draw purposeful meaning from these encounters.

Summary points

- Building strong relationships and making connections is one of the most important aspects when we support the development of young children. Allowing children to build a life with meaning and purpose in companionship with significant others, human and other-than-human, is intrinsic to wellbeing and human flourishing.
- Developing caring apprenticeships fosters authentic relationships with self, others and the planet. Children develop deep understandings for how to function as the *cared for* and *the one caring*.
- Drawing on the notions of multiplicity, curiosity, awe and wonder reconceptualises opportunities within ECEC and allows ECPs and children to see and experience the world differently, in ways that are more socially just and equitable for self, others and the world.
- Being open to the ways in which children wonder *at*, wonder *about* or wonder *how*, promotes a slow pedagogic approach, were ECPs listen with all of the senses and act as role models to support children's learning and development both now and in the future.

Recommended reading

Ellyatt, W. (2020) *The ecology of wellbeing: Introducing the flourish model*. Available at www.flourishproject.net/uploads/1/8/4/9/1849450/introducing_the_flourish_model__optimized_.pdf (Accessed 4 February 2025).

L'Ecuyer, C. (2014) The wonder approach to learning. *Hypothesis and Theory Article*, 8(764), pp. 1–8. Available at https://doi.org/10.3389/fnhum.2014.00764 (Accessed 4 February 2025).

Unicef (nd) *What make me? Core capacities for living and learning*. Available at www.unicef.org/innocenti/reports/what-makes-me (Accessed 4 February 2025).

References

Biesta, G. (2012) The educational significance of the experience of resistance: Schooling and the dialogue between child and world. *Other Education: The Journal of Educational Alternatives*, 1(1), pp. 92–103.

Bjerknes, A., Wilhelmsen, T. and Foyn-Bruun, E (2023) A systematic review of curiosity and wonder in natural science and early childhood education research. *Journal of Research in Childhood Education*. https://doi.org/10.1080/02568543.2023.2192249

Bowlby, J. (1988) *A Secure Base: Clinical Applications of Attachment Theory*. Abingdon: Routledge.

Bronfenbrenner, U. (1974) Developmental research, public policy, and the ecology of childhood. *Child Development*, 45(1), pp. 1–5.

Clark, A. (2023) *Slow Knowledge and the Unhurried Child: Time for Flow Pedagogy in Early Childhood Education.* Abingdon: Routledge.

Cliffe, J. and Solvason, C. (2023) What is it that we still don't get? – Relational pedagogy and why relationships and connections matter in early childhood. *Power and Education*, 15(3), pp. 1–15.

Csíkszentmihályi, M. (2014) *Flow and the Foundations of Positive Psychology: The Collected Works of Mihaly.* Berlin: Springer.

Deleuze, G. (1994) reprinted (2014) *Difference and Repetition.* 2nd ed. London: Bloomsbury.

Deleuze, G. and Guattari, F. (1987) reprinted (2013) *A Thousand Plateaus.* London: Bloomsbury.

Eichsteller, G. and Holthoff, S. (2011) Conceptual foundations of social pedagogy: A transnational perspective from Germany. In C. Cameron and P. Moss (Eds) *Social Pedagogy and Working with Children and Young People Where Care and Education Meet.* London: Jessica Kingsley Publishers, pp. 33–52.

Hayes, N. and Filipović, K. (2018) Nurturing 'buds of development': From outcomes to opportunities in early childhood practice. *International Journal of Early Years Education*, 26(3), pp. 220–232.

Intergovernmental Panel on Climate Change (2018) *Global warming of 1.5°C.* Available at: www.ipcc.ch/sr15/ (Accessed 26 September 2023).

L'Ecuyer, C. (2014) The wonder approach to learning. *Hypothesis and Theory Article*, 8(764), pp. 1–8. Available at https://doi.org/10.3389/fnhum.2014.00764 (Accessed 4 February 2025).

Mcphie, J. (2019) *Mental Health and Wellbeing in the Anthropocene.* Singapore: Palgrave Macmillan.

Moore, T. (1993) Care of the soul: The benefits – and costs – of a more spiritual life. *Psychology Today*, 26(3), pp. 28–29.

Moss, P. and Cameron, C. (2020) *Transforming Early Childhood in England: Towards a Democratic Education.* London: University College Press.

Narvaez, D. (2014) *Neurobiology and the Development of Human Morality.* New York: Norton and Company.

Noddings, N. (2013) *Caring: A Relational Approach to Ethics and Moral Education.* London: University of California Press.

Rinaldi, C. (2006) *In Dialogue with Reggio Emilia: Listening, Researching and Learning.* Abingdon: Routledge.

Ritchie, J. (2017) Fostering eco-cultural literacies for social, cultural and ecological justice: A perspective from Aotearoa (New Zealand). *International Journal of Early Childhood*, 49, pp. 287–302.

Robert-Holmes, G. (2020) Towards a pluralist and participatory accountability. In P. Moss and C. Cameron (Eds) *Transforming Early Childhood in England: Towards a Democratic Education.* London: University College Press, pp. 170–187.

Rodríguez-Carrillo, J., Mérida-Serrano, R. and González-Alfaya, M.E. (2020) A teacher's hug can make you feel better: Listening to U.S. children's voices on high quality early childhood teaching. *European Early Childhood Education Research Journal*, 28(4), pp. 504–518. https://doi.org/10.1080/1350293X.2020.1783925.

Rosa, H. (2020) *The Uncontrollability of the World.* Cambridge: Polity Press.

Schinkel, A. (2019) Wonder, mystery, and meaning. *Philosophical Papers*, 48(2), pp. 293–319. https://doi.org/10.1080/05568641.2018.1462667.

Sellers, M. (2013) *Young Children Becoming Curriculum: Deleuze, Te Wh_ariki and curricular understandings (Contesting Early Childhood).* Abingdon: Routledge.

Sellers, M. and Imig, D. (2021) Pestalozzi and pedagogies of love: Pathways to educational reform. *Early Child Development and Care*, 191(7–8), pp. 1152–1163. https://doi.org/10.1080/03004430.2020.1845667.

Taylor, A. and Giugni, M. (2012) Common worlds: Reconceptualising inclusion in early childhood communities. *Contemporary Issues in Early Childhood*, 13(2), pp. 108–119.

Trevarthen, C. (2005) Stepping away from the mirror: Pride and shame in adventures of companionship. In: C.S. Carter, L. Ahnert, K.E. Grossmann, S.B. Hrdy, M.E. Lamb, S.W. Porges and N. Sachser (Eds) *Attachment and Bonding: A New Synthesis.* 1st edn. London: MIT Press, pp. 55–84.

4 Adopting social pedagogical values to support children with SEND

Sue Baylis

Introduction

As humans, we have needs that are special and unique to us, and we crave to have those needs met. Neurotypically developing humans communicate their needs in a wide range of ways. However, when working with children and young people (CYP) who are neurodivergent, or atypical, it can be a challenge to fully understand their needs, regardless of the severity of them. Difficulty frequently arises when the young person struggles to express those needs or to accept the support offered to meet them. As a result, they frequently feel disempowered.

Practitioners and researchers often speak about 'empowering children', but as Charfe and Gardner (2019, p.13) remind us, 'empowerment is not ours to give'. When considering relationships through a social pedagogical lens, equality and mutuality are fundamental. Charfe and Gardner (2019) remind us that it is essential to maintain a balanced distribution of power within these relationships. There is a need to walk *alongside* those we work with, providing resources and support to enable individuals to act for themselves, to develop their own strength. Rather than 'doing for' the child, we work with them in partnership to identify what their needs are and to consider ways that *they* might address them.

Identifying exactly what is meant by 'need' is rarely considered within daily life in the Western World. However, we all have needs that require attention; they contribute to our very existence. Wearmouth (2017) explains that 'need' refers to a situation where something essential is required to achieve a desired goal. She continues to highlight that needs can vary widely, from basic life necessities to preferences in music and social interactions, differing across cultures, locations and age groups due to societal norms. Based on my work with children, I would add that a child's needs, and the variety of those needs, can differ significantly depending on the severity of their SEND and the challenges these create. What is important to remember, however, is that there is always something the child can do for themselves. We, as practitioners, are not always aware of this, and we need to collaborate with the child to set small but achievable tasks for them so that they can achieve a sense of fulfilment. It would be hugely challenging if we had to climb to the top of a long ladder with enormous spaces between each rung. If, however, there are small spaces, the ascent to the top is more achievable, given the right support. Finding the right spacing between the rungs of the ladder is a challenge, but it should be at the forefront of our minds as we develop meaningful opportunities for progression and learning.

It is important to remember that this does not happen only in schools, learning needs must be considered across the whole of a child's life experiences. This aligns with Petrie's (2020) assertion

DOI: 10.4324/9781003533276-4

that social pedagogy seeks to promote education in the broadest sense, reaching beyond traditional classroom environments. She goes on to highlight that learning happens whenever the social pedagogue interacts with the child, whether during leisure activities or other non-classroom settings. Because of this I focus on both within school and outside school contexts below. Petrie (2020) emphasises the need for us to *walk alongside* the individual we are working with, to provide them with learning opportunities in an environment that is of interest to them; it is important, therefore, that we understand what that might look like.

Relationships with CYP within the classroom

Social pedagogues supporting children with a specific learning need regard adopting a creative approach almost as a moral obligation. When working in Ofsted registered settings it is also necessary to consider Government policy requirements, including the Children and Family Act 2014. In Section 20 (*no page*) of this document, it explains what the parameters of a child with SEND are, stating that '(1) A child or young person has special educational needs if he or she has a learning difficulty or disability which calls for special educational provision to be made for him or her'. It also goes on to explain that a CYP has 'a learning difficulty or disability if he or she—(a) has a significantly greater difficulty in learning than the majority of others of the same age, or (b) has a disability which prevents or hinders him or her from making use of facilities of a kind generally provided for others of the same age'. When considering the 'facilities' that a child with SEN might need, practitioners in educational settings must also consider the requirements of the Special Educational Needs and Disability Code of Practice (DfE, 2015).

The SEND Code of Practice (DfE/DoH, 2015) states that special educational provision should align with the child's identified special educational needs. The needs are divided into four broad categories: (i) communication and interaction; (ii) cognition and learning; (iii) social, emotional and mental health; and (iv) sensory and/or physical needs. The DfE (2015) acknowledges that individual children often have needs that span multiple areas, and that needs may evolve over time. What is important is that we do not mistake a need in one area for total incapacity. For example, speech, language and communication needs can be present in various SEN categories, but it would be a mistake to assume that the child cannot communicate at all—they may just need a different approach. This draws attention to the need for special educational provision to be tailored to a child's specific strengths and needs, utilising evidence-based interventions. It is important to recognise that these needs can only be recognised and fully understood within a secure relationship. Knowing and understanding the needs of the individual child is another key factor in unlocking their capabilities.

When meeting the holistic needs of CYP it is important that we reflect on models of disability, as this can impact on the way we work with individuals, as well as how we interpret statutory guidance documents. Our '*Haltung*' can have an impact on both of these. Charfe and Gardner (2020) explain that *Haltung* is a German term that roughly translates as a person's mindset, or ethos. It forms the foundation of one's moral compass and guides us through life, shaping our perceptions and values. While we often discuss the values and beliefs that underpin our practice, *Haltung* goes a step further, recognising that these values are embedded in our very being. Eichsteller (2010, no page) emphasises that 'Haltung is like a skin, not a jacket'; you can remove a jacket, but your skin remains an integral part of you, just as Haltung should'. We need to be mindful of our own values and beliefs (or *Haltung*) and the impact this could have on the CYP that we work with.

Zaks (2023) suggests that when considering a child's 'needs', some may (perhaps inadvertently) adopt a perspective that emphasises what is 'wrong' with the child and how to address the problem. This approach aligns with a medical model of disability, which implies that a child with SEND is inferior to the neurotypically developing child. Viewing needs in this way hinders a positive approach to meeting the unique needs of each child. (Although it is also important to acknowledge that there are occasions when a child has a medical condition that does need to be 'fixed'; for example, a positive relationship cannot 'solve' a diabetic child's need for insulin.)

The social pedagogical approach aligns more closely with the social model of disability, emphasising the significance of social inclusion and individual rights and wellbeing (Rothuizen and Harbo, 2017). For example, Goering (2015) identifies disability as a difference arising from the mismatch between an individual's needs and their social environment. When considering disability through this lens the focus is on how the environment creates barriers, making it difficult for individuals with specific needs to integrate into society; the deficit is not with the individual, but their surroundings.

Employing the social model of disability and creating a supportive learning environment for children with SEND demands professionals who are patient, caring, empathetic and understanding, regardless of the severity of a child's needs. It requires professionals who value the child's uniqueness, rather than categorising them by their needs, using terms like 'they are Downes' or 'they are ADHD'. It is crucial to recognise that every child, irrespective of their SEND needs, is an individual. While children with conditions such as Downes and ADHD may share certain traits, they are, first and foremost, unique individuals who can flourish when given the right opportunities to reach their full potential.

> **Reflection point**
>
> Consider your own values concerning the capability of CYP with disabilities.
> What beliefs shape your expectations when working with CYP with SEND?
>   Create a representation of your 'Haltung' and consider how you are going to express these values within your practice.

Eichsteller and Holthoff (2011, p. 33) highlight the need for us to provide a 'thriving garden for children which allows them to flourish and grow'. They use the analogy of offering 'a fertile environment' to ensure all are provided with the greatest opportunity to develop. This inclusive view emphasises the need for us, as professionals, to focus on the needs of the individual CYP we are working with to ensure our environment meets *their* needs and promotes their learning, wellbeing and confidence. Beazidou's (2023) work, relating to inclusive education, highlights that practitioners can create nurturing environments where children are *valued* because of their differences and feel comfortable participating in activities. Such a culture was found in Solvason *et al.*'s research (2020), when a nursery school leader discussed the opportunity that each child with unique needs provided for them, as practitioners, to expand their professional understanding. She specifically mentioned how much the adults working with him had learned, when they supported a child who was deaf and blind.

Relationships with CYP beyond the classroom

Such positive approaches to working with children with SEND equally relate to any environments *outside* of a formal learning context. Rothuizen and Harbo (2017) highlight the importance of social pedagogues fostering environments where they can engage in meaningful actions. As was mentioned at the start of this chapter, a social pedagogical approach to working with children with SEND enables us to take a more holistic and flexible approach to practice. To achieve this, practitioners need to recognise that successful practice begins by considering the individual needs of children within their daily lives. Eichsteller and Holthoff (2011) stress that valuing a child's 'life world orientation' relates to practitioners unconditionally valuing each child's life experiences and the context in which these occur. They also highlight that practitioners should show unconditional respect for the CYP, acknowledging the experiences that have shaped the CYP's identity, not merely their disability. Relationship-based practice, and taking a holistic approach, is at the heart of finding the unique key that unlocks the magic in the minds of individual children with SEND.

> **Reflection point**
>
> When you begin working with a CYP what approaches do you (or could you) take to finding out more about their lives, their interests, their strengths and their personal goals?

Pestalozzi, cited in Rothuizen and Harbo (2017), proposed that education involves three essential components: the head, heart and hands. The head pertains to acquiring knowledge, the heart to emotional engagement with that knowledge and the hands to applying what we've learned to take action. Social pedagogues excel in using these three dimensions—head, heart and hands—to create a dialogue between a child and their environment, thereby enhancing the child's comprehension of it. Furthermore, social pedagogues help create environments that encourage individuals to engage in meaningful actions, which this can only occur when there is a secure, respectful relationship that acknowledges the individual's autonomy in their daily life.

Page *et al.* (2013) concur that to provide the best possible support for CYP it is essential to build respectful and caring relationships with them, maximising the opportunity for positive experiences for all involved. The adult's commitment to understanding and interpreting children's needs is vital and is the foundation stone of a secure and respectful relationship which honours the individual's autonomy. Page and Elfer (2013) go further and highlight the importance of 'attachment interactions' in forming secure relationships, promoted in early years policy in England through the key person approach. The relationship forms the secure base for positive attachments to flourish and is a central tenet of practice when working with all CYP. Fox and Thiessen's (2019) research highlights that the integration of social pedagogical practice and attachment theory is fundamental to building trusting relationships. They assert that trust, empathy and authenticity are essential to fostering effective relationships that enables children to feel empowered to express themselves.

It should be acknowledged, however, that those who have additional needs may sometimes appear to resist our attempts to form a relationship with them. This is due to them not always appreciating the *need for* and *nature of* social interactions that neurotypically developing adults see as expected behaviours. Sreckovic *et al.* (2018), when they highlight the importance of forming strong relationships with all children, recognise that this can sometimes be challenging for those who have SEND. Time is required to slowly interact with the child, taking cues from the child's responses to inform your actions; knowing when to interact and when to step back is an important skill to master.

Fox and Thiessen (2019, p. 3) stress that the 'role of the social pedagogue is to develop 'positive growth' relationships with the clients/child we are working with' and remind us that this approach underpins the development of a reciprocal relationship. Noddings (1996) explains that all relationships between a child and practitioner are relational, they are unique to the partnership and dependent upon the context in which they are taking place. She highlights that caring can be identified as a set of relational practices which foster mutual recognition, realisation, growth, development, protection, empowerment, human community, culture and possibility; all of which underpin a successful relationship being formed. Noddings (2013) explains how a reciprocal relationship is based upon the *sharing* of experiences, whereby each can learn from the other. This, she adds, provides opportunity for 'receptivity and joy' (Noddings, 2013, p. 135) for all involved. Similarly, Rinaldi (2005) refers to the practitioner and child as fellow researchers, highlighting that we are *learning from* children when working effectively in partnership with them. Identifying the many integral, though often unnoticed, elements of reciprocal relationships, helps us to prioritise making time to establish them.

Noddings (2002) puts the notion of *caring* as central to positive relationships. In 2013 she stated that, 'it is certainly true that 'caring' can be seen as a professional attribute or disposition shown by behaving as a moral agent. Caring is a relationship that involves another person, the cared-for' (Noddings, 2013, p. 18). She suggests that these relationships are 'reciprocally dependent' (Noddings, 2013, p. 18), in that both parties contribute to the building of the relationship. Social pedagogical practice centres on the importance of working with CYP and encouraging a shared relationship where there is a suitable balance of power. Charfe and Gardner (2019) remind us that social pedagogical relationships are based upon equality and respect for one another, and that this underpins the balance of power within the relationship.

However, such an approach can pose challenges when working with a non-speaking child, or a child with processing difficulties and limited levels of understanding. Taking time to work out the best and most effective ways to communicate can be of enormous benefit when forming a secure relationship with the child. This cannot be achieved in a day, and needs may change over time; it must be continually worked on. Children with SEND still have ideas, values and feelings of their own, and it is our responsibility to discover what these are and how we can best support that child to reach their goals.

Professional love

Page (2011) highlights that discussing and practising love within professional roles is challenging, especially given the emphasis on safeguarding. Although policies do not explicitly require practitioners to 'love' children, Page (2011) argues that practitioners' responsibilities include education, care and the expression of professional love. Love is seldom addressed in professional discourse and certainly not in policy. However, Page et al. (2013, p. 196) cite Page (2011) who asserted that 'love truly matters; children need love and affection to develop strong minds, bodies, and souls, to be prepared to learn and to build emotional resilience throughout their lives'.

So, how does 'professional love' intersect with the values of social pedagogy? For practitioners to feel confident in showing professional love they need to have an awareness of their professional, personal and private selves. Fox and Thiessen (2019) propose that within social pedagogy relationships are formed based on the 'Three Ps' approach. This approach requires professionals to 'give of themselves' while still maintaining suitable professional and private boundaries. Thempra (2024) states that, the *professional* strand focuses on the following rules, regulations and policy to undertake your role, and the *personal* strand involves engaging with others in an authentic manner. By revealing who we are as individuals, we can build deeper, more genuine relationships. When we are comfortable being ourselves and showing our personality—including our imperfections—we create a space where those whom we support are free to be themselves as well. Employing our personal self in a social pedagogical context demands significant professional reflection (which is where the professional self comes into play); we need to understand our goals for the relationship, how it can benefit the individual, why authenticity is essential, and how we ensure that this approach is ultimately helpful to the person.

Thempra (2024) goes on to explain that the conscious, *private* self, distinguishes between what is personal and what is private, recognising when our own needs take precedence. While it is important to be genuine in what we share and to reveal aspects of our experiences that have shaped us, these should be well-processed and shared with the intention of benefiting the other person. The private self also has a subconscious element, where our needs and emotions can unexpectedly surface, leading to impulsive reactions instead of thoughtful responses. Reflecting on our experiences in practice helps us identify when our reactions may be influenced by our private self.

Reflection on practice is important as it helps you to recognise when you are calm and in control and under what circumstances you become agitated. The reason that this is important is because the child you are working with will also pick up on this, and it can have a detrimental impact on your experiences with them. Never be afraid to call for support or ask for someone to take over from you for a few minutes so that you can recompose yourself. You need to be calm before you can successfully engage with a child. There is a need for consistency when supporting children, particularly if we are to enable them to feel empowered and equipped with the tools required to fulfil their potential.

Supporting self-determination and agency

Emerson (2016, p. 107) asserts that she wants a 'call for blanket adoption of positive approaches to relationship building with children who have SEND as this underpins the development of self-determination and agency'. Why is this so important? Self-determination theory (Deci and Ryan, 2002) is a framework for understanding human motivation which focuses on self-determined behaviour and freely chosen actions that align with a person's true self. This contrasts with impulsive actions that are later regretted or behaviours driven mainly by the expectations of others, such as parents, teachers, or peers. True self-determination involves willingly engaging in actions that contribute positively to society, underpinned by a personal commitment to creating a better world for all.

Self-determination theory identifies three innate psychological needs that all people, not just CYP, strive to fulfil. When these needs are met, individuals thrive and experience a sense of wellbeing.

Conversely, if these needs are unmet, it can lead to psychological consequences, often reflected in behaviours such as anxiety, lack of empathy, or aggression. The three psychological needs are relatedness, autonomy and competence. Relatedness involves feeling safe, special and valued, which leads to having a sense of belonging. Autonomy is the need to explore and learn about the world independently within certain boundaries, while still desiring love and support from those working with them. Competence is the need to feel capable of making a difference and to be understood by others. Children need opportunities to practise paying attention, waiting and managing impulses to develop these competencies.

> **Reflection point**
>
> Consider ways that you already do, or that you might support the development of these three psychological needs in your practice.

No matter how severe or minimal their level of SEND, all CYP will have these innate underlying needs. On occasions we can forget that inappropriate behaviour might be connected to these needs remaining unmet, or not being addressed in a way that is appropriate to the individual child. Reflecting on my own practice I am aware that sometimes my expectations of children were too high, and that at other times they were too low. Remembering that ladder that was mentioned at the start of the chapter, we need to set small, achievable steps for the CYP to take if they are to flourish and gain a sense of relatedness, autonomy and competence.

Conclusion

All CYP we work with are like diamonds, they are not always bright and polished, but given the right conditions and opportunities to shine, they can become unique, dazzling gems. How we work with them to create this environment and the relationships we build with them will depend on their individual needs. Drawing on The Diamond Model (Eichsteller and Holthoff, 2012) can remind us of the various facets that can impact on a child's growth, development and learning (for an illustration see Chapter 2).

When considering The Diamond Model, Eichsteller and Holthoff (2012) highlight that *happiness* refers to the here and now, while *wellbeing* encompasses a more enduring sense of physical, mental, emotional and social health. It is crucial to recognise that both wellbeing and happiness are deeply personal; what brings happiness varies greatly from person to person. Therefore, as discussed earlier, social pedagogical practice must be tailored to the specific context and needs of the individual, rather than following a uniform approach. This can only be achieved by establishing a *secure and trusting relationship* between the CYP and the practitioner. Emerson (2016, p. 106) reminds us that a positive relationship with the child is required 'for the development of self-determination or agency or, indeed, the adoption of positive attitudes towards behaviour and learning for their own sake'. Relationships lie at the heart of all positive development.

As was established earlier, learning extends well beyond the confines of school; it is a comprehensive process of recognising and nurturing the potential for individual growth, which can occur in any situation that presents a learning opportunity. Fox and Thiessen (2019, p. 3) stress that the 'role of the social pedagogue is to develop 'positive growth' in relationships' with the client/ CYP they are working with and remind us that this approach underpins the development of a reciprocal relationship. The relationship is both professional and personal, requiring the social pedagogue to engage in continuous reflection. Thus, appropriate relationships, and continual reflection on these, lead to *positive experiences* for CYP.

By establishing a secure relationship and taking a *holistic* approach to learning in the broadest sense, the CYP we are working with are provided with opportunities to feel empowered for themselves. This is essential for ensuring that an individual gains a sense of control over their life, is involved in decisions that impact them and can understand their own world and their place within it. *Empowerment* involves the individual taking ownership and responsibility for their learning, wellbeing and happiness, as well as their relationships within the community. Charfe and Gardner (2019, p. 49) highlight that this also contributes to CYP having a sense of control in life. Social pedagogy is, therefore, focused on providing the tools for CYP to feel empowerment for themselves, promoting both their independence and interdependence.

This approach to working with CYP with SEND highlights that to be successful social pedagogues we must engage our whole self, as individuals who want to make a difference. We need to think beyond a mere practical role and see ourselves as pedagogues working in partnership with CYP with SEND, to search for the key that unlocks the magic in their minds. There is no quick fix, but with time this can happen. As CYP deeply connect with their educators, the bond nurtures the child's growth, and in this fertile space, their minds can blossom. Remember, 'It's absurd to suppose that we are educating when we ignore those matters that lie at the very heart of human existence' (Noddings, 2013, p. 172). As human beings, positive relationships lie at the heart of our existence, and only through these can we reach our full potential.

Summary points

- Every CYP with SEND is unique and has unique needs.
- Taking time to 'grow' a trusting, secure and reciprocal relationship with CYP will build a foundation from which they can flourish.
- Adopting positive approaches to relationship building with CYP who have SEND underpins the development their self-determination and agency.
- Effective communication is crucial. It is essential to consider the type of communication approaches required to meet the individual needs of the CYP you are working with.
- Practitioners and CYP (including those with SEND) are fellow researchers; we both learn from one another when we effectively work in partnership with them.

Recommended reading

Eichsteller, G. and Holthoff, S. (2011) Conceptual Foundations of Social pedagogy: A Transnational Perspective from Germany. In C. Cameron and P. Moss (Eds) *Social pedagogy and working with children, where care and education meet.* London and Philadelphia: Jessica Kingsley, pp. 33–52.

Hellawell, B. (2019) *Understanding and challenging the SEND code of practice.* London: Sage.

Leadbeater, C. (2020) *Lover Meets Power*, White Paper. Available at www.tacsi.org.au/file/kl39q3m8z/TACSI_Love%20Meets%20Power_Whitepaper_2020.pdf: TACSI (Accessed 22 August 2024).

Tutt, R. and Williams, P. (2015) *The SEND code of practice 0-25 years: Policy, provision and practice*. London: Sage.

References

Beazidou, E. (2023) Socio-pedagogical practices towards inclusive education implemented by teachers in their classrooms. *International Journal of Social pedagogy*, 12(1), pp.1–11.

Charfe, L and Gardner, A. (2019) *Social pedagogy and social work*. London: Sage.

Charfe, L. and Gardner, A. (2020) Does my Haltung look big in this?: The use of Social pedagogical theory for the development of ethical and value-based practice. *International Journal of Social Pedagogy*, 9(1), pp. 1–10.

Deci, E. L. and Ryan, R. M. (2002) The 'what' and 'why' of goal pursuits: Human needs and self-determination behaviour. *Psychological Inquiry*, 11(4), pp. 227–268.

Department for Education/Department for Health (2015) *Special educational needs and disability code of practice: 0 to 25 years (2015)*. Available at: https://assets.publishing.service.gov.uk/media/5a7dcb85ed915d2ac884d995/SEND_Code_of_Practice_January_2015.pdf (Accessed 20 January 2025).

Eichsteller, G. (2010). *The notion of 'Haltung' in social pedagogy*. Available at https://thetcj.org/in-residence/the-notion-of-haltung-in-social-pedagogy

Eichsteller, G. and Holthoff, S. (2011) Conceptual Foundations of Social Pedagogy: A Transnational Perspective from Germany. In C. Cameron and P. Moss (Eds) *Social pedagogy and working with children and young people*. London: Jessica Kingsley, pp. 33–52.

Eichsteller, G. and Holthoff, S. (2012) *Thempra's Diamond Model*. Available at www.thempra.org.uk/social-pedagogy/key-concepts-in-social-pedagogy/thempras-diamond-model/ (Accessed 29 August 2024).

Emerson, A. (2016) Applying the 'least dangerous assumption' in regard to behaviour policies and children with special needs. *Pastoral Care in Education*, 34(2), pp. 104–109. http://dx.doi.org/10.1080/02643944.2016.1154095

Fox, D. and Thiessen, S. (2019) Social pedagogy as relational attachment practice. *International Journal of Social pedagogy*, 8(1):, pp. 1–14. https://doi.org/10.14324/111.444.ijsp.2019.v8.x.004

Goering, S. (2015) Rethinking disability: The social model of disability and chronic disease. *Current Reviews in Musculoskeletal Medicine*, 8(2), pp. 134–138. https://doi.org/10.1007/s12178-015-9273-z

Noddings, N. (1996) The Cared for. In S. Gordon, P. Benner and N. Noddings (Eds) *Caregiving: Readings in knowledge, practice, ethics, and politics*. Philadelphia, PA: University of Pennsylvania Press, pp. 21–39.

Noddings, N. (2002) *Starting at home. Caring and social policy*. Berkeley, CA: University of California Press

Noddings, N. (2013) *Caring: A relational approach to ethics and moral education* (2nd edn). Berkeley, CA: University of California Press.

Page, J. (2011) Do mothers want professional carers to love their babies? *Journal of Early Childhood Research*, 9(3), pp. 310–323. https://doi.org/10.1177/1476718X11407980

Page, J., Clare, A. and Nutbrown, C. (2013) *Working with babies and children from birth to three*. London: Sage

Page, J. and Elfer, P. (2013) The emotional complexity of attachment interactions in a nursery. *European Early Childhood Educational Research Journal*, 21(4), pp. 553–567. https://doi.org/10.1080/1350293X.2013.766032

Petrie, P. (2020) Taking social pedagogy forward: Its fit with official UK statements on promoting wellbeing. *International Journal of Social Pedagogy*, 9(1), pp. 1–13.

Rinaldi, C. (2005). *In dialogue with Reggio Emilia*. London: Routledge Falmer.

Rothuizen, J. J. and Harbo, L. J. (2017) Social pedagogy: An approach without fixed recipes. *Internation Journal of Social Pedagogy*, 6(1), pp. 6–28.

Solvason, C., Webb, R. and Sutton-Tsang, S. (2020) What is left...?: The implications of losing maintained nursery schools for vulnerable children and families in England. *Children and Society*, 25(1), pp. 75–89. https://onlinelibrary.wiley.com/doi/full/10.1111/chso.12391

Sreckovic, M. A., Schultz, T. R. and Kenney, C. K. (2018) Building community in the inclusive classroom: Setting the stage for success. *YC Young children*, 73(3), pp. 75–81.

Thempra (2024) *Key Concepts in Social Pedagogy*. Available at www.thempra.org.uk/social-pedagogy/key-concepts-in-social-pedagogy/the-3-ps/ (Accessed 19 August 2024).

Wearmouth, J. (2017) *Special educational needs and disabilities in schools. A critical introduction*. London: Bloomsbury.

Zaks, Z. (2023) Changing the medical model of disability to the normalization model of disability: Clarifying the past to create a new future direction. *Journal of Disability and Society*, 39(12), pp. 3233–3260.

5 The potential of art to break down barriers and draw together

Kaytie Holdstock

Art in education and childhood

In Europe, the visual arts play a central role in the professional development of practitioners within education and those supporting families in the community (Petrie et al., 2006). Within these approaches, education is seen as so much more than traditional schooling; rather it is developing the whole child through the 'cultivation and elevation of character' (Stephens, 2009, p. 344). Yet here in England the state of the arts has never been so precarious. Despite the government espousing a broad and balanced curriculum (Department for Education, 2014, p. 2), creative opportunities for our children and young people continue to be eroded by a culture of testing and an ideology that more formal, academic education is the road to success (Spielman, 2017). Arts and crafts form a fundamental part of the training of the social pedagogue in continental Europe (Cameron and Moss, 2011), yet in the UK, trainee teachers receive on average less than one and a half hours of art-based instruction throughout their entire initial teacher education (Gregory, 2017). Many early years practitioners enter the profession with little or no training in arts and crafts at all (Petrie et al., 2006), resulting in a workforce with limited understanding of the positive impact that art can have on child development. This results in many educators feeling ill prepared to support children with their artistic endeavours (Cooper, 2018) and contributes to the narrowing of educational opportunities within both schools and early years settings (Ofsted, 2019).

> **Reflection point**
>
> Why do you think the place of art within education can be such a divisive topic?

The time and resources devoted to art education in the UK have been consistently reduced, not only due to the erosion of government funding for education generally, but also as a result of the fundamental lack of understanding of the multifaceted value of art. A social pedagogical approach to the much-needed reform of education would see art fully re-integrated into children's educational lives (Stobbs et al., 2023) ensuring that children explore the asset of creativity as an entitlement. The Cultural Learning Alliance (CLA) outlines the benefits of an art-rich life in their Key Research Findings of 2017, which serves as a compelling call to arms for all social pedagogues (CLA, 2017). This report outlines the many benefits of arts engagement, citing empirical improvements in the health, social mobility and life chances of artistically engaged individuals, as well as identifying the positive impact that art has on community engagement and social activism (CLA, 2017, p. 2). It is for these reasons that arts and crafts have always been fundamental to the social pedagogical approach. Through the magic of art, children are exposed to the beauty, creativity and wonder of the world around them. Understanding the value of these wider dimensions of existence supports practitioners in recognising the infinite possibilities available within society (Petrie and Chambers, 2009, p. 3) and encourages a more nuanced understanding of the way that individuals might be supported to fulfil their great potential.

Even the opportunities to engage with art at home during those precious, formative years of a young child's life have been reduced due to increasing societal pressures on parents to return to work. Year on year, a record number of children live in households where both parents work full time (Office for National Statistic, 2022, p. 3) and this, coupled with the government introduction of free childcare from age two, means that children find themselves in education and care settings earlier and for longer (Erikson, 2018). For many young children, sitting around a table at home engaging with painting, colouring or junk modelling with a caregiver is no longer a staple experience whilst growing up, reducing the many valuable opportunities for connection, playful adult-child relationships, shared attention and eye contact that mutual engagement in art can command (Armstrong and Ross, 2022, p. 1). This leads to generational decline in arts engagement at home, where parents who have not experienced an arts-rich childhood themselves are less likely to prioritise creativity with their own children.

The increasing financial pressure on families also means that the provision of extra-curricular art opportunities and the availability of art resources at home are increasingly beyond the budget of many families (Hodgson, 2023). Children's attendance at educational settings from an increasingly young age not only erodes opportunities that children may once have had to engage in unrestricted creativity within their own homes, but it also places onto educators increased responsibility for a child's art engagement and development. A social pedagogical approach to early art experiences would help redress this imbalance, recognising that holistic education, including opportunities for creativity, provides children, like flowers, with the optimum conditions to grow (Eichsteller and Holthoff, 2011, p. 20).

With art becoming ever more underfunded, undervalued and overlooked in education settings (Cooper, 2018), it is, like so many other experiences, becoming a luxury experienced only by middle-class children whose parents have the resources to provide (often expensive) art materials or access to extra-curricular art opportunities. This means that the benefits derived from a richly artistic upbringing, like so many other enriching activities, are retained only for those who can afford it (Warwick Commission, 2015). Social pedagogues need to recognise their responsibility to bring back this missing ingredient to a child's experiences, and to ensure that the opportunity of creativity enhancing an individual's life chances is experienced by everyone (Hatton, 2020, p. 2).

Reflection point

Reflect upon your experience of art as a child. What artistic opportunities did you have? Were there any limitations to the art experiences that you were able to access?

As Malaguzzi (1996) observed, the way that children think and understand is nuanced, rich and impossible to define in just one, singular way. Art is often a child's first method of communication, even before their vocabulary and writing develop (Adu and Kissiedu, 2017). Limiting children's self-expression to just words and numbers ignores the wealth of communication that can be conveyed through brush strokes, mark-making and sculpting in both two and three dimensions. This is the premise at the heart of the integration between social pedagogy and art; holistic experiences are needed for the positive development of the child.

In their formative years children will naturally seek out opportunities for creativity without encouragement (Ershadi and Winner, 2020). Sticks become pencils in mud, food is an exploration of colour and texture, discarded cartons and packaging become robots, houses and rockets. This is a child's first language and one that they openly and willingly share with those around them. A social pedagogue ensures that children have access to and make the most of these creative opportunities as they know that within these experiences children are also learning the social skills they need for successful lives (Warwick Commission, 2015). In group activities like these, children will be learning to collaborate, negotiate, compromise, articulate and imagine: fundamental traits that will accelerate them on their journey towards the fulfilment of their limitless potential. Schools should design their curriculum with arts and creative media at their core to provide opportunities to empower and embolden all children (Stobbs et al., 2023).

Social pedagogy is underpinned by the principles of a truly holistic education that redirects the traditional flow of learning from teacher to student, instead acknowledging the child's autonomous role in their discovery and understanding of the outside world (Eichsteller and Holthoff, 2011). It is impossible for a child to develop as a rounded and socially competent being when raised on a diet of reading, writing and maths. We need to rethink the value of artistic and creative learning activities, and recognise their value alongside STEM (Science, Technology, English and Maths, frequently seen as areas that are core to a child's future success) subjects, if we are to provide child-centred opportunities that speak to the interests of *all* children, and support the fulfilment of *all* children's unlimited potential (Smith and Whyte, 2008).

The argument for arts-rich experiences during childhood is gaining traction (National Society for the Education of Art and Design, NSEAD, 2023) but an additional challenge for the social pedagogue is what comes after. Evidence demonstrates that the inclination to innovate and create deteriorates rapidly as we grow older (Land and Jarman, 1996) and for most of us, we see the evidence of this in our own lives, where art is frequently forgotten after childhood. Society teaches us that art is something that children do, and our own lack of engagement in art as adults, in turn, then teaches children that art is something that they will grow out of (Eisner, 2002).

Art in adulthood

A social pedagogue recognises the role that art can play in the magical relationship between a human and their world, and how it can be valued as a tool to reengage both children and adults with their own existence. It should be recognised, however, that this is no easy task for many adults, as feelings of self-consciousness and self-doubt in ones' capabilities as an artist can set in during adulthood. This can present significant challenges for social pedagogues attempting to reconnect adult learners with art, and to nurture relationships using art activities as a '*Common Third*', as I discuss later in the chapter. There is no shortage of evidence to support the ongoing health and social benefits of art at all stages of life (CLA, 2017; Warwick Commission, 2015) but very few maintain their enthusiasm for creativity into adulthood without significant intervention. This leaves a wealth of untapped potential that can be explored and nurtured though a social pedagogical approach.

> **Reflection point**
>
> Did creative opportunities play a significant role in your own education? Do you still engage with art as an adult? Why, or why not?

Johann Heirich Pestalozzi conceptualises holistic education in his 'head, heart and hands' model (Pestalozzi, cited in Heafford, 1967, p. 61). This model describes how an individuals' mental, moral and physical development should be perfectly balanced throughout all pedagogical practices. Engagement in art lends itself organically to all three of these aspects of development. The 'head', or cognitive understanding, is encouraged as art encourages the acquisition of knowledge that transcends simple facts and figures, and instead creates alternative learning opportunities to create with culture, heritage and the world around us. Art appeals to the 'heart', or the emotions, by not only bringing joy in creating, but by encouraging socially active practices that shape an individuals' moral compass through strong examples of art as activism (Dufour, 2002). Using art can be a powerful means to respond to societal issues and social injustices and can give a voice to individuals who would otherwise be silenced. Art transcends the boundary of different languages, encouraging connections with the wider world as global citizens (Juntunen and Partti, 2022). The physicality of experiencing art through a wide range of media and scale allows development of 'the hands', or physical skills, as individuals engage their whole bodies through sensory exploration, manipulation of materials and the learning of new techniques and processes that rely on both gross and fine motor control (James, 2013). In the same way that social pedagogues open their minds to the whole person, art can open our minds to the world around us (Eisner, 2002).

The benefits of art transcend the physical act of making or doing. By utilising art as a tool that engages us with our own existence, we open ourselves up to the joy that comes from noticing, appreciating beauty in its many different forms, and being present, experiencing the awe and wonder that occurs naturally within our own environments. Art activities can provide a unique opportunity for us to balance our head, heart and hands by providing strength, focus and discipline to our thoughts; warmth, imagination, originality and enthusiasm to our hearts and giving order and resolve to our will (James, 2013, p. 5).

Social pedagogy, with art as a key approach, provides opportunity for human interaction and experiences that can gently take people experiencing them to a place of emotional self-sufficiency and resourcefulness. It provides opportunity for challenges where the tools, and the solutions to problems can be accessed from within (Böhnisch, cited in Eichsteller and Holthoff, 2011). Similarly, engaging with creative, artistic practice encourages the notion of process over product, and develops resilience and critical thinking, skills that are invaluable to creating a mind-set of self-reliance (Zarobe and Bungay, 2017); one of the fundamental aims of the social pedagogical approach.

The potential of art to foster connections within diverse communities

The need to create is a fundamental part of what makes us human (Golden, 2015). Since time began there is historical evidence of humankind's pursuit for outlets of aesthetic expression. Although there have been nuances in style and medium, the need to create has been a constant, transcending geographical, cultural, and socioeconomic boundaries. In an increasingly diverse world, the creation of art has the power to connect communities through a shared language that allows a two-way transfer of skills and knowledge (Bublitz, 2019).

Within art there has always been a predisposition for historians and educators to label different artists and movements, thus creating segregation between the people and cultures from whom the art is conceived. As formal education in England moves ever further away from a holistic approach in favour of a knowledge-based curriculum (Hirsch, 2006), so the tendency for educators to put art genres into clearly defined boxes has been exacerbated. Whilst art education moves towards knowledge of individual artists, art genres and timelines, many educators have lost sight of the fundamental concept of art for art's sake (See and Kokotsaki, 2016); art as a process, not a product. Social pedagogy sees most value in those opportunities for creativity with no fixed start or end point. The value of the endeavour is not found in a 'product', but in the shared experience of the making, the risks taken, and the solutions found; the connections and collaborations created through a collaborative art activity cannot be separated from the artwork itself (McLennan, 2010). It is in this place that we develop holistically, in the safe space that art creates, where the tools for resilient and emotional self-sufficiency can be practised and eventually honed (Böhnisch, cited in Eichsteller and Holthoff, 2011).

Using art to connect diverse communities is distinctly more nuanced than simply teaching learners about the artistic contribution of the many cultures of the world. Social pedagogues are far less concerned with the product of a culture's aesthetic history, than they are the people within it (Eichsteller and Holthoff, 2011). Art is at its most powerful when it brings people together through projects based on understanding, collaboration and empathy (Peloquin, 1996). A common theme in community art projects used by social pedagogues is that of identity (White and Ricarte, 2023). This could be using art to explore one's own identity, create curiosity and empathy with the identity of others, or examine the parallels between the evolving identities of participants within a group, by making connections between everyone's heritage and identifying shared futures. Looking at the artwork of a culture in isolation encourages analysis of difference, whereas examining the artistic preferences and experiences of the individuals within the project itself, encourages connection and understanding of our commonality (Lowe, 2000).

> **Refection point**
>
> Why do you think understanding identity is an important theme within social pedagogy?

As an example of such an approach, Anna Hickey-Moody and Mia Harrison (2018) led on a project exploring how the facilitation the articulation of social and cultural values through creative activities could build relationships between children and families from different faith backgrounds. This concept of socially engaged arts practice (Bishop, 2012, p. 7) can be used as an 'affective pedagogy' (Hickey-Moody, 2012, p. 79), that aligns with social pedagogy in its underlying principles of relational education. Within such an approach the artist practitioner uses art to create feelings of empathy and understanding, providing participants with a new sense of shared resourcefulness that emerged from belonging within a community of practice with common goals and aspirations (Wenger, 1998).

Hickey-Moody and Harrison's (2018, p. 2) project engaged children and their parents in collaborative art that encouraged participants to explore an 'intrafaith future' built on discovering shared values and cultural connections. Participants were asked to create papier mâché sculptures that displayed key values in the form of 'special stickers' that represented the ideals fundamental to each of their cultural beliefs (Hickey-Moody and Harrison, 2018, p. 6). Quickly, individuals recognised that despite the myriad of different cultures and religions represented within the group, the key themes that emerged shared commonality such as 'service' and 'faith'. The shared art project gently encouraged children and their parents to engage in open, honest and empathetic dialogue that shaped new ways of thinking and built lasting relationships that transcended class and culture. Through the activity, feelings of 'otherhood' were eroded, as participants focused instead on their many similarities. The materiality of the process of creating art provided a mechanism for cultivating friendship and belonging where individuals instinctively sought to find common ground and connection (Hickey-Moody and Harrison, 2018).

The success of such a project may seem the product of chance, but the role of the social pedagogue is integral to the planning and implementation of such an endeavour. Activities must be carefully planned to incorporate all participants' 'direct experiences, their living contexts, their life skills and the strength of their self-responsibility' (Grunwald and Thiersch, 2009, p. 132), creating a predictable space where mutual decision-making values both individuals and the collective (Eichsteller and Holthoff, 2011, p. 20). The social pedagogue must know 'when to persist and when to back off', whilst carefully balancing the authentic and meaningful development of relationships alongside the maintenance of appropriate boundaries (Eichsteller and Holthoff, 2011, p. 27). The practitioner inevitably maintains a degree of pedagogical responsibility, which creates a power imbalance between practitioner and subject, but this responsibility must be maintained to safeguard all within the experience, whilst respecting the individuality, dignity and free will of those involved (Husen, 2022, p. 8). This means that the social pedagogue must choose activities carefully to recognise participants as experts in their own lives and to meet them in their everyday realities (Grunwald and Thiersch, 2009, p. 132).

Art as the *Common Third*

Art is used by many social pedagogues as a way of strengthening relationships through a mutually appreciated, fully accessible activity that encourages collaboration between practitioner and individual working at the same level. This activity is described as 'the *Common Third*' in social pedagogy, where the shared purpose or experience bridges the gap between individuals who are brought together in pursuit of a common interest (ThemPra, 2015, p. 2). This could be an external problem or issue to be solved where individuals work together to achieve a common goal, or a new skill to be learned where all parties approach the activity as novices ready to learn together. This principle exemplifies social pedagogy's commitment to learning and personal development as indistinguishably important from the development of long-lasting, healthy relationships (Hadi and Johansen, n.d., p. 3).

Choosing art as the *Common Third* encourages the development of cooperative relationships where all parties have permission to be vulnerable and all voices can be equally heard. The artistic process also encourages a mutual understanding and mobilisation of each individual's available, internal resources and encourages a shared appreciation and discovery of life's many dimensions (Dworak-Peck, 2024, p. 9). The visual arts naturally support the expression of unconscious emotions that can then be explored in the safe space of a collaborative activity (Stobbs *et al.*, 2023). Selecting an art process in which both parties are novices creates opportunities for communication, problem solving and negotiation, all of which are significant from a social pedagogical stance in the holistic development of the individuals within the experience. By employing a shared art activity as the *Common Third*, 'personal development through purposeful engagement' is encouraged alongside the cultivation of trusting relationships (Parker, 2020, p. 7).

Social pedagogy and community art

Although the *Common Third* can be used between two individuals to harness the therapeutic benefits of the artistic process, the affiliation between art and social pedagogy has fostered many tangible benefits within larger groups to build belonging and cohesion within communities. As Lowe (2000, p. 1) explains, 'Community art serves as a catalyst for community because it is both the setting for group solidarity building and the symbol of group identity'. Participation in a shared visual art project can encourage communities to discover things about themselves whilst fostering understanding of the group's collective identity (Flood, 1982).

Lowe discusses an example of a community development project in which an artist facilitated communities working together through the *Common Third* of designing and installing a mural to enhance their local environment (Lowe, 2000). Through this project, residents who previously described themselves as individually isolated and disconnected, came together to create a mutual piece of art that represented the diversity of cultures within the community. The benefits of this project were overwhelmingly positive with participants describing the social bonds, solidarity, collective identity and common mood that emerged from the experience (Lowe, 2000, p. 1). The sense of belonging that developed through the process of planning, designing and painting the mural encouraged the inclusive and connected community described by Tönnies as 'Gemeinschaft' (Tönnies, 1967, p. 1) where social relationships develop organically and are built on shared ideals and values (Lowe, 2000, p. 380). The project developed this sense of community through the coexistence of Tönnies' three types of Gemeinschaft: kin, neighbourhood and friendship (Tönnies, 1967) and in doing so enhanced participants independence as well as interdependence (Eichsteller and Holthoff, 2011, p. 25).

Lowe (2000) attributes the success of this project to the way that the social pedagogue created opportunities for structured interactions within the community setting, establishing a culture of inclusive decision making, developing a shared goal with a physical outcome and ensuring that the common mood was both playful and light-hearted (Lowe, 2000, p. 381). This project illustrates a set of foundational principles that could be used by any social pedagogue to develop similar projects that, likewise, could harness the power of art to empower individuals from diverse communities to become connected, collaborative and interrelated. Through this focus on the human element of art, communities can be encouraged to learn and grow together whilst exploring and promoting the potential of each individual (Romeo, 2018).

> **Reflection point**
>
> Considering Lowe's criteria for the success of a community art project, do you know of any, or do you have any, ideas for other creative projects that could support individuals to come together through a shared artistic purpose?

Conclusion

Art and social pedagogy are natural allies, encouraging participants to embark on a journey of self-discovery that connects them to their own lives in the present and encourages optimism for the future (Seligman and Csikszentmihalyi, 2000). Only by prioritising genuinely holistic human development, can education fulfil its true purpose – to improve quality of life for all and create engaged, responsible and self-sufficient citizens. By creating connections within communities and a sense of belonging within diverse populations, a social pedagogical approach to art can be a powerful tool to encourage individuals to draw on the resources and attributes that exist within themselves, as well as their contemporaries. Creative activities can serve as a tool for emancipating members of the community who feel isolated and working towards a more balanced society. However, the lack of value ascribed to art within all phases of education prevents individuals from accessing the many proven health and social benefits that art participation can bestow (CLA, 2017) and the absence of a holistic approach to education contributes to a society that is becoming less connected and more divided.

Effective use of art within a social pedagogical context prioritises the value of community and recognises the power and potential of the people within it. Encouraging shared creativity and explorations of our own heritage by identifying the things that bring us together as global citizens empowers communities to seek social change and challenge injustice through their own self-reliance and resourcefulness. Whereas approaches to education in England increasingly encourage competition and comparison, social pedagogy and art encourage connection, collaboration and the value of uniqueness. Embracing the freedom of self-expression harnessed by 'art for art's sake', the social pedagogue can create authentic connections between themselves and participants, that evolve through shared understanding and purpose. By creating artistic opportunities that engage head, heart and hands through a mutually purposeful '*Common Third*', the social pedagogue can provide rich opportunities to nurture self-understanding and empathy towards others, self-esteem and the resourcefulness of all participants at both individual and community level. The potential for art to bring about meaningful change is limitless.

Summary points

- Access to art should be a fundamental ingredient of a holistic education experience, yet time given to it has diminished in favour of other subjects recognised as key to future success.

- Creative activities have proven health and social benefits at all stages of life.
- The use of art as a *Common Third* activity strengthens relationships between individuals and within communities.
- The use of art within social pedagogy must be carefully planned to engage all aspects of the head, heart and hands. It is the process of exploration through art where the journey of self-discovery and relationship building exists.
- Exploring themes of identity and cultural heritage through art can encourage individuals to gain a greater sense of self-awareness, and draw parallels between themselves and other members of society.

Recommended reading

Chambers, A. and Petrie, P. (nd) *A Brief Learning Framework for Artist Pedagogues*. Available at https://static.a-n.co.uk/wp-content/uploads/2016/09/abbreviated_learning_framework_for_artist_pedagogues.pdf (Accessed 5 February 2025).

CLA (n.d.) *Key Research Findings: The Case for Cultural Learning, Cultural Learning Alliance:* Available at www.culturallearningalliance.org.uk/wp-content/uploads/2024/01/CLA-key-findings-2017.pdf (Accessed 5 February 2025).

Hickey-Moody, A. and Harrison, M. (2018) *Socially Engaged Art and Affective Pedagogy: A Study in Inter-faith Understanding*. Available at www.tate.org.uk/research/tate-papers/29/socially-engaged-art-and-affective-pedagogy (Accessed 5 February 2025).

References

Adu, J. and Kissiedu, K. (2017) Exploring children's communication through art in the early years: The role of the teacher. *Journal of Education and Practice*, 8(35), 34–42.

Armstrong, V. G. and Ross, J. (2022) The experiences of parents and infants using home-based art intervention aimed at improving wellbeing and connectedness in their relationships. *Frontiers in Psychology*, 13(732562), 1–21.

Bishop, C. (2012) *Artificial Hells: Participatory Art and the Politics of Spectatorship*. London: Verso Books.

Bohnisch, L. (2017) Social Work: A problem-oriented introduction. Berlin: Walter de Gruyter.

Bublitz, M. G., Rank-Christman, T., Cian, L., Cortada, X., Madzharov, A., Patrick, V. M., Peracchio, L. A., Scott, M. L., Sundar, A., To, N. and Townsend, C. (2019) Collaborative art: A transformational force within communities. *Journal of the Association for Consumer Research*, 4(4), 313–331.

Cameron, C. and Moss, P. (2011) Social Pedagogy: Current Understandings and Opportunities. In S. Holthoff (Ed.) *Social Pedagogy and Working with Children and Young People*. London: Jessica Kingsley, pp. 7–32.

Cooper, B. (2018) *Primary Colours: The Decline of Arts Education in Primary Schools and How It Can Be Reversed*. Available at: https://fabians.org.uk/wp-content/uploads/2019/01/FS-Primary-Colours-Report-WEB-FINAL.pdf (Accessed 26 June 2024).

Cultural Learning Alliance (2017) *Key Research Findings: The Case for Cultural Learning*. Available at: www.culturallearningalliance.org.uk/wp-content/uploads/2024/01/CLA-key-findings-2017.pdf (Accessed 20 June 2024).

Department for Education (2014) *The National Curriculum in England*. Available at: https://assets.publishing.service.gov.uk/media/5a81a9abe5274a2e8ab55319/PRIMARY_national_curriculum.pdf (Accessed 2 July 2024).

Dufour, K. (2002) Art as activism, activism as art. *Review of Education, Pedagogy, and Cultural Studies*, 24(1–2), 157–167.

Dworak-Peck, S. (2024) *Social Work and the Arts*. Available at: https://dworakpeck.usc.edu/social-work-and-the-arts#:~:text=The%20artistic%20process%20enhances%20the,lives%20are%20and%20can%20be. (Accessed 25 June 2024).

Eichsteller, G. and Holthoff, S. (2011) Conceptual Foundations of Social Pedagogy: A Transnational Perspective from Germany. In S. Holthoff (Ed.) *Social Pedagogy and Working with Children and Young People*. London: Jessica Kingsley, pp. 33–52.

Eisner, E. (2002) *The Arts and the Creation of Mind*. New Haven: Yale University Press.
Erikson, J. (2018) *Measuring the Long-Term Effects of Early Extensive Day Care*. Available at: https://ifstudies.org/blog/measuring-the-long-term-effects-of-early-extensive-day-care (Accessed 20 June 2024).
Ershadi, M. and Winner, E. (2020) Children's Creativity. In M. Runco and S. Pritzker (Eds) *Encyclopedia of Creativity*, 3(1). Cambridge: Academic Press, pp. 144–148.
Flood, W. (1982) Animation: Socio-cultural community development in Europe and the United States. *Master's Thesis*, Pennsylvania State University.
Golden, J. (2015) *Mural Arts Program Engages Community Members in Murals That Improve Aesthetics and Transform Neighborhoods*. Available at: www.preventioninstitute.org/sites/default/files/editor_uploads/images/stories/Documents/Philadelphia_Mural_Arts_Program.pdf (Accessed 24 June 2024).
Gregory, P. (2017) *Art and Design in Primary ITE*. Available at: www.nsead.org/files/19547770509429df26fe1118e98e2795.pdf (Accessed 20 June 2023).
Grunwald, K. and Thiersch, H. (2009) The concept of the lifeworld orientation for social work and social care. *Journal of Social Work Practice*, 23(2), 131–146.
Hadi, J. and Johansen, T. (n.d.) *The Common Third: A Kindred Spirit to Youth Work?* Available at: https://sppa-uk.org/the-common-third/ (Accessed 24 June 2024).
Hatton, K. (2020) A new framework for creativity in social pedagogy. *International Journal of Social Pedagogy*, 9(1), 16.
Heafford, M. (1967) *Pestalozzi*. Bungay: The Chaucer Press.
Hickey-Moody, A. (2012) Affect as Method, Feelings, Aesthetics and Affective Pedagogy. In R. Coleman and J. Ringrose (Eds) *Deleuze and Research Methodologies*. Edinburgh: Edinburgh University Press, pp. 79–95.
Hirsch, E. D. (2006). *The Knowledge Deficit: Closing the Shocking Education Gap for American Children*. Boston: Houghton Mifflin.
Hodgson, S. (2023) *Art Now Enquiry*. Available at: www.nsead.org/files/13a555d0c7a3c66da64bfb8049a4dae1.pdf (Accessed 20 June 2024).
Husen, M. (2022) *The Common Third*. Available at: https://michaelhusen.dk/the-common-third/ (Accessed 25 June 2024).
James, V. (2013) Art and the integration of head, heart and hand. *Journal for Waldorf Education*, 15(1), 3–7.
Juntunen, M. L. and Partti, H. (2022) Towards transformative global citizenship through interdisciplinary arts education. *International Journal of Education and the Arts*, 23(13), 1–28.
Land, G. and Jarman, B. (1996) *Breaking Point and Beyond*. San Francisco: HarperBusiness.
Lowe, S. (2000) Creating community: Art for community development. *Journal of Contemporary Ethnography*, 29(3), 357–386.
Malaguzzi, L. (1996). *The Hundred Languages of Children: The Reggio Emilia Approach to Early Childhood Education*. Norwood, NJ: Ablex Publishing Corporation.
McLennan, D. M. P. (2010) Process or product? The argument for aesthetic exploration in the early years. *Early Childhood Education Journal*, 38, 81–85.
National Society for the Education of Art and Design (2023) *Art Now: An Inquiry into the State of Art and Design Teaching in Early Years Foundation Stage, Primary and Secondary Education*. Available at: www.nsead.org/files/13a555d0c7a3c66da64bfb8049a4dae1.pdf (Accessed 8 July 2024).
Office for National Statistics (2022) *Families and the Labour Market, UK: 2021*. Available at: www.ons.gov.uk/employmentandlabourmarket/peopleinwork/employmentandemployeetypes/articles/familiesandthelabourmarketengland/2021 (Accessed 20 June 2024).
Ofsted (2019) *Ofsted Inspection Framework*. Available at: https://assets.publishing.service.gov.uk/media/6034be17d3bf7f265dbbe2ef/Research_for_EIF_framework_updated_references_22_Feb_2021.pdf (Accessed 26 June 2024).
Parker, C. (2020). Creative mentoring: A creative response to promote learning and wellbeing with children in care. A service developed by Derbyshire County Council's Virtual School. *International Journal of Social Pedagogy*, 9(1), 5.
Peloquin, S. M. (1996) Art: An occupation with promise for developing empathy. *American Journal of Occupational Therapy*, 50(8), 655–661.
Petrie, P., Boddy, J., Cameron, C., Simon, A. and Wingfall, V. (2006) *Working with Children in Residential Care: European Perspectives*. Buckingham: Open University Press.
Petrie, P. and Chambers, H. (2009) *Richer Lives: Creative Activities in the Education and Practice of Danish Pedagogues*. Available at: www.thempra.org.uk/wp-content/uploads/2022/03/Petrie-Chambers-Richer-Lives.pdf (Accessed 26 June 2024).

Romeo, L. (2018) *Social Pedagogy... social what?* Available at: https://socialworkwithadults.blog.gov.uk/2018/12/19/social-pedagogy-social-what/#:~:text=Social%20pedagogy%20is%20based%20on,recognise%20and%20promote%20individual%20potential. (Accessed 24 June 2024).

See, B. and Kokotsaki, D. (2016) *Impact of Arts Education on the Cognitive and Non-cognitive Outcomes of School-Aged Children. A Review of Evidence*. Available at: https://durham-repository.worktribe.com/output/1607361/impact-of-arts-education-on-the-cognitive-and-non-cognitive-outcomes-of-school-aged-children-a-review-of-evidence (Accessed 24 June 2024).

Seligman, M. and Csikszentmihalyi, M. (2000) Positive psychology: An introduction. *American Psychologist*, 55(1), 5–14.

Smith, M. and Whyte, B. (2008) Social education and social pedagogy: Reclaiming a Scottish tradition in social work. *European Journal of Social Work*, 11(1), 15–28.

Spielman, A. (2017) *HMI's Commentary: Recent Primary and Secondary Curriculum Research*. Available at: www.gov.uk/government/speeches/hmcis-commentary-october-2017 (Accessed 2 July 2024).

Stephens, P. (2009) The nature of social pedagogy: An excursion in Norwegian territory. *Child and Family Social Work*, 14(3), 343–351.

Stobbs, N., Solvason, C., Gallagher, S. and Baylis, S. (2023) A human approach to restructuring the education system: Why schools in England need social pedagogy. *International Journal of Social Pedagogy*, 12(1), 1–11.

Tönnies, F. (1967) *Community and Society*. East Lansing, MI: Michigan State University Press.

Warwick Commission (2015) *Enriching Britain: Culture, Creativity and Growth*. Available at: https://europaregina.eu/wp-content/uploads/2015/03/warwick_commission_report_2015.pdf (Accessed 21 May 2025).

ThemPra (2015) *The Common Third*. Available at: www.thempra.org.uk/social-pedagogy/key-concepts-in-social-pedagogy/the-common-third/ (Accessed 24 June 2024).

Wenger, E. (1998) *Communities of Practice: Learning, Meaning, and Identity*. Cambridge: Cambridge University Press.

White, B. and Ricarte, J. (2023) *Harnessing the Power of Identity and The Arts for Social Transformation: Practitioner Toolkit*. Available at: https://oicd.net/wp-content/uploads/UNESCO-OICD-TOOLKIT-WITH-COVER.pdf (Accessed 24 June 2024).

Zarobe, L. and Bungay, H. (2017) The role of arts activities in developing resilience and mental wellbeing in children and young people in a rapid review of the literature. *Perspectives in Public Health*, 137(6), 175791391771228.

6 Harmony and connection
Integrating social pedagogy with music education

Kate Howen

Introduction: music and connection

Social pedagogy recognises that individuals are moulded by their experiences in society, and music will, inevitably, have played a part in that experience, whether through the nursery rhymes of our childhood or the music libraries of our adulthood. Social pedagogues view individuals holistically and recognise that they are constantly evolving, and that each has huge potential. The wide-ranging benefits of engaging with music have long been documented, whether it is listening to, participating in, or creating music (Bilhartz et al., 1999; Butzlaff, 2000). One challenge with research into the benefits of engaging in musical activities is the difficulty in excluding other factors that enhance academic success, such as having supportive parents and a study-friendly home environment (Hallam, 2010), factors that social pedagogy recognises as being vital to an individual's life chances. There are strong connections made in research between music and the enhancement of skills across disciplines (Campabello et al., 2002; Gordon et al., 2015; Degé, 2021). Music is recognised as enhancing learning and boosting self-esteem (Hallam, 2010).

Human learning presupposes a social nature, children grow their abilities with and through those around them (Vygotsky, 1978). Knowledge is created through collective action and social experience (Dewey, 1916), individuals interact with their environment and live within a social context that mediates their learning (Wandersee et al., 1994). People enter any learning experience with prior knowledge, they are not simply empty vessels to be filled with information (Gilbert et al., 1982). Supportive learning spaces are where individuals can grow and develop through their experiences, which are simultaneously shared with others, leading to the cultivation of knowledge and values that are mutually accepted and embraced by others (Kelly, 1963). These concepts which are widely accepted in the Western world's approach to education are explicitly linked to the values of social pedagogy.

Whether working in early years, higher education or social services, social pedagogy applies, because human development is a lifelong process (Petrie, 2015). Regardless of the age-range, appropriate activities and trusting relationships are central to all successful learning and development. And this is where music activities as a learning opportunity can be problematic. Music activities can place learners in a place of hyper awareness of the skills or knowledge they consciously do not have yet, with the potential pressure of 'performing' to their peers, too. The first step of all learning is a willingness to lean into this vulnerable position, the position of not knowing, not understanding. And this can be a huge step to take, which is why social pedagogy recognises that

DOI: 10.4324/9781003533276-6

being 'alongside' learners is so important. Establishing trust is a vital first step. To know areas for development can be shared without judgement, to make mistakes without feeling a failure, and to trust that the practitioner believes that the goal for success is achievable are key foundations in this practitioner-learner relationship. It is this social connection that lays the cornerstone for everything else to follow.

The music education context

The challenges faced by music education over the decades are well documented in the literature (Swanwick, 1988; Philpott and Plummeridge, 2001; DFES, 2006). Following decades of shifting educational landscape and funding for the arts, the contemporary context for music practitioners is challenging. Most recently, following a period of a relatively supportive music education environment fostered by initiatives such as *Every Child Matters* (DFES, 2003), the *Music Manifesto Reports* (DFES, 2005, 2007), 'Sing Up!' campaign (DFES, 2011), music hubs and free instrumental teaching opportunities, funding issues and shifts in government policy (Dufour and Griffiths, 2019) now present obstacles to the quality of opportunity that a learner can experience. Added to this, many educators lack confidence in this area. For example, Ofsted has found that primary teachers often have low self-esteem as musicians (Ofsted, 1993/1994, p. 4) which can negatively affect the standard of music activity that the learner experiences. In this chapter I explain how all practitioners, regardless of their own training or resources available, can create a supportive environment where musical experiences can be shared, diverse musical traditions can be explored and stereotypes can be challenged. And I hope, by doing so, that more practitioners will be encouraged to incorporate music into their practice (Hall et al., 2012).

As part of the arts, music is seen by many to be a creative subject. However, just as the core subjects also require creative skills (such as innovation in scientific inquiry, designing solutions in maths and self-expression in English), creative subjects can require elements that are less creative and more technical. For example, anyone who has learned to play an instrument through formal tuition may have a story to tell about how uninspiring musical theory can be. The repetition of practicing for a perfect performance or a dry experience of learning about music history are the types of experiences that lead people to disengage with music. There are elements of every subject that can be experienced negatively, and music is no exception. Creative subjects can be approached in less than creative ways.

Losing sight of the motivation for creating music can remove the context and purpose for learning from music experiences. Music soothes, lifts and transports us to memories we cherish, and moments of great sorrow, and it is important to make the connection with the composer's motivation behind the music. Asking questions about the personal, geographical and historical context for the creation of music allows us to see the humanity of the composer and offers a chance for connections to be made between life experiences. When we discuss music history and performance, we must hold onto this dimension that drives the music. The passion behind the sounds and the connection to emotion from the storyteller to their captivated audience is what brings music to life, whether Beethoven or Ed Sheeran. We must remember the purpose. Music is a point of connection.

> **Reflection point**
>
> Think of a song, or a piece of music that you love to hear when it comes on the radio- why is that? What memories do you connect with that song? What emotions does it provoke?

Encouraging individuals to interrogate how music has played a role in their own lives, how it has formed their own musical journey, enables them to recognise their own musicality, even when they are not a musician in the traditional sense of the word. Using an open-minded approach to the language chosen to express emotion, self-identity and cultural connection, life narrative allows us to provide an understanding of the historical and geographical context of the music and the message the composer is communicating to their intended audience; we must remember that music is there to tell a story. And as social pedagogues, this is something that we can tap into, music can serve as a common third as we explore the emotions and experiences of the composer, and how each interrelated dimension creates a connection to the listener and their experience of the music. Exploring music provides the opportunity to appreciate the meaning and the messages that it holds and to investigate what some sounds mean to us, collectively and individually. As social pedagogues our role is to highlight similarities in our connections with musical creations and to explore differences, to better understand the human experience through the messages of the music.

Integration of social pedagogy into music education

Music education has long divided learners and has a history of being seen through a cultural divide (Deloughry, 2014; Kallio, 2021). There has been a dominant perception that music is not for all. Learning a musical instrument takes time, and financial investment, and exists within a generally culturally accepted narrative that not everyone was born to be musical (Kirnarskaya, 2009; Gaztambide-Fernández, 2010). There are opposing societal views regarding musical ability where ability is seen as either fixed or acquired through learning experiences (Molden and Dweck, 2000). The notion of fixed musical ability has been devastating to children's opportunities in music and many adults have been educated out of feeling they are musical, creative and imaginative (Young, 2009). However, the barrier of musicianship or musicality is a fiction, and with some focused work on challenging and developing ideas of what it really means to be musical, learners can be released from the emotional and social barriers and find joy in engaging in music-focused activities (Figure 6.1).

In my experience as an educator with expertise in music, the phrase I hear most often is a variation on a theme of "I'm not musical". My heart sinks every time, and I advocate a very clear message to all educators: you do not have to be a musician to be musical.

Loving music, connecting with music and understanding how music forms parts of your identity is key, not only to unlocking our skills for encouraging musical appreciation in the next generation, but also to making connections with others. Musicality is global and transcends cultures, whilst yet allowing cultural, social and individual expressions of self-identity. Offering learners the opportunity to connect with a diverse range of composers and musicians allows them all to find themselves reflected somewhere in their study of music.

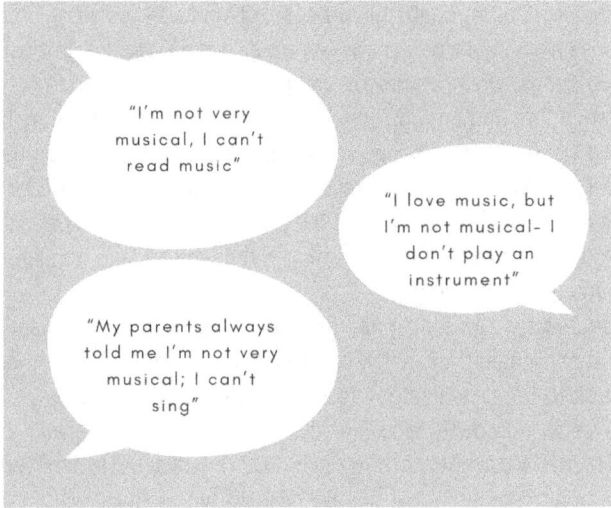

Figure 6.1 Typical comments made about not being musical.

Reflection point

Do you see yourself as musical? Does that influence whether you volunteer to take part in, or facilitate, musical activities?

The goal of music education is not to produce the next generation of recording artists; the reality is that very few will ever sellout stadium tours, but this is not to limit the dreams of our musical learners. By focusing on musicality, the barrier to facilitating musical activities when you are not a musician could be broken down. Practitioners who feel unable to teach music may be empowered to see that their musicality is enough for them to facilitate music-focused activities. The aim of inclusive practices, such as Universal Design for Learning (UDL), is that they meet a range of needs, through multiple means of engagement, representation, action and expression (Hall et al., 2012; Rose, 2000). The same can apply to approaches to music. Addressing musicality before musicianship can enable practitioners to see the potential of music activities to draw together and to empower individuals through this universal language.

There are vast opportunities for engagement with music to develop learners' sense of self and to facilitate social connection and cultural celebration, as music transcends culture, gender, class, race and religion. The job opportunities of the children and young people that we work with today may not exist yet, and by advocating musicality, we enable them to both dream and see potential in their own musical futures. Many music industry opportunities from sound technicians to music supervisors in television and film do not require adeptness as a musician. In considering the holistic development of *all* children, and providing opportunity for all to fulfil their potential, we should provide opportunities for those that we support to explore their own musicality, as they explore the many aspects and potentialities of themselves.

An awareness of the diverse range of people behind the *global* history of music can bring us together with our learners through the process of mutual discovery and expansion of our understanding. Music is a uniting force and, as we are all human, we are all musical. Each one of us remembers childhood songs, when we discovered popular music, the first music gig we attended, the first t-shirt we owned that had a group's name, or a group's lyrics. All of us have memories that are sparked when we hear a certain song, sometimes positive, sometimes negative. Most of us will have memories of how similar tastes in music drew us to friends. Music has been influential in all of our lives, if not centrally, then at least on the periphery, and our experiences with music can provide a powerful 'common third' when interacting with learners, and a valuable source for us to better understand ourselves and others.

A note about vocabulary. Facilitating the activity of musical composition through technical aspects alone can be challenging for many, but it is worth mentioning that these 'building blocks' are part of enabling all to have clear steps to success. Using the related vocabulary as a 'list of key ingredients' may suit individuals who find the potentially 'blank canvas' of musical creation overwhelming. The Model Music Curriculum (DfE, 2021) outlines the key terms such as pitch, tempo and timbre amongst others, that should be used when discussing music, however, it is important to understand that this is the agreed language of *Western* musical traditions. There are numerous forms of music and numerous names to describe it, as I'm sure children and young people will be happy to share with you. The process required to decolonise our musical lexicon is to understand that we have a very basic set of vocabulary as a starting point, but with an inclusive and open approach, in partnership with our learners, we can add to and enrich this. As social pedagogues we learn with, and that means listening to, and valuing the lived experiences, and culture-specific languages, of those that we work with.

> **Reflection point**
>
> In facilitating learning activities with others think about the extent to which you dictate the vocabulary of others or whether you are open to the new vocabulary emerging from diverse cultural contexts.

A world of possibility: teaching through a global perspective of music

Culturally responsive education is key to social pedagogy. Enabling an authentic and active social consciousness that recognises the intersections of culture and social experience in the learning space enables the crossing of cultural and social boundaries (Villegas and Lucas, 2002). As we enable individuals to achieve within music, we should encourage self-expression through their own cultural or social vocabulary. Welcoming alternative styles of music and sharing the stories of composers and musicians who follow a range of traditions in musical creation offers a well-rounded experience for developing musical literacy. It is useful to note that there are lists of musicians and composers (Hall, 2021) who never learned how to read traditional musical notation, from Hans Zimmer to Danny Elfman, Arethra Franklin to Taylor Swift and from Jimmy Hendrix to Elvis Presley, and through recognising this it provides inspiration that anyone can be a musician, even without any formal training.

It is important that social pedagogues understand their own purpose and the purpose of the musical activity that they are facilitating. For example, musical activities can be based upon and spark discussions around social injustices that have been challenged through music (Holder, 2023). Shevock (2018) advocates for an eco-literate pedagogy, integrating indigenous and spiritual knowledge: the links with social pedagogy are clear. Orr (2020) calls for innovative musical practices that inspire environmental awareness and action, urging collaboration across disciplines to protect the Earth. One needs to only consider the enormity of an event like Band Aid (1984) to see the potential of this.

Martusewicz et al. (2015) argue for a radical re-envisioning of music education to emphasise interdisciplinary and experiential learning. They stress the importance of helping children maintain wonder in nature, develop sensory capacities fully, address mental health needs when necessary, and align more closely with their innate nature and life purpose. Furthermore, they place these individual concerns within the broader context of relationships and community, suggesting that music education can also contribute to stewardship and the regeneration of environmental and cultural resources (Martusewicz et al., 2015). Whether through instruments, dance, or speech, uncovering multiple layers of musical representation can provide varied channels through which children and young people can communicate effectively (Holder, 2023). Plotkin (2008) argues that Western and Westernised cultures promote values such as social conformity, materialism and self-centredness over authenticity, intimate relationships and creative exploration. Music can be a way of challenging this narrowness and providing forms of expression for those who may not be able to express themselves in other ways.

Boyce-Tillman (2020) argues that music-making is a powerful tool to challenge and transcend the destructive sociopolitical norms that endanger humanity, offering pathways to spiritual connection and wonder, and there is an increasing awareness of how ideas of stewardship come through cultures outside of the dominant western discourse, particularly indigenous cultures (Elliott and Rodenburg, 2019; Boyce-Tillman, 2020). Once we have a global perspective in our pedagogy for teaching the social history of music, we can extend this into other areas of self-expression, with children and young people exploring song and their own musical identities. We can tackle stereotypical viewpoints by embracing representative resources, challenging social barriers, and enabling **everyone** to find their voice.

> ### **Reflection point**
>
> Many songs which tackle societal issues such as racism and class divides have made it into our music charts... can you think of any?

Our role as social pedagogues is to explore music in all of its diversity, including who makes it, how they make it, where you can find it and the value of it. We can guide individuals to unravel the complexities of the interrelated dimensions of music to focus on the purpose behind it, and to acknowledge a global perspective whilst finding connection with the people behind the music. Music is, by nature, a social practice to be understood in context (Hess, 2015) and social pedagogy allows each person to see themselves in music and to find purpose, passion and drive for their own musical responses, appreciating that their lived musical experience matters.

> **Reflection point**
>
> You want to find out more about your learners, what music-based activity might enable that?

Conclusion

This chapter explored the intersection of social pedagogy and music education, emphasising the imperative of fostering belonging and affirming the intrinsic value of everyone within musical learning environments. By integrating social pedagogy when facilitating musical activities, practitioners can create inclusive spaces where people can authentically engage with music, drawing upon their lived experiences to cultivate musical identities and lifelong connections with music.

Central to this discussion is the recognition of music's transformative potential beyond its technical aspects. Music enhances cognitive abilities and academic skills and serves as a vehicle for emotional expression and social interaction. Through a social pedagogical lens, practitioners view the individuals they work with holistically, recognising their social contexts and personal narratives, narratives which will have included music at some point in their development. Openness can only be achieved through a relationship built upon trust between educator and learner, this means fostering environments where mistakes are opportunities for growth and where diverse forms of expression are celebrated.

This chapter has also underscored the importance of cultural responsiveness. By embracing diverse musical traditions and narratives, practitioners empower others to explore their musicality in ways that resonate with their own cultural backgrounds. This inclusive approach not only enriches musical experiences but also challenges stereotypes and broadens perspectives on what it means to be musical. Looking ahead, the chapter advocates for a global perspective in music pedagogy, where practitioners guide individuals to understand music as a universal language that transcends boundaries. By highlighting the stories and contexts behind musical creations, educators can inspire others to connect deeply with music's purpose and meaning in their lives. Despite funding cuts in the education context, practitioners are encouraged to advocate for the value of music, emphasising its role in nurturing creativity (Liu, 2023), critical thinking (Aycicek, 2021) and emotional wellbeing (Smith, 2021).

In summary, when viewed through the lens of social pedagogy music offers a pathway for people to develop not only musical skills but also a sense of belonging, resilience and cultural awareness. By prioritising inclusive practices, practitioners can create transformative learning experiences that empower others to explore their musical potential and cultivate a lifelong love and appreciation for music.

Summary points

- Musicality vs. musicianship: Understanding and valuing musicality over musicianship can help practitioners feel more confident in facilitating musical activities. Emphasising that one does not need to be a musician to appreciate and teach music allows for a broader and more inclusive approach.

- Social pedagogy and music: Integrating social pedagogy and music promotes a sense of belonging and values each person's individuality through the concept of mattering. This approach uses people's lived experiences to explore music, helping them develop skills and a lifelong love for music.
- Importance of trust and connection: Establishing trust between practitioners and the people they work with is vital. Trust allows everyone to feel safe in sharing their areas for development, make mistakes and believe in their success, which lays the foundation for a strong relationship.
- Challenges in music education: The fluctuating support and funding for music education present significant challenges. Despite various initiatives to promote music in schools, issues like inconsistent training and low self-esteem among practitioners affect the overall quality of music facilitation.
- Global and inclusive perspective: Approaching music from a global perspective and incorporating diverse musical traditions can be enriching. This approach helps dismantle stereotypes and encourages self-expression, enabling a connection with various musical forms and finding their unique musical identity.
- Music as a social tool: Music can promote social awareness and empathy. Collaborative musical experiences and inclusive practices in facilitating musical activities can foster social and emotional development, helping people become socially conscious citizens who understand the power of music to drive social change.

Recommended reading

Hess, J. (2019) *Music Education for Social Change: Constructing an Activist Music Education*. Abingdon: Routledge.

Smith, T. D. (2021) Music education for surviving and thriving: Cultivating children's wonder, senses, emotional wellbeing, and wild nature as a means to discover and fulfil their life's purpose. In *Frontiers in Education* (Vol. 6, p. 648799). Frontiers Media SA.

References

Aycicek, B. (2021) Integration of critical thinking into curriculum: Perspectives of prospective teachers. *Thinking Skills and Creativity*, 41, pp.100895.

Band Aid (1984) Do They Know Its Christmas? Available at www.youtube.com/watch?v=RH-xd5bPKTA (Accessed 3 February 2025).

Bilhartz, T. D., Bruhn, R. A. and Olson, J. E. (1999) The effect of early music training on child cognitive development. *Journal of Applied Developmental Psychology*, 20(4), pp. 615–636.

Boyce-Tillman, J. (2020) An ecology of eudaimonia and its implications for music education. In G. Dylan Smith and M. Silverman (Eds) *Eudaimonia*. New York: Routledge. pp. 102–125.

Butzlaff, R. (2000) Can music be used to teach reading? *Journal of Aesthetic Education*, 34(3/4), pp. 167–178.

Campabello, N., De Carlo, M. J., O'neil, J. and Vacek, M. J. (2002) Music Enhances Learning. Masters thesis published online. Available at: https://files.eric.ed.gov/fulltext/ED471580.pdf (Accessed 20 January 2025).

Degé, F. (2021) Music lessons and cognitive abilities in children: How far transfer could be possible. *Frontiers in Psychology*, 11, p. 557807.

Deloughry, C. (2014) Who pays and who plays? Music school research ii. In M. Hahn, and F.-O. Hofecker (Eds) *Music School Research II. The Future of Music Schools – European Perspectives*. St. Pölten: Musikschulmanagement Niedrösterreich. pp. 151–168.

Dewey, J. (1916)(1997) *Democracy and Education: An Introduction to the Philosophy of Education*. New York: The Free Press.

DfES (Department for Education and Skills) (2003) 'Every Child Matters' Green Paper, Cm. 5860. London: The Stationery Office (TSO).

DfES (2005) The Music Manifesto Report No 1. Norwich. Crown Publications.
DfES (Department for Education and Skills) (2006) Departmental Report No 2. Available at https://assets.publishing.service.gov.uk/media/5a7ef89de5274a2e87db30b5/DFE_Departmental_Report_2006.pdf (Accessed 14th February 2024).
DfES (Department for Education and Skills) (2007) Music Manifesto Report No 2 (Every Child's Music Matters). Available at https://webarchive.nationalarchives.gov.uk/ukgwa/20100612004747/ www.musicmanifesto.co.uk/research/details/music-manifesto-report-no-2/19085 (Accessed 14th February 2024).
Department for Education [DfE]. (2021) Model music curriculum: Key stages 1 to 3: Non-statutory guidance for the national curriculum in England. https://assets.publishing.service.gov.uk/government/uploads/system/uploads/attachment_data/file/974366/Model_Music_Curriculum_Full.pdf
Dufour, B. and Griffiths, A. (2019) 'Not enough music': A critique of music education in schools in England.
Elliott, P. and Rodenburg, J. (2019) Supporting new teachers in environmental and sustainability education: The pathway to stewardship and kinship. In D. D. Karrow and M. DiGiuseppe (Eds) *Environmental and Sustainability Education in Teacher Education: Canadian Perspectives*. New York: Springer International Publishing.
Gaztambide-Fernández, R. (2010) Wherefore the musicians? *Philosophy of Music Education Review*, 18(1), pp. 65–84.
Gilbert, J., Osborne, R. and Fensham, P. (1982) Children's science and its consequences for teaching. *Science Education*, 66, pp. 623–633. http://dx.doi.org/10.1002/sce.3730660412
Gordon, R. L., Fehd, H. M. and McCandliss, B. D. (2015). Does music training enhance literacy skills? A meta-analysis. *Frontiers in Psychology*, 6, p. 1777.
Hall, T. E., Meyer, A. and Rose, D. H. (Eds) (2012) *Universal Design for Learning in the Classroom: Practical Applications*. New York: Guilford Press.
Hallam, S. (2010) The power of music: Its impact on the intellectual, social and personal development of children and young people. *International Journal of Music Education*, 28(3), pp. 269–289.
Hess, J. (2015) Decolonizing music education: Moving beyond tokenism. *International Journal of Music Education*, 33(3), pp. 336–347.
Holder, N. (2023) Challenging attitudes towards race and representation in music education *Orff Schulwerk International Journal of IOFSF*, 2(2). Available at: www.iosfsjournal.com/2-2 (Accessed 3 July 2024).
Kallio, A. A. (Ed.) (2021) *Difference and Division in Music Education*. New York: Routledge.
Kelly, G. (1963) *A Theory of Personality: The Psychology of Personal Constructs*. New York: W. W. Norton and Company.
Kirnarskaya, D. (2009) *The natural musician: On abilities, giftedness, and talent*. New York: Oxford University Press.
Liu, Y. (2023) The Influence of Music Activities on Children's Creative Thinking Development. In *SHS Web of Conferences*, 180, p. 04001. EDP Sciences.
Martusewicz, R. A., Edmundson, J. and Lupinacci, J. (2015) *Ecojustice Education: Toward Diverse, Democratic, and Sustainable Communities*, 3rd edn. Abingdon: Routledge.
Molden, D.C. and Dweck, C.S. (2000) Meaning and motivation. In *Intrinsic and extrinsic motivation*. Academic Press, pp. 131–159.
OfSTED (1993/1994) *Inspection of Instrumental Music Services*. London: HMSO Publications.
Orr, D. W. (2020) Musicophilia, biophilia, and the human prospect. In G. Dylan Smith and M. Silverman (Eds) *Eudaimonia: Perspectives for Music Learning*. Abingdon: Routledge, pp. 50–59.
Petrie, P. (2015) Social justice and social pedagogy. In C. Cooper, S. Gorvally and G. Hughes (Eds) *Socially Just, Radical Alternatives for Education and Youth Work Practice: Re-imagining Ways of Working with Young People*. London: Palgrave Macmillan UK, pp. 85–106.
Philpott, C. and Plummeridge, C. (2001) *Issues in Music Teaching*. London: Routledge Falmer.
Plotkin, B. (2008) *Nature and the Human Soul: Cultivating Wholeness in a Fragmented World*. Novato, CA: New World Library.
Rose, D. (2000). Universal design for learning. *Journal of Special Education Technology*, 15(4), pp. 47–51.
Shevock, D. J. (2018) *Eco-Literate Music Pedagogy*. Abingdon: Routledge.
Sing Up! (2011) Executive Summary. Available at www.singup.org/fileadmin/user_upload/Blog/PDFs/Sing_Up_2007-11_Executive_Summary_01.pdf (Accessed 14th February 2024).
Smith, T. D. (2021) Music education for Surviving and Thriving: Cultivating children's wonder, senses, emotional wellbeing, and wild nature as a means to discover and fulfil their life's purpose. *Frontiers in Education*, 6, p. 648799. https://doi.org/10.3389/feduc.2021.648799
Swanwick, K. (1988) *Music, Mind and Education*. London: Routledge.
Villegas, A. M. and Lucas, T. (2002) *Educating Culturally Responsive Teachers: A Coherent Approach*. New York: Suny Press.

Vygotsky, L. S. (1978) *Mind in Society.* Cambridge MA: Harvard University Press.
Wandersee, J. H., Mintzes, J. J. and Novak, J. D. (1994) Research on alternative conceptions in science. In D. L. Gabel (Ed.) *Handbook of Research on Science Teaching and Learning.* New York: Simon and Schuster and Prentice Hall International, pp. 177–210.
Young, S. (2009) *Essential Guides for Early Years Practitioners: Music 3–5.* Abingdon: Routledge.

Website resource

Hall, S.A. (2021) '10 legendary musicians who never learned to read music' Classic FM.com. Available at www.classicfm.com/discover-music/famous-musicians-who-cant-read-music/ (Accessed 10 November 2024)

7 Taking a social pedagogical approach to including Gypsy, Roma and Traveller communities in a setting

Stacey Hodgkins

Introduction: Gypsy, Roma and Travellers in the UK

It is estimated that there are approximately 300,000 Gypsies and Travellers and 200,000 Roma in the UK (Friends Families and Travellers, FFT, 2023), although the term Gypsy, Roma, Traveller encompasses various groups within these umbrella terms. These groups include English Gypsies, Welsh Gypsies, Irish Travellers, Romany Gypsies, Roma, Scottish Travellers, Bargee and New Age Travellers amongst others. All these groups have different roots but 'have been traditionally associated with a nomadic way of life' (Bhopal, 2011, p. 466). Some groups have been in the UK since 1000CE, with migration of Romany Gypsies in 1500. Regardless of group, all communities within this umbrella term face challenges accessing basic needs such as health, housing and education, contributing to limitations in life aspirations (House of Commons, 2019, p. 22). They also face prejudice and racism stemming back over centuries, with the creation of a negative stereotypical version of culture and communities which has become a fixed perception (FFT, 2023, p. 20). Despite this, a report by the House of Commons (2019, p. 3) stated 'Gypsy, Roma and Traveller communities have every right to live their lives according to their values and beliefs within the law that applies to every UK resident'.

With complete nomadism becoming more of a challenge due to changing wider societal factors including legislation and a lack of stopping places, communities have been forced to change. This has resulted in only a small number of families travelling all year round or for set seasonal work patterns. Traditional ways of life are passing away and work constraints make it more of a challenge. Many GRT families are now settling in bricks-and-mortar houses, and due to a shortage of site provision some families become displaced from extended family members. This then creates the misconception that because they are settled, they are no longer GRT. This is not the case at all: they do indeed fiercely hold onto their cultural identity. They do this by living the same way in bricks and mortar as they would live on the roadside or in a trailer on a site. It is a way of life that stays with you always.

Many GRTs struggle to access healthcare. In 2024 (p. 9), a report by the Roma Support group and partners stated:

> Gypsy, Roma and Traveller people face chronic exclusion across the social determinants of health causing high risk of poor health. Increasing evidence highlights wide inequalities in accommodation, education and employment, impacting on the mental wellbeing of Gypsies, Roma. Over 90% of Gypsies, Roma and Travellers experience racism and discrimination in their everyday life, exacerbating health inequalities.

DOI: 10.4324/9781003533276-7

The barriers faced by GRTs accessing healthcare include the stigma attached to mental health issues, not knowing how to access a GP and not being able to read correspondence due to literacy barriers, to name just a few. In a country that boasts of accessible welfare services for all, these communities should not still be experiencing such inequality. Although this chapter cannot tackle the range of issues in our social structure, it can consider the messages that future generations receive about GRT people and their community.

Historical context of Gypsy, Roma and Traveller engagement with education

The UK has championed education for all dating back to the 1944 Education Act. Reports and policies written since this time have recommended that local authorities should try to improve access to education for GRT pupils, with Bhopal (2011, p. 175) observing how 'The educational underachievement of Gypsies and Travellers has been a cause for concern as far back as The Plowden Report 1967 and the Swann Report 1985'. There were common themes in both reports that highlighted the following:

- Local authorities needed to improve access to school for Gypsy, Roma and Traveller Pupils.
- Prejudice was not only faced by these communities but by all ethnic minority communities.
- No child should be expected to keep their home language and culture separate from school.

One solution to try to end this cycle of disadvantage in education came in the form of the funded Traveller Education Service that worked closely with GRT families to engage them in education. I remember seeing this service delivered via a mobile bus going onto sites or pulling up on the roadside. Children could then be taught with their parents nearby. Within schools at this time, if it was known that GRT children were not staying long, they often were put onto a separate table with no attempt made to provide them with meaningful learning opportunities.

From the 1990s onwards, conscious attempts were made to dispel barriers to inclusion for GRT children. These came in the form of policymaking, initiatives and legislation. Education for these communities was no further forward than it was in the 1960s. In 2003 the Advisory Council for Education of Romany and other Travellers (ACERT, undated) requested that the Government add a 'Gypsy, Roma and Traveller' category to the school admission form. There was still limited progress in their access to education, and funding continued to be cut to services to these communities. However, in the years that followed publications were produced on what was best practice by organisations, including Ofsted and the Department for Children, Schools and Families. These included topics such as: *Raising the Achievement of Gypsy and Traveller Children* (DCSF, 2009) and *Raising the Attainment of Gypsy, Roma and Traveller Children* (NATT, 2011).

The publications stated that more needed to be done to support GRT engagement with education. However, there continued to be no requirement to ensuring inclusion. GRT communities always appeared to be last on the list of priorities, and funding gradually disappeared for Traveller Education Support Services. Attainment and engagement gaps became wider which resulted in marginalisation becoming more apparent and engagement with education more sporadic (Foster and Cemlyn, 2012).

The current education landscape

Moving forward to the present day, a report carried out by Friends, Families and Travellers (2023) highlighted that GRT children have the lowest educational attainment at all key stages. This included primary education up to secondary education and included all ethnic groups in the UK. Marginalisation in education is clearly still a challenge, despite all legislation, policies and publications. It is vital to recognise that if poor educational attainment is addressed, then it will significantly impact upon other inequalities in GRT communities, such as health and housing. However, disengagement does not wholly rest on the inadequacies of educational provision, it also stems from the communities themselves. Parents fear that education will take their children away from their culture. Foster and Cemlyn (2012, p. 63) explain:

> People who have been marginalised and subjected to prejudice for generations look to their own communities to equip children with the skills they need as adults, believing learning these skills come by working alongside their relatives.

It is useful to unpack the many barriers to education that GRT families can face to fully understand the reluctance to engage. These might include, but are not limited to:

- Parents have had negative experiences of education so do not feel schools are safe places for children.
- Parents have a fear that children will lose a sense of who they are and their culture.
- Children do not attend school due to being bullied and experiencing racism. In 2019 statistics showed that 86 per cent of Gypsy, Roma and Traveller pupils reported bullying and 73 per cent racism (FFT, 2023, p. 6).
- There is a stereotypical stigma whereby it is assumed that because they come from Gypsy, Roma and Traveller heritage, they are going to leave school anyway.
- There can be a lack of understanding from educational establishments about culture. This can include not acknowledging important cultural celebrations and history of the heritage.
- There are no formal requirements for a Traveller Education Service in every area. It is the decision of local authorities to decide how to share funding between schools and services (House of Commons, 2024).

Coming from a Romany Gypsy family, although I hid my heritage while at school, it was still apparent to some teachers and other children around me that I was different. I did experience really challenging school days with some of these barriers, including bullying, which impacted on the experience I had right through to high school. This feeling of not belonging also impacted negatively upon my achievement in my schoolwork and exams.

In the 2019 House of Commons report *Tackling Inequalities for Gypsy, Roma and Traveller Communities* it was recognised that one of the reasons for poor outcomes was due to 'lack of co-operation between local authorities, schools, regulators and families which has led to a perfect storm of poor outcomes' (Women and Equalities Committee, 2019, p. 23). Poor outcomes have persisted. In 2023 only 18 per cent of Gypsy and Roma children and 21 per cent of Irish Travellers met the expected educational standard (House of Commons, 2024).

Despite these factors, it should not be assumed that all Gypsy, Roma and Travellers have a negative perception of education. In the 2022 ONS census it revealed that some members of the GRT communities do value education and want their children to attend school. They want them to receive a good education as it is an experience they never had. There is no easy explanation as to why, in a cultural climate that seems to be increasingly accepting of 'difference', the barriers outlined above still exist. However, it is possible that with greater awareness practitioners may be able to alleviate some of them and make a difference to the individuals they work with. In the following sections I explain how a social pedagogical approach might be implemented to challenge inequities.

> **Reflection point**
>
> Consider your existing knowledge of GRT families. Have you had previous interactions with them, or is this a new area for you? What are your existing views about GRT families?

The role of social pedagogy

hThe sections that follow focus on various social pedagogical approaches that could be taken to support individuals and families from the GRT community. Pestalozzi, who was born in the eighteenth century, suggested that every individual had the right to an education and had the ability to learn, adding that this could be achieved through using a *ead, heart and hands* approach (Charfe and Gardener, 2019). This approach, I believe, is a useful framework for those working with GRT, or any marginalised community. Below I explore each aspect, and how this approach might look in practice.

Awareness and self-awareness

As practitioners we use knowledge (of topics and people) as the basis of our professional practice. That is, we use our 'head'. This is then combined with self-awareness regarding our practice and those around us. When considered within the context of working with Gypsy, Roma and Traveller communities, a good starting point is to reflect upon your own existing bias. It may be that you are already aware of this bias, or perhaps you have never really considered it before: perhaps it is subconscious, but you will have existing preconceptions of the GRT community, whether positive or negative. In order to take an authentic approach, it is important that you are self-aware enough to endeavour to set aside any existing prejudice while working with children and families from this heritage.

Thempra (2024, *no page*) explains that 'Building trust and authentic relationships with the people we support is very important in social pedagogy'. Change cannot come about if we, as professionals, are not willing to build authentic relationships and gain a deeper understanding of the communities around us. For some of us that might mean acknowledging our limited understanding of GRT communities, for others it might be avoiding unhelpful 'labelling' of this group based on past experiences. As social pedagogues, it is important that we use our head, our ability to reflect, and our academic skills, to gather information about these communities and their heritage. This might be your first stepping stone to informing good practice and could look something like this:

- Researching and being familiar with the history of GRT culture.
- Having an awareness of any existing policies, publications and legislation related to GRT, including education, which may support you with strategies.
- Becoming aware of research about GRT children and families as a basis for asking informed questions when you meet them.
- Finding out if there are any support services available for GRT families in the local area that you may be able to contact.

These are just a few suggestions, and any practitioner will know that each family is unique and set within a context of unique circumstances. By combining what we know with self-awareness, it is possible to connect more authentically with those we support.

> **Refection point**
>
> Of course this does not only apply to GRT families; can you think of other contexts where it would be useful to do some research and find out more about the experiences of the community before working with them?

As Pestalozzi informed us, effective, holistic pedagogy requires 'heart' (Charfe and Gardener, 2019). This closely relates to our '*Haltung*', in that the framework of values and beliefs that underpin our practice will be palpable to those that we work with and will affect 'our relationships and communications with others' (Petrie, 2011, p. 8). Emotions, or heart, are central to this, a key aspect of which is our ability to empathise with those we work with. As has already been explored, many GRT families have faced ongoing issues related to prejudice, racism and adverse life experience, and for them sending their children to school is a significant, progressive step. It is important to acknowledge, and to be able to empathise with, the fear and anxiety that these families may be experiencing during this time.

Pollock and Barrow (2021, p. 115) define a sense of community as 'A feeling that members matter to one another and that members' needs will be met through their commitment to be together'. It is important to consider how you reassure the families that you are working with that you are 'on the same side' and share the same goals for the child.

> **Reflection point**
>
> Building trusting relationships requires a degree of openness. How, and what type of information might you share about yourself to the families that you work with?
>
> To aid your reflection it might be useful to look at Thempra's discussion of '*The Three Ps*', the professional, the personal and the private.

To consider these concepts in a practical way I would like you to imagine that the family in the case study below have arrived in your local area and would like to enrol their children at your school. To enable the successful integration of the children into your school, it is important to consider the following.

- The family's background
- Living conditions
- The children's interests
- Educational support that may be needed
- Factors that may affect attendance.

As you read through the case study that follows consider these aspects and some of the challenges that may arise in supporting this family.

Part 1 – The Butler family

Dad – Henry – Works 12 hours a day
Mum – Annie – Currently 30 weeks pregnant.
Child 1 – Elsie-Lou, Age 13. Not attending secondary school. Struggles with anxiety and does not want to return. She wants to be at home and learn skills this way.
Child 2 – Billy, Age 9. Loves to be outside and helps with family horses. He goes to work with Henry and really enjoys gardening.
Child 3 – Mary-Ann, Age 5. Loves to help in house and likes to cook. She enjoys playing with her dolls house and looking at books.
Nana – Diana, and Grampy – Jim, raises horses on the site.

The family come from Romany Gypsy heritage. Henry and Annie have recently moved to Annie's mother and fathers' private site in a semi-rural area. They have moved from a house 100 miles away to be closer to extended family after feeling isolated and experiencing prejudice.

Diana and Jim, the grandparents, live in a chalet on the site. Annie and Henry live in a static caravan with access to a separate kitchen and shower block. Jim and Diana rear horses, which are in stables on site with their own field next to the site for exercise.

Henry and Annie have decided that they will only travel in the summer months, May until September, due to Henry having seasonal work in other areas. They would like Billy and Mary-Ann to attend at least primary school. However, they feel nervous and apprehensive due to them having negative experiences when they were children, and also due to their own reading and writing difficulties.

The parents withdrew Elsie-Lou from education at age 11 due to bullying and racism in their last area and would like her to be home schooled. Henry and Annie did approach the school about issues faced but felt they were unsupported and that the school did not want to deal with it, labelling Elsie-Lou as the problem.

Billy started primary school elsewhere, but the parents felt that he was unsupported and faced difficulties while learning in the classroom environment. He was withdrawn at age 7.

Annie has recently noticed that Mary-Ann is struggling with their recent move and that her behaviour has started to change, becoming quieter than usual.

Annie has also faced difficulties through her pregnancy, but due to literacy difficulties and moving areas she currently is not registered with a doctor.

Considering how life looks for this family, it is clear that there will be many challenging aspects:

- The family have faced prejudice and racism in the last area and are (understandably) apprehensive about encountering this again. It will take time to build trust.

- Members of the family are dealing with heightened anxiety as a result of their transition.
- Annie (Mum) needs medical support, and future issues with her pregnancy may affect the children's attendance.
- There is unlikely to be any communication with the father due to his long working hours.
- The parents will need support with the administrative side of settling the children into school, filling out forms, providing information in an accessible way.

You may have noticed other challenges inherent in this situation, such as Billy's love for outdoor activities and the incongruence of this with the sedentary nature of schooling. Fully engaging this family into a school community, which is so foreign to their previous experience, will take time and commitment. But the first step for practitioners working with this family would be simply getting to know them. By finding out what a day may look like, what life looks like from their perspective, practitioners can work in a professional and compassionate way to build a trusting relationship. This will take time and may be built from many small, hands-on experiences, such as those explored below.

Practical engagement and motivation

Having explored how head and heart come into practice, it is the 'hands' that combine all elements together to bring about engagement in a practical way. When considering how to embed the principles into practice and be as inclusive as possible, support needs to be tailored (to the extent possible) to individual need. However, this does require input from both parties. For a positive experience for everyone, not only is there the need for empathic understanding of GRT culture by the practitioners, but GRT communities also need to understand, and empathise with, the aims of the school and wider community. Any effective relationship requires mutual engagement. Gould (2017) provides a simplified outline of how the stages of this might look in practice:

1. Gypsy, Roma and Traveller families voluntarily engage with education and other services.
2. Practitioners invest resources to support the inclusion of Gypsy, Roma and Traveller pupils.
3. Gypsy, Roma and Traveller families engage with the strategies implemented by practitioners.
4. A mutually supportive, trusted school environment is created.

Of course, markers of success would have to be witnessed by stage 2 to enable further progress, and it is interesting to consider what this 'success' might look like.

> ### Reflection point
>
> What would the successful integration of GRT children into a school and its wider community look like? You might want to consider attendance, achievement and social aspects. How would your expectations of GRT children compare to your expectations of the other children?

Consider the aspects of practical engagement as you read part two of the case study.

Part 2 – The Butler family

After reading the initial information about the family as lead practitioner you meet with the relevant school staff to discuss how to welcome the family into the community. You also contact Henry and Annie and invite them to meet with you. They feel apprehensive at first, but after talking things through with you both agree to visit the school with Billy and Mary-Ann.

On the day you warmly welcome them at the entrance and start by introducing them to other staff and show them some of the facilities. Billy and Mary-Ann are welcomed by the other children and seem to enjoy the experience.

You then all go to a quieter area and tell the parents a little more about the inclusive culture of the school.

You go through some of the administrative information with Henry and Annie. The information pack contains forms, school uniform information and a visual timetable of how the school day would look. Unsure of their literacy skills you offer to read the forms for Henry and Annie. You then help them with the information that needs to be completed and give practical advice about obtaining school uniforms and so on.

You share some information about yourselves with Henry and Annie, such as how long you have been working with the school and the ages of your own children. By touching on your own experiences as parents you are able to establish common ground and with parents whose life experience is very different to your own, important for building a foundation of trust.

They seem to be happy at the end of your meeting and agree for the children to start school the following week.

> **Reflection point**
>
> To what extent could you recognise aspects of head, heart and hands in the encounter above? Which were the actions taken that demonstrated each?

It is vital, of course, that such behaviours are not only a 'one off', but that they are conscientiously maintained. With the Butler family this would include ensuring that all information given to them is in accessible format or is shared verbally with them. Also, that the initial connection created during this meeting is maintained and further developed through regular dialogue, showing interest and inviting openness. Ensure communication is not reduced to instructions, or worse, criticisms. Make regular space to share positive aspects of their child's experience with an aim of lessening initial anxieties. Be human and show empathy, parent to parent, or carer to carer, where the wellbeing of the child is always your '*Common Third*'.

> **Reflection point**
>
> Veale (2013, p. 243) defines inclusive education as 'The provision of a framework which encompasses and values all children regardless of their backgrounds and circumstances'. Reflect on the extent to which your own setting, your own practice or both embody this.

Conclusion

For genuine inclusion to take place it is important for practitioners and families to work more closely together to narrow the chasm of misunderstanding that causes the marginalisation of certain groups. The suggestions given in this chapter relating to GRT families could, and should, apply to any marginalised groups. When you read the recommendations outlined below, consider how they reflect a *ead, heart and hands* approach, and the varied and complex communities to which they could apply:

- Become aware of events that are significant to Gypsy, Roma and Traveller communities and why.
- Collect storybooks reflecting GRT culture.
- When discussing concepts such as 'home' be mindful of the variations in all communities, but particularly ethnic minority communities such as Gypsy, Roma and Travellers.
- Recognise Gypsy, Roma and Traveller Month in June, maybe with storytelling events and inviting families to explain more about their culture.
- Be clear and transparent with parents of GRT parents and children of any interventions that may be needed and provide the information step by step and in a reassuring way.
- Find out if the local area has a GRT education team or a general inclusion education team. This will be a good source to form links with for accessing resources, advice and support for both school and the families that you work with.

Summary points

- Gypsy, Roma and Travellers have been present in UK since 1000 with Romany Gypsies arriving in the 1500s.
- Gypsy, Roma and Travellers face many challenges related to health, housing and education.
- Gypsy, Roma and Travellers have tended to have poor engagement with services, particularly education, because of factors including (but not limited to) prejudice, fear of losing culture, being highly mobile, and previous lack of support from professionals.
- It is useful to consider a *ead, heart and hands* approach to working with Gypsy, Roma and Traveller communities as this allows consideration of the whole person and provides opportunity for their unique abilities to be supported. Building strong relationships may in time also help to narrow the gap of marginalisation.
- True inclusion of Gypsy, Roma and Traveller communities and other marginalised ethnic groups can take place when settings and families work closely together.

Recommended reading

Gould, S. (2017) Promoting the social inclusion and academic progress of Gypsy, Roma and Traveller children: A secondary school case study. *Educational Psychology in Practice*, 33(2), pp. 126–148.

LeBas, D. (2018) *The Stopping Places, a Journey Through Gypsy Britain*. London: Penguin.

References

Advisory Council for the Education of Romany and other Travellers (undated). Available at http://acert.org.uk (Accessed 14 September 2024). (Accessed 5 February 2025).

Bhopal, K. (2011) This is a school, it's not a site: Teachers attitudes towards Gypsy and Traveller Pupils in schools in England UK. *British Educational Research Journal*, 37(3), pp. 465–483.

Charfe, L. and Gardener, A. (2019) *Social Pedagogy and Social Work*. London: Sage.

DCSF (2009) *Moving Forward Together: Raising Gypsy, Roma and Traveller Education*. London: DCSF.

Foster, B. and Cemlyn, S. (2012) Education Inclusion and Government Policy. In J. Richardson and A. Ryder (Eds) *Empowerment and Inclusion in British Society*. Bristol: Policy Press, pp. 61–81.

Friends, Families and Travellers (2023) *Education Inequalities Facing Gypsies, Roma and Travellers in England*, pp. 1–10. Brighton: FFT. Available at: www.gypsy-traveller.org/news/new-briefing-on-education-inequalities-faced-by-gypsies-roma-and-travellers/ (Accessed 1 June 2024).

Gould, S. (2017) Promoting the social inclusion and academic progress of Gypsy, Roma and Traveller children: A secondary school case study. *Educational Psychology in Practice*, 33(2), pp. 126–148.

House of Commons. (2024) *House of Commons Libraries (2024) Research Briefing Gypsies and Travellers Educational Outcomes*. UK Parliament. Available at: https://commonslibrary.parliament.uk/research-briefings/cbp-10016/

NATT. (2011) *Raising the Attainment of Gypsy, Roma and Traveller Pupils*. London: NATT.

Office for National Statistics (2022) *Gypsies and Travellers Lived Experiences, Overview England and Wales 2022*. Available at: www.ons.gov.uk/peoplepopulationandcommunity/culturalidentity/ethnicity/articles/gypsiesandtravellerslivedexperiencesoverviewenglandandwales/2022 (Accessed 30th May 2024).

Petrie, P. (2011) *Communication Skills for Working with Children and Young People, Introducing Social Pedagogy Third Edition*. London: Jessica Kingsley Publishers.

Plowden, B. (1967) *Children and Their Primary Schools: A Report of the Central Advisory for Council for Education England*. London: HMSO.

Pollock, L. and Barrow, W. (2021) There's a school community but not everyone is happy about it: Experiences of school as a community among Gypsy, Roma and Traveller children. *Educational and Child Psychology*, 38(2), pp. 113–125.

Swann, M. (1985) *Education for All: The Report of the Committee of Inquiry into the Education of Children from Ethnic Minority Groups*. London: HMSO.

Thempra (2024) The Three Ps. Available at www.thempra.org.uk. (Accessed 20 January 2025).

Veale, F. (2013) *Early Years for Level 4 and 5 and the Foundation Degree*. London: Hodder Education.

Women and Equalities Committee. (2019) *Tackling Inequalities Faced by Gypsy, Roma and Traveller Communities*. London: House of Commons. Available at: https://publications.parliament.uk/pa/cm201719/cmselect/cmwomeq/2411/2411.pdf (Accessed 30 June 2024).

8 Creativity and the common third
Approaches in education

Nicola Watson and Rosemarie Hill

Introduction: a values-based approach to creativity

Creativity is a slippery concept. Everyone knows the term and most have something to say about its relevance and its place in the twenty-first century majority world. People will often identify as either 'creative', or 'definitely not creative'. The perceived value of creativity divides the crowd. For example, it can be characterised as intrinsic to what it means to be human, derided as a route for the non-academic, or associated with leisure or self-expression for the privileged few. As a socially constructed concept, (that is, a concept the meaning of which is dependent upon the prevailing culture and ideology at any particular time and place in history), creativity defies universal definition. By exploring the concept of creativity in the context of social pedagogy, we aim to elucidate how and why creativity deserves its position as central to the meaning and aims of social pedagogy theory and practice.

Our starting place is values. Social pedagogy is a person-centred approach which emphasises the personal, social and moral elements within each individual (Charfe and Gardner, 2019, p. 7). Fostering creativity helps to optimise these elements. Supporting the creative expression of individuals, can provide insights into their unique experience of the world. Sharing and acknowledging our uniqueness offers the opportunity to make connections and deepen our understanding of one another. This approach necessitates the framing of creativity as a democratic, rather than an elite, phenomenon.

An elite definition would suggest that creativity requires exceptional talent or genius and is the preserve of the gifted few. Taylor (2024, p. 7), points out that this perspective has some value in that it acknowledges 'creative achievements which are of historic originality, which push back the frontiers of human knowledge and understanding'. However, for the social pedagogue, this view precludes the recognition of the importance of the creative *process* rather than any outcome, respecting that which is meaningful and of value to individuals rather than foregrounding its cultural value. A democratic conception of creativity is grounded in the belief that everyone can be creative given the right conditions (National Advisory Committee on Creative and Cultural Education; NACCCE, 1999, p. 29).

> **Reflection point**
>
> Do you consider yourself creative? Do you see creativity as something innate to all, or a gift to some?

Defining creativity

Although creativity defies a singular definition, this is not merely because of ideas which prevail in any particular time or place. We also encounter the problem of language and its subjective interpretation. The search for detached, objective meanings of subjective concepts can be intriguing but is ultimately futile. The twentieth-century philosopher Ludwig Wittgenstein (1953, p. 32), likened the rules of language to games. A game is instantly recognisable and yet when we analyse the properties of games, 'similarities crop up and disappear'. Wittgenstein suggested that it is more useful to look for 'family resemblances' rather than definitions (1953, p. 32). We recognise similarities in the features of members of a particular family, overlapping or in details. However, they are not the same. Therefore, in teasing out elements of what for us, constitutes creativity, we are aiming to provoke your thinking and consideration of what creativity means to you: those features that you recognise across different fields of creativity, rather than asking you to adopt our ideas. We hope, however, that our thinking can act as a useful springboard for yours and support the synthesis of ideas across creativity and social pedagogy, thereby finding points of connection and widening understanding.

Reflection point

Before you read on, if you were to define creativity now, what would your definition be?

In creating a provisional understanding of what defines creativity, it is useful to distinguish between outcomes, processes and dispositions. These are not discrete categories but overlap and resemble one another. However, by teasing out characteristic elements and recognising their distinctions and similarities, we can hone our understanding of creativity. Below, we consider each of these aspects of creativity.

Creativity as outcomes

Many commentators regard creativity as *producing* something which is original and of value (Robinson, 2011, Bruce 2011). This may be regarded as an outcome-focused perspective which foregrounds creativity in terms of cultural value. Indeed, Sawyer (2003, p. 240, cited in Glăveanu, 2011) exemplifies an elite rather than a democratic definition of creativity in distinguishing between adult and child creativity thus:

> Some of us are willing to retain a residual notion of small c creativity – the everyday cleverness that makes us smile or makes life easier – for the novel, unusual actions of children, but we all distinguish this from big C Creativity, the creation of culture-transforming products that is found only in adults.

In contrast, a democratic definition would not distinguish between adult and child in this way but would align with the social pedagogy principle of the Diamond Model, (introduced in Chapter 2).

Holtoff and Eichsteller (2009, p. 60) recognise the Diamond Model as embodying the fundamental principle that,

> every human being has intrinsic value. We are all precious and possess unique knowledge, skills and abilities. But as with a diamond, not all of this richness is necessarily visible. Not all diamonds are polished and sparkly, but all of them have the potential to be.

Through this lens, a child's hand-made birthday card or an adult's upcycled piece of furniture satisfies the criteria of a creative outcome in that each is original, not a reiteration of something already in existence and each is of value, either culturally, or to individuals who deem them so. In addition to artistic outcomes, other examples from a democratic perspective would include curating or arranging objects, inventing something or solving a problem in a novel way.

Creativity as dispositions and processes

This view of creativity involves identifying dispositions and behaviours which can be characterised as resembling or comprising creativity. One such characteristic is imagination which can be both a disposition: an imaginative person, and a process: the process of imagining. Many commentators regard imagination as the foundation of creativity. Vygotsky, 'defined imagination as using experience to create ideas rather than repeat or imitate an experience' (Hedges, 2020, p. 5). Robinson (2011) regarded creativity as applied imagination. For him, imagination is 'being able to think about what's not there, being able to step out of the here and now and see things differently' (Charfe et al., 2020, p. 2). Imagination is a prerequisite to a range of creative behaviours such as flexible or possibility-thinking. Possibility-thinking involves thinking 'about what *could* be possible, as opposed to what *is* or *should* be possible, [and therefore] involves applied imagination' (Cooper, 2013, p. 4).

Imagination can also support empathy; the capacity to imagine the experience of another and to identify with them even when personal prior experience is lacking. The capacity to apply imagination, and thereby think creatively, requires a disposition of open-mindedness; the ability to entertain differing and multiple perspectives rather than a rigid, rule-bound way of thinking (Cooper, 2013, Duffy, 2010, Stewart, 2011). A non-judgemental approach is a core value in social pedagogy (Charfe and Gardner, 2019, p. 7). This disposition acts as a brake on a rush to judgement. It provides opportunity for the development of empathy and respect, which can act as a basis for positive relationships.

Another disposition which aids creativity is the ability to tolerate uncertainty. Tolerance of uncertainty facilitates processes or behaviours such as open-ended thinking, risk-taking, exploring and experimenting. From an education perspective, Kirby and Webb (2023, p. 17) see the value of uncertainty as offering an 'invitation' for creativity, and for the mentor and mentee to be 'uncertain together'. Roseneil (2023, p. X111), points out that in an uncertain world, 'our ability to shape our shared future rests on our ability to acknowledge and lean into the uncertainty'.

A further disposition we regard as fundamental to creativity is curiosity. Over a century ago, John Dewey (1910, p. 34) recognised curiosity as an innate characteristic in children. He suggested that the educator's task was to 'keep alive the sacred spark of wonder and to fan the flame that already glows'. In writing about the social pedagogical principle of *Bildung*, a German term broadly translated into English as a 'holistic, humanistic concept of education', Cleary (2019, p. 1), includes curiosity as a skill or quality 'that the practitioner/client develops in the pursuit of meaning' suggesting that in order 'to live a dignified life, all humans need to undertake this struggle for existential meaning' (Cleary, 2019, p. 4).

The dispositions which enable creativity may or may not be apparent in individuals with whom social pedagogues work, but by applying the principles and values of social pedagogy, individuals, groups and communities can benefit from the conditions which enable creativity to germinate and grow.

Reflective point

Do you view supporting curiosity in those with whom you work as part of your role?

The alignment between creativity and social pedagogy

In our view, understanding the value of creativity is core to social pedagogy. Rather than relying on a technical, rule-bound approach, the social pedagogue 'is encouraged to think more laterally and speculatively as a way of moving beyond the obvious' (Charfe and Gardner, 2019, p. 37). In other words, social pedagogical practice itself is intrinsically creative.

Social pedagogy involves forging positive relationships with others from diverse backgrounds. Many people are disadvantaged by normative societal structures which favour the white, able-bodied, adult (but not elderly), neurotypical male. Exploring and applying creativity in practice can promote inclusion by seeking to ensure the marginalised have a voice. Malaguzzi, the educator and architect of the Reggio-Emilia approach to early education, recognised the value of creativity in enabling practitioners to gather finely-grained insights into children engaged in the creative processes. He observed that, 'Creativity becomes more visible when adults try to be more attentive to the cognitive processes of children than to the results they achieve in various fields of doing and understanding' (Malaguzzi, 1993, p. 77). The insights gained from such attentiveness are rich in their potential to nurture the growth of understanding and empathy, thereby strengthening the person-centred nature of the professional relationship.

The social pedagogue who values creative expression invites those with whom they work to communicate what might otherwise, remain unsaid. Ellyat (2010, p. 91) recognises the potential for empowerment through creativity when she states that creativity 'is about tapping into who we really are and how we express it'. In addition, the social pedagogue is given privileged access and insights into the experience and life-world orientation of those with whom they work. They are seeking to better understand those whom they are supporting, a concept explored in Chapter 5.

Creativity and wellbeing are inextricably linked. Bruce (2011, p. 4) explains that creativity can help children understand 'how they contribute to the world as well as finding the fulfilment that creativity brings into their lives'. Crucially, she goes on to say that 'Fulfilment is deeper than happiness or enjoyment – it helps us through the difficult times as well as the easier side of our lives' (ibid). In saying this, she illustrates powerfully that creativity can be a source of empowerment for those in distress. Fisher (2005, p. 35) echoes this in observing that creativity requires *feeling* as well as thinking.

The connections between personal fulfilment, wellbeing and creativity are well established (these were also discussed in Chapter 5). For creativity to flourish, the environment must feel emotionally safe to enable imagination, curiosity and uncertainty. It is the role of the social pedagogue to create this 'space' by fostering what psychologist, Carl Rogers (1967) termed, 'unconditional positive regard', a concept reflected in the Diamond Model which recognises the 'unconditional value of human beings' (Kaska, 2016, cited in McCreadie 2020, p. 6). Claxton (2018, p. 46) points out that 'how successfully [children] respond to novelty or difficulty, depends as much on acquired attitudes as on any immutable kind of intelligence'. Roseneil, (2023, p. X11) explains that 'psychoanalysis has expanded on the idea that the ability to sit with uncertainty, to not rush to close down uncomfortable experiences of not knowing, is important both in the therapeutic relationship, and to psychic health and well-being'. The nurturing of creativity supports wellbeing and recognises the synergy between the two.

Reflection point

Is the link between creativity and wellbeing something that is already well embedded in your practice, or something new to you?

Education policy and creativity

The education policy context in England reveals a tension within the early years and primary sectors. The Statutory Framework for the Early Years Foundation Stage (Department for Education, 2023, p. 11) provides for children's appreciation of artistic and cultural aspects of experiences, thereby providing a glimmer of the recognition of the need for pleasure and an appreciation of beauty. It also recognises that children learn through play (DfE, 2023, p. 7). However, play is not mentioned in the National Curriculum (DfE, 2013), which sets out education policy for the over-fives. Although it does mention the importance of giving opportunities for creativity and harnessing curiosity of children, current government policy still favours a knowledge-rich approach. This emphasis can close opportunity for curiosity, playfulness and creativity as children move through primary school years. This reflects a normative approach to teaching which frames the child as passive and in receipt of expert tuition from the educator (Cushing, 2023). This approach assumes that there is a 'right' way to learn and to be (Biesta, 2015, Cushing, 2023).

Social Pedagogy offers a welcome antidote to the transmission mode of educating, with its emphasis on creativity and meaningful relationships. It has a focus on the creation of opportunities for children of all ages to explore, question, wonder and play with their learning, whilst developing relationships with their peers and the adults around them. Such an approach is not new. Vygotsky (1978) rejected the behaviourist model of the child as an empty vessel. He suggested that learning is socially constructed in collaboration with others so that 'Learning awakens a variety of internal development processes that are able to operate only when the child is interacting with people in his environment and in cooperation with his peers' (p. 90). Likewise, Bruner (1999, cited in Glăveanu, 2011, p. 3) promoted a shift away from the image of the child as passive and responsive, towards the 'informationally active, socially interactive infant mind'.

Vygotsky (2004, p. 11) also emphasised the importance of play and imagination, regarding it as inherently creative, explaining:

A child who sits astride a stick and pretends to be riding a horse; a little girl who plays with a doll and imagines she is its mother; a boy who in his games becomes a pirate, a soldier, or a sailor, all these children at play represent examples of the most authentic, truest creativity.

Unfortunately, it is this type of authentic and imaginative play which appears to be increasingly discouraged as children move through the school system in England.

The *Common Third*

Whilst social pedagogy has slightly different traditions depending on the culture, society and country implementing it, the guiding principles of relationships, creativity and the person being central are common to all (Kirkwood *et al.*, 2017). One key approach to nurturing both relationships and creativity is the *Common Third*. This is a shared activity which all participants enjoy, have a shared interest in and where the purpose is to use the activity to develop and deepen relationships (ThemPra Social Pedagogy, 2024). The *Common Third*, a concept touched upon in previous chapters, is a holistic approach where traditional hierarchies of 'expert-subject' are broken down, and creative activities are used to develop relationships (Hatton, 2020, p. 5). The emphasis is on the process of creating rather than the final outcome. It is the co-operation, teamwork, shared experiences and process of being creative on an equal footing which makes a *Common Third* activity meaningful (Moss and Petrie, 2019). Within this space, there is no right or wrong answer (Stobbs *et al.*, 2023, p. 5). There is no judgement, and learning can become adaptable and organic (Charfe *et al.*, 2020). Here the expert, usually an adult in a position of authority, learns and develops *alongside* the novice, often a child or young person. Traditional hierarchies loosen their hold and the child or young person can take more of an active role and develop a greater sense of agency as they engage in the activity.

The Common Third space is an ideal environment to explore all forms of creativity, not only that which is commonly attributed to the Arts. There is no ceiling, limit or list of *correct* Common Third activities. They can range from everyday activities such as preparing meals to traditionally creative processes such as composing music or creating a sculpture to outdoor residential trips and project work. The key theme is that a creative activity is chosen so both expert and student become learners together. They become 'fellow travellers in journeys of growth' (Smith, 2012, p. 52).

> **Reflection point**
>
> Is the idea of creativity in your own practice now gaining relevance? What formats might that creativity take within your own work?

The relinquishing of power could create some uncomfortableness in the educator and for the novice when moving from a passive to an active role in their learning (Charfe *et al.*, 2020, p. 3). However, qualitative research conducted by Charfe *et al.* (2023) found most participants (both experts and subjects) found this to be a liberating experience, taking the pressure off the mentor, and a positive and engaging one for the mentee. The experience becomes about exploring a topic and sharing knowledge (Charfe *et al.*, 2023, p. 8). However, professional boundaries and mutual respect still do need to exist within such a context, and using the '3Ps Model' may provide a helpful scaffold to enable this to occur (McCreadie, 2020).

The 3Ps refer to the professional, personal and private selves of the expert and allows the social pedagogue to evaluate how much of themselves they share with others (Kirkwood et al., 2017). By sharing some professional and personal aspects of themselves, relationships can begin to build and develop with learners. These professional, respectful and trusting relationships could be helpful for drawing in learners (Anderberg, 2020, p. 1). With the focus on relationships, co-operation, teamwork and sharing of knowledge, the role of the professional or expert also changes. In the Common Third, the educator is also allowed the freedom to learn, to explore, to be curious and creative alongside the children. This concept of learning together and learning from each other further breaks down the barriers formed by traditional hierarchical relationships and develops more meaningful ones.

The Common Third provides the ideal space for the elements intrinsic to creativity to flourish. By removing barriers such as the need for a 'right' answer, the omniscient expert, judgement or fear of making a mistake, creativity can be nurtured. Curiosity for both the expert and the subject can flourish. When this gateway opens, adults, young people and children can play with knowledge, skills and creativity. They can apply their imagination and explore it. Through the removal of barriers imposed by traditional learning, possibility-thinking can occur: 'what will happen if…?' Focusing on the creative process itself for only itself can engage the disengaged and excluded, it can develop and build 'self-confidence, self-knowledge and self-awareness' of all (Hatton, 2020, p. 5). Applying the *Common Third* in practice offers a more democratic and creative process whereby learning can be developed in its broadest sense: learning how to be oneself, learning how to interact with others, learning to explore and to be curious and ultimately to be creative.

Case study

The following case study is drawn from a real scenario which took place in a higher education setting in England. Time was set aside in each session of their module on creativity over a period of six weeks, before an evaluation of the experience took place.

The eight students and their tutor began by generating ideas before arriving at a consensus on what they would like to do within the confines of the environment. They chose to learn how to crochet, since no-one in the group had any previous experience. Yarn and hooks were provided together with a YouTube instructional video. The outcomes were mixed. Some, but not all, participants managed to produce some basic crochet. However, the focus was on the experience of the participants and the process of learning together as equals. The following reflection from the tutor offers a template for consideration when planning, applying and evaluating a Common Third activity.

Practitioner reflection:

Thinking about the Common Third activity, I found myself addressing some difficult questions about *my* pedagogy. Firstly, why were we doing it at all? My idea was that it represented an opportunity for creative collaboration. Collaboration in the Common Third theoretically entails strengthening bonds by removing the 'expert' from the interactions between the participants, so that they are on a more equal footing. My working definition of creativity involves doing, making, expressing or thinking something as a curious, motivated participant who adds something new and of value for themselves and/or others. It takes innumerable and diverse forms such as exploring, experimenting, risking being wrong, curating, problem solving, crafting et cetera.

Applying the *Common Third* for part of each session was intended to invite students' reflections on whether adopting the *Common Third* facilitated our creative thinking (irrespective of what we were actually doing together: in this case, crochet).

Here are some other questions that arose:

- Was the activity really a choice or was it imposed by me or by the restrictions of the environment?
- Did we have the right tools for the activity?
- Was everyone's voice heard or did the group nature make a difference?
- Did I discover more about the young people that I was working with through the process?
- How did it relate to supporting creative thinking?
- Could I see any benefits to it?
- Could the students?

It may be that such questions guide your thinking as you venture into more creative activities where you work 'side by side' with those that you are supporting.

Conclusion

In this chapter, we have explored some of the innate human dispositions which we believe comprise creativity, and some of the processes which can be enabled by the skilled social pedagogue in order to support human flourishing. We highlighted the alignment between creativity and social pedagogy built upon a foundation of the values of respect, inclusion and empowerment. We also highlighted the potential power of creativity in collaboration with others. We set out our own current conception of creativity and invited you to explore your own, whilst acknowledging that any definition will be tentative and provisional. In considering more creative approaches to working alongside others, we suggest that this, in itself, is an act of creativity, since we become knowledge creators, engaged in a cycle of evaluating, experimenting refining and imagining possibilities to enhance our practice.

Creativity as core to social pedagogical practice invites us to regard uncertainty as a strength to be guided by a commitment to supporting the wellbeing of others (and ourselves), our ethical values and our professional curiosity. Creative practice goes further than promoting inclusion; it recognises that diversity is essential to creativity and celebrates diversity as a strength, offering the potential for us to extend our understanding of what it is to be human and enhance our own lives and the lives of others.

Summary points

- The meaning of creativity is hard to define, it will mean different things to different people. It is variously perceived as product or process.

- Creativity is linked to imagination, curiosity, risk-taking, open-mindedness, empathy and wellbeing.
- Social pedagogical approaches and creativity are intrinsically linked as they respect the individual identity, needs and methods of expression of the individual.
- Creative activities enable a more democratic and balanced approach to support, where the practitioner works alongside those whom they are supporting on a shared goal.

Recommended reading

Charfe, L., Gardner, A., Greenhalgh, E., Marsden, H., Nester, D. and Simpson, L. (2020) Creating a learning space: Using experiential learning and creativity in the teaching and learning of social pedagogy. *International Journal of Social Pedagogy.* 9(1), pp. 1–9.

Glăveanu, V.P. (2011) Children and creativity: a most (un)likely pair? *Thinking Skills and Creativity*, 6 (2). pp. 122–131. ISSN 1871-1871 DOI: 10.1016/j.tsc.2011.03.002

Kirby, P. and Webb, R. (2023) *Creating with Uncertainty, Sustainability education resources for a changing world.* University of Sussex Library. Available at: https://openpress.sussex.ac.uk/creatingwithuncertainty/#:~:text=Book%20Description%3A%20This%20set%20of,loss%20in%20their%20everyday%20lives. (Accessed 6 February 2025).

References

Anderberg, A. (2020) In search of social pedagogical profession in schools. Missions and roles under reconsideration. *International Journal of Social Pedagogy.* 9(1), pp. 1–19.

Biesta, G. (2015) What is education for? On good education, teacher judgement, and educational professionalism. *European Journal of Education*, 50(1), pp. 75–87.

Bruce, T. (2011) *Cultivating creativity for babies, toddlers and young children* (2nd ed.). Abingdon: Hodder Education.

Charfe, L. (2023) Ethical and relational leadership in a complex world: The use of the human learning systems and social pedagogical leadership framework to navigating complexity. *International Journal of Social Pedagogy*, 12(1), p. 16. DOI: https://doi.org/10.14324/111.444.ijsp.2023.v12.x.016

Charfe, L. and Gardner, A. (2019) *Social pedagogy and social work.* London: Sage.

Charfe, L., Gardner, A., Greenhalgh, E., Marsden, H., Nester, D. and Simpson, L. (2020) Creating a learning space: Using experiential learning and creativity in the teaching and learning of social pedagogy. *International Journal of Social Pedagogy*, 9(1), pp. 1–9.

Claxton, G. (2018) Deep rivers of learning. Available at: https://kappanonline.org/claxton-deep-rivers-learning/ (Accessed 6 February 2025).

Cleary, B. (2019) Reinterpreting bildung in social pedagogy. *International Journal of Social Pedagogy*, 8(1), pp. 1–12.

Cooper, H. (2013) *Teaching history creatively.* Abingdon: Routledge.

Cushing, I. (2023) The knowledge-rich project, coloniality, and the preservation of whiteness in schools: A raciolinguistic perspective. *Educational Linguistics*, 2(1), pp. 51–71. https://doi.org/10.1515/eduling-2022-0018

Department for Education (2013) National curriculum in England: Primary curriculum. Available at: www.gov.uk/government/publications/national-curriculum-in-england-primary-curriculum (Accessed 26 September 2024).

Department for Education (2023) Early Years Foundation Stage Statutory Framework. Available at: https://assets.publishing.service.gov.uk/media/65aa5e42ed27ca001327b2c7/EYFS_statutory_framework_for_group_and_school_based_providers.pdf (Accessed 26 September 2024).

Dewey, J. (1910) *How we think.* New York: Heath Publishing Company.

Duffy, B. (2010) Using creativity and creative learning to enrich the lives of young children at the Thomas Coram Centre. In C. Tims (Ed.), *Born creative.* London: DEMOS, pp. 19–28.

Ellyat, W. (2010) A science of learning: New approaches to thinking about creativity in the early years. In C. Tims (Ed.), *Born creative.* London: DEMOS, pp. 89–98.

Fisher, R. (2005) *Teaching children to think.* Cheltenham: Nelson-Thomas.

Glăveanu, V. P. (2011) Children and creativity: A most (un)likely pair? *Thinking Skills and Creativity*, 6(2). pp. 122–131. https://doi.org/10.1016/j.tsc.2011.03.002

Hatton, K. (2020) A new framework for creativity in social pedagogy. *International Journal of Social Pedagogy*, 9(1), pp. 1–9.

Hedges, H. (2020) The place of interests, agency and imagination in funds of identity theory. *Mind, Culture, and Activity*, 28(2), pp. 1–14.

Holtoff, S. and Eichsteller, G. (2009) Social pedagogy: The practice. *Every Child Journal*, 1(1), pp. 58–63.

Kirkwood, S., Roesch-Marsh, A. and Cooper, S. (2017) Evaluating social pedagogy in the UK: Methodological issues. *Qualitative Social Work*, 18(1), pp. 8–23. https://doi.org/10.1177/1473325017699266.

Malaguzzi, L. (1993) History, ideas, and basic philosophy: An interview with Lella Gandini. In C. Edwards, L. Gandini and G. Forman (Eds.), *The hundred languages of children: The Reggio Emilia approach – Advanced reflections* (2nd ed.). Greenwich: Ablex Publishing, pp. 49–97.

McCreadie, E. (2020) Utilising the 'common third' to enhance social work education. *International Journal of Social Pedagogy*, 9(1), pp. 1–11. Moss, P. and Petrie, P. (2019) Education and social pedagogy: What relationship? *London Review of Education*, 17(3), pp. 393–405.

National Advisory Committee on Creative and Cultural Education (NACCCE Report) (1999) *All our futures: Creativity, culture and education*. London: DCMS and DfEE

Robinson, K. (2011) *Out of our minds: Learning to be creative* (2nd ed.). West Sussex: Capstone.

Rogers, C.R. (1967) *On becoming a person: A therapist's view of psychotherapy*. London: Constable.

Roseneil, S. (2023) Stilling the voices that know, cultivating those that don't know. In P. Kirby and R. Webb (Eds.), *Creating with uncertainty, sustainability education resources for a changing world*. University of Sussex Library. pp. X11–X1V Available at: https://openpress.sussex.ac.uk/creatingwithuncertainty/#:~:text=Book%20Description%3A%20This%20set%20of,loss%20in%20their%20everyday%20lives (Accessed 6 February 2025).

Sawyer, K. (2003) Emergence in creativity and development. In R.K. Sawyer et al. (Eds.), *Creativity and Development*. Oxford: Oxford University Press, pp. 12–60.

Smith, M. (2012) Social pedagogy from a Scottish perspective. *Journal of Social Pedagogy*, 1(1), pp. 46–55.

Stewart, N. (2011) *How children learn: The characteristics of effective learning*. St. Albans: BAEC.

Stobbs, N., Solvason, C., Gallagher, S. and Baylis, S. (2023) A human approach to restructuring the education system: Why schools in England need social pedagogy. *International Journal of Social Pedagogy*, 12(1) pp. 1–11.

Taylor, S. (2024) *Creativity in the early years: Engaging children aged 0-5*. London: Sage.

ThemPra Social Pedagogy Community Interest Company (2024) Available at: www.thempra.org.uk/thempra/ (Accessed: 26 September 2024).

Vygotsky, L. (2004) Imagination and creativity in childhood. *Journal of Russian and East European Psychology*, 42(1), pp. 7–97.

Wittgenstein, L. (1953) *Philosophical investigations* (3rd ed.). New York: Macmillan.

9 Managing emotions and maintaining wellbeing as an empathic social pedagogue

Angela Hodgkins and Suzanne Allies

Introduction

Social Pedagogy is a values-led approach to practice, where relationships are key, and its focus is to holistically support a person's wellbeing, learning and social inclusion. In this chapter, we focus on the wellbeing aspect of practice. We acknowledge social pedagogy as an art form, rather than a skill, where relationships are formed authentically with each empowered person being present and genuinely themselves (Eichsteller and Holthoff, 2012a).

Having a relationship with someone we trust and can rely on is one of the underpinning principles of social pedagogy. Feeling known, having confidence in the fact that the people around you understand who you are, your characteristics and your needs, is a basic human need (Purvanova, 2013). For practitioners, knowing our clients and allowing our clients to know us allows us to create an environment in which everyone can reach their potential. Social pedagogy encourages us, as professionals, to bring our personality into the relationship with those in our care. Knowing a person, valuing and respecting their own personality and uniqueness, is the key to self-actualisation.

In social pedagogy, the Diamond Model describes the way that practitioners can facilitate individuals to reach their potential. The philosophy is based on a belief that every human being is precious and possesses skills and talents which make them unique. Eichsteller and Holthoff (2012b) explain,

> There is a diamond within every one of us. Not all diamonds are polished and sparkly, but all have the potential to be. Similarly, every person has the potential to shine – and social pedagogy is about how we can support people to uncover and recognise their potential, to draw out their inner richness.

This view of human beings as having within themselves the resources for change and growth is both positive and affirming (Prowle and Hodgkins, 2020).

Learning is an emotional process; emotions and learning cannot be separated. For instance, it is clear that emotions can both enhance and interfere with development depending on which emotions drive or colour the experience. In addition, emotions can be contagious, and these positive or negative emotional states are able to impact others in the learning environment (Osika et al., 2022). The role of the practitioner is to support and empower individuals to take ownership for their own life through positive experiences.

> **Reflective point**
>
> Reflect on your own experiences of learning; think about a teacher (assistant, mentor, etc.) from your past who inspired you. What was it about them that encouraged you to succeed? How did they make you feel? What aspects of good practice can you take from this in your work?

Emotion and transitions

One way that a practitioner can support their learners is to aid them to cope with transitions in their lives. A transition is a process of change, which can be environmental or emotional. Young children are particularly vulnerable at times of transition, often feeling a degree of anxiety and insecurity (Early Education, 2021). For a young child, a transition can be a significant change, such as moving from home to an early years setting or from nursery to school. Additionally, transitions within a setting, like moving from one room to another, or changes in caregivers, or even shifts from one part of the day to another, can be equally significant (Klette and Killen, 2019). Datler et al. (2010, p. 82) describe the intensity of a child's emotion during this critical time; here, they reflect on their research:

> Within the framework of our research project we were obliged, repeatedly, to witness the experience of how hard and disturbing it is to be confronted so intimately with the primitive and often catastrophic emotions of very young children during their process of transition from home care to out-of-home care.

In early years settings, transitions should be managed sensitively, involving a partnership between the child, the child's family and practitioners, to ensure as smooth a changeover as possible. The EYFS guidance (DfE, 2024, p. 28) advocates a key person approach, to 'help the child become familiar with the setting, offer a settled relationship for the child and build a relationship with their parents and/or carers'. Close practitioner-child relationships are essential in the early years and significantly impact on child development. As Gerhardt (2015, p. 40) notes, 'being lovingly held is the greatest spur to development'. Recognising the importance of these relationships, Page (2018) coined the phrase 'professional love' to describe the loving care required by young children and the strong feelings experienced by practitioners.

Throughout childhood, there are many transitions to manage. Rouse et al. (2023, p. 724) suggest that these transitions are not merely points in time, but processes that occur over time, 'beginning well before children move into a new … environment and extending to the point where they, their families and practitioners recognise a sense of belonging in that space'. These transitions require ongoing emotional support and acknowledgement of their significance in children's lives. Although on the brink of adulthood at this point, the transition from school to university is particularly complex and particularly challenging, involving multi-faceted life-changes (see Figure 9.1).

In the higher education (HE) context some students are more vulnerable and at risk of academic failure, particularly those from backgrounds with little or no experience in HE (McMillan, 2014) and mature students (Kahu et al., 2015). Emotions, however, are subjective and dependent on

84 Social Pedagogy in Education

Figure 9.1 The multi-faceted transition to university.

individual perspectives. Learning and achievement are emotional processes, encompassing positive dimensions, such as interest, enjoyment and success, as well as challenging ones. Emotions affect attention, memory, motivation and self-regulation (Kahu et al., 2015), significantly impacting learning. Kahu et al.'s (2015, p. 487) research with mature students highlighted many stresses but also revealed a profound love of learning; students expressed sentiments like, 'I am absolutely loving studying', 'the more I learn, the more I want to learn', and 'it's like I'm addicted to learning'. When approached the right way, and properly supported, learning can be a joyful and empowering experience.

The range of emotions experienced in all settings extends to the practitioner as well. Education and care rely heavily on communication and relationships. For example, Naylor and Nyanjom (2021, p. 1238) describe teaching in classrooms as 'a complex, dynamic and idiosyncratic phenomenon that represents an emotional experience'. Beyond possessing subject knowledge, pedagogical skills, classroom management and a range of instruction techniques, education and care practitioners also need communication skills, commitment, care and motivation. They should 'create positive and nurturing learning environments; treating students as individuals and promoting enthusiasm' (Dolev and Leshem, 2017, p. 22). Many of these attributes are features of emotional intelligence, which Mayer and Salovey (1997, p. 10) define as:

The ability to perceive accurately, appraise and express emotions, the ability to access and/or generate feelings when they facilitate thought; the ability to understand emotions and emotional knowledge and the ability to regulate emotions to promote emotional and intellectual growth.

Positive and nurturing relationships can be fostered by initiating one-to-one interactions, genuinely listening to those in our care, showing interest in their lives, using positive language, engaging in dialogues rather than lecturing, asking open-ended questions, and focusing on their strengths (Dolev and Leshem, 2017). Building good relationships with those that we support is at the heart of the social pedagogical approach.

Relational universe

The Relational Universe encapsulates our understanding of relationship-centred practice in social pedagogy and illustrates how meaningful connections support individuals in creating robust social support networks. In the vast expanse of social pedagogy, the concept of the Relational Universe focuses on interdependency amongst people and the power of connection. The universe metaphorically represents an individual's relationships and, in particular, their support networks.

At its core, the Relational Universe embodies the essence of relationship-focused pedagogy, highlighting the profound interconnectedness of individuals within a dynamic network of human connections. It recognises that within the tapestry of human relationships lies the potential for significant growth, empathy, and understanding. By fostering meaningful connections, social pedagogues cultivate robust social support networks that provide individuals with the scaffolding necessary to navigate life's challenges and triumphs.

Central to this concept is the acknowledgement that human beings thrive in relationships, drawing sustenance and support from the intricate web of connections that surround them. Drawing inspiration from the insights of renowned scholar Brené Brown (2010), the *Relational Universe* underscores the transformative power of connection. Brown highlights how meaningful relationships can profoundly impact individuals by cultivating a sense of belonging and purpose. She argues that for practitioners, vulnerability and authenticity are essential in forming deep connections that promote wellbeing and resilience in those that we work with (Brown, 2010). This perspective aligns with social pedagogy's emphasis on relationship-centred practice, which seeks to nurture supportive and authentic relationships between practitioners and those in their care.

Maclean and Harrison's (2015) exploration of systems theory further enriches our understanding of the *Relational Universe*. They demonstrate how these networks sustain individuals, offering a reservoir of support and belonging. However, they also caution that life's tumultuous currents may exert pressure upon these networks, challenging their resilience and integrity. Yet, even amidst adversity, the *Relational Universe* endures, adapting and evolving to meet the fluctuating needs of individuals. Embedded within the *Relational Universe* are the stories of countless relationships, each imbued with its own unique narrative arc. From the tender bonds of familial love to the camaraderie forged in shared collaborations, these relationships shape and define the human experience. Yet, they are not static entities but rather fluid and dynamic, constantly evolving in response to the ebb and flow of life. There is a story attached to every relationship and all relationships evolve and are in a constant state of flux.

As practitioners, there are several practical strategies that can be employed to improve relationships with those in our care within this relational framework:

- Cultivating empathy using active listening giving full attention to the what the person has to say, allow them to feel heard and valued. Role-play scenarios can also be used to better understand and articulate the perspectives of others (Gordon, 2005).
- The process of mentalising (Cooper and Redfern, 2015), by, for example, reflecting back to the other how you think they are feeling, rather than assuming, can build effective relationships. Mentalising refers to the ability to read self or other people's thoughts and feelings using our imagination, knowing that it is impossible to read someone else's mind because it is separate and distinct from our own mind.
- Building authentic connections that encourage practitioners to model vulnerability and authenticity by sharing personal stories and experiences, which can create a safe space for others to do the same (Brown, 2010).
- Designing collaborative projects and group activities that require cooperation and mutual support, reinforcing the value of interdependence (Johnson and Johnson, 2009).
- Incorporate holistic approaches that address the emotional, social, and cognitive aspects of learning, recognising the whole person (Noddings, 2015).
- Integrating mindfulness and wellbeing practices into the daily routine to enhance self-awareness and emotional regulation (Kabat-Zinn, 1990).

In the realm of social pedagogy, the *Relational Universe* serves as an illustration of hope and possibility, guiding practitioners toward a deeper understanding of the transformative power of relationships. By nurturing connections, fostering empathy, and embracing the inherent interdependence of human existence, we embark upon a journey of collective growth and discovery. As we navigate the expanse of the Relational Universe, let us remember that within its embrace lies the potential to cultivate a more compassionate, interconnected world — one relationship at a time.

> **Reflective point**
>
> Which relationship that you formed as a practitioner has had the most significant impact on you? Once you have identified someone, please reflect on the reason for this and how this may have changed your life course or decisions.

The role of empathy

The work of psychologist Carl Rogers (1942) first brought the study of empathy into renown. Rogers established core conditions for therapeutic relationships, the most important of which included empathy, congruence and unconditional positive regard. Rogers deemed these core conditions to be essential in therapy interactions (Rogers, 1959). The concept was developed for the counselling profession and still forms the basis of person-centred counselling and therapy today (Brown, 2007). However, Rogers had a strong conviction that, although the conditions are essential in a therapeutic setting, they are equally important in any interpersonal relationship. Rogers (1980) described empathy as the 'sensitive ability and willingness to understand the client's thoughts, feelings and struggles from their point of view', being able to 'see through the client's eyes' (Rogers, 1980, p. 85). The terms 'empathy' and 'compassion' are sometimes mistakenly used interchangeably

(Singer and Klimecki, 2014); however, they are very different concepts. Empathy is the capacity to understand or share the feelings of others, whereas compassion is a desire to act, which is one of the consequences resulting from empathy (Maibom, 2017).

In social pedagogy, Rogers' (1959) core conditions are characterised in the concept of *Haltung*. *Haltung* is a German term, roughly translated as ethos, mindset or attitude. It describes how we bring our values and beliefs into our practice in a congruent manner, with 'empathic understanding and regard for human dignity' (Thempra, 2024, no page). In social pedagogy, the *Haltung* of the professional is based on an emotional connectedness to others. In an education and care context, supportive and trusting relationships are paramount in ensuring the emotional wellbeing of those whom we support. Empathy is a crucial aspect of such a relationship.

Another social pedagogical concept which recognises the importance of empathy is 'head, heart, hands'. The concept combines cognitive knowledge (head), emotional and spiritual learning (heart) and practical and physical skills (hands). Dachyshyn (2015, p. 32) suggests that 'heartful practice', rather than being a new alternative idea, is a return to our roots to find 'wisdom to guide, inspire and challenge us'. Dachyshyn's (2015, p. 37) definition of 'heartful practice' is 'responding from the heart, from a place of deep compassion and empathy'. In our work with others, heartful practice advocates *being with* them rather than *doing to* them. This requires a shift of thinking from the professional as an expert towards being a skilled facilitator (Monteux and Monteux, 2020), from dependence to independence to interdependence. Covey (1989, p. 11) famously defined these terms:

> Dependent people need others to get what they want. Independent people can get what they want through their own effort. Interdependent people combine their own efforts with the efforts of others to achieve their greatest success.

An example of this in an educational context might be an early career teacher working in a primary school, struggling to manage the multitude of tasks during the working day. Examples from a range of teacher job descriptions have been used to create a word cloud, showing some of these tasks and responsibilities (see Figure 9.2).

The teacher may, at first, be dependent on another person to take on some of the daily tasks: for example, asking a teaching assistant to prepare all resources or using another teacher's plans, rather than writing their own. Relying on each other is challenging; people naturally strive for independence and want to be able to manage things on their own. The teacher would rather not have to be dependent on others, as most advanced societies value self-sufficiency and professional distance from others (Monteux and Monteux, 2020). The move to independence for the teacher may develop over time with experience; the teacher may develop tools and strategies to manage and organise aspects of the day. However, independence can come at a high cost, and has been found to contribute to mental health disorders (Junger, 2016). Statistics show that, among UK teachers, stress, insomnia and burnout are all rising with 78 per cent of teachers reporting high levels of stress (Harrison, 2024). Independently trying to manage alone can be isolating, as well as stressful.

In contrast, Isaacson (2020, p. 381) points out the fact that 'there is remarkably little evidence of depression-based suicide in tribal societies'. Such societies, with high group cohesion and shared resources also have high levels of resilience. These are societies where multiple people are mutually dependent on one another. Lisak et al. (2022, p. 4) defines interdependence as:

Figure 9.2 Words to describe a teachers' responsibilities.

a critical social characteristic of work that affects relational and emotional mechanisms such as perceived impact, interpersonal cohesion, and affective interpersonal commitment, all of which are linked to outcomes of motivation and performance, attitudes, team coordination, and cognition.

As Covey asserted, interdependence is the interplay between individuals in community. Our ability to be interdependent enables us to solve problems and succeed at challenges much greater than we would be able to conquer alone.

The teacher in our example may develop interdependence in a variety of ways, but these all require empathy and relationship building. Building a close working relationship with the class teaching assistant (TA), for example, may reveal the TA's skills in, and passion for, specific areas, technology, for example. This might be an area of the curriculum that the TA would enjoy, and their individual skill could be employed to enhance the experience for the children. This would not only benefit the pupils, however, as taking on responsibility could also provide motivation through a sense of accomplishment for the TA, and relieve one area of stress from the teacher's workload. An effective whole setting 'interdependent' approach is one where people know one another, value one another's skills, and care for each other. In an environment that is fast-paced and ever-changing, a collective effort based on empathy and 'heartful practice' is a healthy way forward (Table 9.1).

> **Reflective point**
>
> Does your organisation/setting embrace interdependence? If it does, what are the benefits? If it does not, what might be some of the barriers?
>   Can you identify examples of empathy within your team? How does this impact on practice?

Table 9.1 Dependence, independence, interdependence

Dependence	Dependence on others to complete some tasks
	Asking someone else to take on menial/ routine tasks
	Copying materials and resources created by others
	Over dependence on mentor
Independence	Coping alone
	Striving for perfection
	Seeing 'coping with stress' as positive
	Successful people do it all by themselves, against all odds
Interdependence	Empathy and compassion for others in the team
	Finding out about people's talents and interests
	Sharing skills and resources
	A group approach to difficult situations

The emotional cost

Practitioners face the dual challenge of nurturing their own wellbeing while endeavouring to help those they support to flourish. As has already been mentioned, the Diamond Model, (for an illustration see Chapter 2), first introduced by Eichsteller and Holthoff (2012a), offers a compelling framework within social pedagogy which emphasises a values-led approach and relationship-focused practice. The metaphor of the diamond symbolises the inherent value and potential within each individual, reflecting a belief that all people possess unique strengths and abilities waiting to be cultivated. The Diamond Model proposes four key principles: wellbeing, learning, relationships and empowerment, encouraging practitioners to consider wellbeing holistically, encompassing psychological, physical, social, and existential dimensions. This holistic perspective acknowledges that wellbeing and happiness are deeply personal and multi-faceted, varying from person to person (Eichsteller and Holthoff, 2012a). It underscores the importance of sustaining long-term wellbeing rather than merely addressing immediate needs, aligning with social pedagogy's commitment to fostering sustainable growth and empowerment.

Social pedagogy emphasises that wellbeing and happiness are interconnected yet distinct concepts — happiness often describing a momentary emotion, while wellbeing encompasses a sustained sense of overall health and fulfilment (Eichsteller and Holthoff, 2012b). Understanding these nuances allows practitioners to tailor their approach, recognising and respecting the unique experiences and needs of each individual that they work with.

By integrating the principles of the Diamond Model into practice, practitioners can cultivate a supportive environment where both personal and professional growth thrive. This approach encourages ongoing reflection, dialogue, and adaptation, ensuring that social pedagogical practice remains responsive, inclusive, and deeply impactful in supporting individuals to unlock their full potential. By adopting these principles, however, practitioners can also better manage the emotional demands of their own roles, ensuring they remain effective, resilient, and fulfilled in their practice. The following examples demonstrate the potential psychological, physical, social and existential advantages of a practitioner employing the Diamond Model to their practice:

- **Psychological dimension**: by cultivating emotional resilience amidst the demands of the role and implementing strategies to foster a positive mindset and manage stress effectively.

- **Physical dimension**: by prioritising physical health within their daily routine and adopting self-care practices to ensure sustained energy and vitality.
- **Social dimension**: by nurturing supportive relationships within the educational community and enhancing a sense of belonging and professional growth through collaborative efforts.
- **Existential dimension**: by Identifying values and beliefs that guide practice, finding purpose and meaning in work, especially during challenging times.

Practitioners' wellbeing and practical steps

Glazzard and Rose (2019) point out what appears obvious but is often overlooked in practice, a practitioner has a greater chance of creating a nurturing and effective environment if they address their own needs and priorities first. Practitioners' own mental ill health can detrimentally impact the quality of support they are able to offer, as well as relationships with both clients and colleagues (Sammons, 2019). Social pedagogy argues that holistic support and sustainable wellbeing, for both carer and cared for, must be embedded in practice if practitioners are to effectively support learners in unlocking their full potential.

Practitioners can engage in a variety of wellbeing practices and actionable steps to increase their resilience, these include:

- **Self-care techniques**, such as mindfulness meditation, exercise, and hobbies that bring joy and relaxation (Boogren, 2019) and prioritising sleep and nutrition to maintain physical health and resilience.
- **Emotional awareness and self-reflection activities,** such as journalling to process experiences and to understand personal emotional triggers and develop strategies to manage stress effectively.
- **Establishing boundaries** to set clear parameters between professional responsibilities and their personal life to prevent burnout, and by scheduling regular breaks and ensuring time is allocated for personal activities and important relationships.
- **Engaging in professional development**, such as participating in ongoing professional development opportunities or attending workshops and seminars focused on stress management, work-life balance, emotional intelligence, and resilience building (Education Support, 2024; Allies, 2021) to stay updated with best practices and new research.
- **Joining peer support networks or professional communities** to share experiences, strategies, and challenges, reducing feelings of isolation and promoting overall wellbeing (Zwart et al., 2007).
- **Creative approaches** to develop self and build relationships with learners by being involved in activities like the arts, music, and drama, which can be therapeutic and foster deeper connections (Cameron and Moss, 2011), facilitate emotional release and build empathy.

Contributing to the wellbeing of others

Social pedagogues contribute to the wellbeing of their clients through relationship-focused practice and holistic support, nurturing the 'whole person' by recognising and responding to their individual strengths, interests and challenges (Cameron and Moss, 2011; Petrie and Calder, 2013). Emphasising meaningful relationships between caregivers and clients is crucial not only in meeting immediate needs but also in fostering a sense of belonging, security, and trust, which are essential for overall wellbeing. Furthermore, empowering people promotes a sense of autonomy, agency and self-confidence, helping them navigate future circumstances and transitions despite any adversity. Building these relationships allows a trusted other to validate and normalise expressions of anxiety without offering interpretation or analysis. This is a powerful approach to building emotional resilience, particularly in vulnerable children. As Ttofa (2017, p. 21) explains:

> to metaphorically walk alongside them – to hold onto hope, like a lantern, so that they will find their way through the darkness of complex emotions, and make their own way out of the tunnel, in their own time. This does not mean that there is no direction, but that the direction comes from the child.

Reflective point

Reflecting on the Wellbeing Diamond Model prompts practitioners to engage in self-reflection and intentional practice to support both themselves and those in their care. Consider the questions below to reflect upon your own self-care in your professional role:

- Psychological Dimension: How do you cultivate emotional resilience amidst the demands of your role? What strategies can you implement to foster a positive mindset and manage stress effectively?
- Physical Dimension: How do you prioritise physical health within your daily routine? What self-care practices can you adopt to ensure sustained energy and vitality?
- Social Dimension: How do you nurture supportive relationships within your educational community? How can collaborative efforts enhance your sense of belonging and professional growth?
- Existential Dimension: What values and beliefs guide your practice? How do you find purpose and meaning in your work, especially during challenging times?

Conclusion

Social pedagogy is a holistic, values-led approach that centres on relationship-based practice to support wellbeing, learning, and social inclusion. Grounded in Carl Rogers' (1959) theory of empathy, congruence, and unconditional positive regard, it highlights the importance of genuine, empowering relationships and interdependence among individuals. The Diamond Model emphasises recognising and nurturing individual potential, while the *Haltung* framework underscores the importance of emotional connectedness. Effective social pedagogy involves managing transitions sensitively, fostering empathy, and promoting the emotional wellbeing of both learners and practitioners.

To effectively manage the emotional costs associated with social pedagogy, practitioners can adopt practical strategies such as self-care techniques, emotional awareness, boundary-setting, and professional development. Engaging in peer support networks and embracing creativity in practice can further enhance resilience and wellbeing. These strategies not only benefit practitioners but also significantly impact the wellbeing and development of the learners they support. By embracing these principles, social pedagogy aims to unlock the full potential of individuals, contributing to their personal and collective growth and resilience. This approach aligns with the broader aims of this book, emphasising the crucial role of relationship-based practice in fostering a supportive and nurturing education and care environment.

Summary points

- The social pedagogy approach emphasises values-led, holistic, and relationship-based practice. It strives for both independence and interdependence within relational frameworks.
- The principles of emotional wellbeing include that authentic relationships are central to our practice, supporting self-actualisation and emotional wellbeing. The Diamond Model highlights every individual's potential and the importance of positive emotional experiences in learning.
- Sensitive handling of transitions is crucial, especially for young children, involving partnerships between children, families, and practitioners.
- The Relational Universe and empathy emphasise interdependence and the power of meaningful connections. Concepts of empathy, congruence, and unconditional positive regard are key, reflected in the social pedagogy *Haltung* and 'Head, Heart, Hands' framework.
- Practitioner wellbeing is essential for creating nurturing environments. The Diamond Model's holistic approach to wellbeing encompasses psychological, physical, social, and existential dimensions, promoting resilience and avoiding burnout.

Recommended reading

Allies, S. (2020) *Supporting teacher wellbeing: A practical guide for primary teachers and school leaders*. Abingdon: Routledge.

Page, J. (2018) Characterising the principles of professional love in early childhood care and education. *International Journal of Early Years Education*, 26(2), pp. 125–141.

References

Allies, S. (2021) A reflection on how a work–life balance can be achieved using professional development. Chartered College of Teaching. Available at: https://my.chartered.college/impact_article/a-reflection-on-how-a-work-life-balance-can-be-achieved-using-professional-development/ (Accessed 17 July 2024).

Boogren, T. (2019) *Self-care for practitioners: A practical guide*. Los Angeles: Solution Tree Press.

Brown, L. (2007) Empathy, genuineness-and the dynamics of power: A feminist responds to Rogers. *Psychotherapy: Theory, Research, Practice, Training*, 44(3), pp. 257–259.

Brown, B. (2010) *The gifts of imperfection: Let go of who you think you're supposed to be and embrace who you are*. Minnesota: Hazelden Publishing.

Cameron, C. and Moss, P. (2011) Social pedagogy and wellbeing: The context of children in care. *International Journal of Social Pedagogy*, 1(1), pp. 7–25.

Cooper, A. and Redfern, S. (2015) *Reflective parenting: A guide to understanding what's going on in your child's mind*. Abingdon: Routledge.

Covey, S. R. (1989) *The seven habits of highly effective people: Restoring the character ethic*. New York: Simon and Schuster.

Dachyshyn, D. M. (2015) Being mindful, heartful, and ecological in early years care and education. *Contemporary Issues in Early Childhood*, 16(1), pp. 32–41.

Datler, W., Datler, M. and Funder, A. (2010) Struggling against a feeling of becoming lost: A young boy's painful transition to day care. *Infant Observation*, 13(1), pp. 65–87.

Department for Education (2024) Statutory framework for the early years foundation stage. Available at: https://assets.publishing.service.gov.uk/media/65aa5e42ed27ca001327b2c7/EYFS_statutory_framework_for_group_and_school_based_providers.pdf (Accessed 28 May 2024).

Dolev, N. and Leshem, S. (2017) Developing emotional intelligence competence among teachers. *Teacher Development*, 21(1), pp. 21–39.

Early Education (2021) Birth to 5 matters: Non-statutory guidance for the early years foundation stage. Available at: www.birthto5matters.org.uk (Accessed 18 July 2024).

Eichsteller, G. and Holthoff, S. (2012a) ThemPra's diamond model. Available at: www.thempra.org.uk/social-pedagogy/key-concepts-in-social-pedagogy/thempras-diamond-model/ (Accessed 15 June 2024).

Eichsteller, G. and Holthoff, S. (2012b) The diamond model: A values-based framework for reflective practice in social pedagogy. *International Journal of Social Pedagogy*, 1(1), pp. 20–32.

Gerhardt, S. (2015) *Why love matters: How affection shapes a baby's brain*. 2nd edn. Abingdon: Routledge.

Glazzard, J. and Rose, A. (2019) The impact of teacher wellbeing and mental health on pupil progress in primary schools. Available at: www.leedsbeckett.ac.uk/carnegie-school-of-education/research/carnegie-centre-of-excellence-for-mental-health-in-schools/school-mental-health-network/-/media/253bcf64213a4a8582a2a0a2be6b1d49.ashx (Accessed 15 June 2024).

Gordon, M. (2005) *Roots of empathy: Changing the world child by child*. Toronto: Thomas Allen Publishers.

Harrison, E. (2024) The mental health crisis crushing teachers – and what it means for schools. *The Independent*, 7th May 2024. Available at www.independent.co.uk/life-style/teaching-mental-health-schools-quit-b2540733.html (Accessed 9 June 2024).

Isaacson, T. (2020) Metaphors of agony: Culture-bound syndromes of hyper-independence, psychoanalysis. *Self and Context*, 15(4), pp. 375–383.

Johnson, D. W. and Johnson, R. T. (2009) An educational psychology success story: Social interdependence theory and cooperative learning. *Educational Researcher*, 38(5), pp. 365–379.

Junger, S. (2016) *Tribe: On homecoming and belonging*. New York: Twelve Publishing.

Kabat-Zinn, J. (1990) *Full catastrophe living: Using the wisdom of your body and mind to face stress, pain, and illness*. London: Delta.

Kahu, E., Stephens, C., Leach, L. and Zepke, N. (2015) Linking academic emotions and student engagement: Mature-aged distance students' transition to university. *Journal of Further and Higher Education*, 39(4), pp. 481–497.

Klette, T. and Killén, K. (2019) Painful transitions: a study of 1-year-old toddlers' reactions to separation and reunion with their mothers after 1 month in childcare. *Early Child Development and Care*, 189(12), pp. 1970–1977.

Lisak, A., Harush, R., Ickeson, T. and Harel, S. (2022) Team interdependence as a substitute for empowering leadership contribution to team meaningfulness and performance. *Frontiers in Psychology*, 13, pp. 1–11.

Maclean, S. and Harrison, R. (2015) Systems theory and family therapy: Beyond structure and process. *Journal of Family Therapy*, 37(4), pp. 445–462.

Maibom, H. (2017) *The Routledge handbook of philosophy of empathy*. New York: Routledge.

Mayer, J. D. and Salovey, P. (1997) What is emotional intelligence? In P. Salovey and D. J. Sluyter (Eds) *Emotional development and emotional intelligence: Educational implications*. New York: Basic Books, pp. 3–31.

McMillan, W. (2014) 'They have different information about what is going on': Emotion in the transition to university. *Higher Education Research and Development*, 33(6), pp. 1123–1135.

Monteux, S. and Monteux, A. (2020) Human encounters: The core of everyday care practice. *International Journal of Social Pedagogy*, 9(1), pp. 1–13.

Naylor, D. and Nyanjom, J. (2021) Practitioners' emotions involved in the transition to online teaching in higher education. *Higher Education Research and Development*, 40(6), pp. 1236–1250.

Noddings N. (2015) Care ethics and caring organisations. In D. Engster and M. Hamington (Eds) *Care ethics and political theory*. Oxford: Oxford University Press, pp. 72–86.

Osika, A., MacMahon, S., Lodge, J. and Carroll, A. (2022) Emotions and learning: What role do emotions play in how and why students learn? *Times Higher Education*. Available at: www.timeshighereducation.com/campus/emotions-and-learning-what-role-do-emotions-play-how-and-why-students-learn (Accessed 19 April 2024).

Page, J. (2018) Characterising the principles of professional love in early childhood care and education. *International Journal of Early Years Education*, 26(2), pp. 125–141.

Petrie, P. and Calder, N. (2013) Social pedagogy in the UK: Gaining a firm foothold? *Education Policy Analysis Archives*, 21, p. 37. https://doi.org/10.14507/epaa.v21n37.2013

Prowle, A. and Hodgkins, A. (2020) *Making a difference with children and families*. London: Red Globe Books.

Purvanova, R. (2013) The role of feeling known for team member outcomes in project teams. *Small Group Research*, 44(3), pp. 298–331.

Rogers, C. (1942) *Counselling and psychotherapy.* Cambridge, MA: Riverside Press.

Rogers, C. R. (1959) A theory of therapy, personality, and interpersonal relationships: As developed in the client-centered framework. In S. Koch (Ed) Psychology: *A study of a science. Formulations of the person and the social context* (Vol. 3, pp. 184–256). New York: McGraw-Hill.

Rogers, C. (1980) *A way of being.* Boston: Houghton Mifflin.

Rouse, E., Garner, R. and Nicholas, M. (2023) Transition into school-aged care – How do services support children starting school? *European Early Childhood Educational Research Journal*, 31(5), pp. 722–738.

Sammons, P. (2019) *The compassionate teacher.* Abingdon: Routledge.

Singer, T. and Klimecki, O. (2014) Empathy and compassion. *Current Biology*, 24(18), pp. 875–878.

Thempra (2024) Welcome to the world of social pedagogy. Available at: www.thempra.org.uk/ (Accessed 6 February 2025).

Ttofa, J. (2017) *Nurturing emotional resilience in vulnerable children and young people: A practical guide.* Abingdon: Routledge.

Zwart, R. C., Wubbels, T., Bergen, T. C. M. and Bolhuis, S. (2007) Experienced teacher learning within the context of reciprocal peer coaching, *Teachers and Teaching*, 13(2), pp. 165–187.

10 Why college-based higher education needs social pedagogy

Olivia Storey and Geoffrey Elliott

Introduction

Several years ago, one author of this chapter (Kadi-Hanifi and Elliott, 2016, p. 7) wrote that CBHE is:

> caught up within an unequal system of education, fast-changing policies and lack of funding, unable even to have the flexibility to do what it has always done very well which is to provide a flexible, multi-faceted, modern and empowering education to the communities that have had (and still do have) faith in its ability to meet their needs.

This underscores the crucial point that CBHE, being part of a wider and complex government-controlled system of HE, is critically constrained in the extent to which it can provide a quality service to its core clientele: typically, mature students, first generation in HE families, disadvantaged and disabled students. Protagonists have strongly maintained that a core value of CBHE is that it is both relevant and responsive to the needs of these students. In fact, CBHE gives priority and prominence to the student in their unique life world, over and above the needs of the economy or the marketplace. This is why so many CBHE courses have developed and flourished in Further Education (FE) colleges that have a very strong tradition of serving the needs of the communities in which they are grounded.

In contrast to this paradigm, contemporary debates around the value of HE, stemming from a highly technical, performative means/ends paradigm, have recently been reinvigorated. This follows the announcement by the Department for Education (DfE, 2023) that student numbers for HE courses that are perceived to be of low quality and with 'poor' employment outcomes were to be capped by the Office for Students (OfS). Despite arguments that such a policy would limit HE opportunities for minority ethnic groups and disabled or disadvantaged adults (Universities UK, 2023), the policy shift was completely in line with the growing policy consensus that the steady increase in widening participation and access to HE achieved over the last 20 years needed to be reversed in favour of more vocational and technical training, typically 'on the job' and more directly linked to perceived labour market skills shortages (Institute for Fiscal Studies, 2023).

This same policy initiative also directly attacks a hugely successful segment of CBHE, the Foundation Year (FY) course, which provides a bridge into higher education for mature, non-qualified students, comparable to access to HE courses. The plans were to significantly reduce the fee charged to FY students from £9,250 to £5,760, making them more accessible to potential students, but economically unviable for many institutions. Hale (2023, no page) argues that the result of this will be that:

DOI: 10.4324/9781003533276-10

high-quality, genuinely transformative foundation years, the ones that equip the most disadvantaged students to succeed at university and beyond, will wither and die, taking the hopes and opportunities of thousands of potential students with them.

CBHE has a long and complex pedigree (Elliott, 2021). It is a significant subsector of HE because around one in ten HE students gain their qualifications via this route prior to attending HE (Association of Colleges, 2022). It is also diverse. CBHE embraces a wide variety of vocational and professional education and training, including 'academic' qualifications. CBHE is important for a number of reasons, for example, most CBHE provision in the UK resides in Further Education Colleges (FECs) which offer further and higher education to their local communities. In addition, CBHE provides an alternative route for students who cannot, or do not wish, to travel to university. Finally, because of their local roots, many CBHE students are characterised as 'widening participation' students, and CBHE has long been recognised as a key driver of widening participation in HE (Gray, 2016; Elliott, 2017).

For the colleges themselves, CBHE provides not only an important and much needed alternative source of fee income, but also accessible and effective HE progression routes for their students. As the traditional model of English HE becomes more vigorously questioned (Bettinson et al., 2023), CBHE provides a compelling alternative, predicated upon an HE offer that is placed in a familiar and supportive setting that meets local employment needs. Not only this, it also provides stimulating higher-level work for college tutors, consolidates partnerships with local universities which may provide validation and quality assurance support and reinforces the idea of a community college spanning entry level courses through to degrees and postgraduate qualifications.

We believe that the socially engaged principles underpinning social pedagogy are fundamental to CBHE. The moral compass that is a foundation stone of social pedagogy (Haltung) is also at the heart of CBHE. This signifies the emergence of a collective Haltung that is characteristic of CBHE, insofar as this alternative mode of HE places a particular emphasis upon the identity and values of the student and operates as 'an interlinked system, based on similar principles, philosophies and visions' (Eichstellar and Holthoff, 2012, p. 32). Scholarly accounts of the recent development of CBHE within a predominantly market-driven HE sector emphasise the centrality of the shared educational values that drive those developments. Tummons' (2019) notion of the ethic of care in CBHE is a pertinent example.

In this chapter, we attempt to develop a social pedagogical theory of CBHE, that is, to conceptualise CBHE as the closest thing we have in the HE sector to a practical embodiment of some of the core principles underpinning social pedagogy. In particular, we focus upon the *Three Ps*, The *Common Third* and *Life World Orientation*. We briefly describe these below, before offering some vignettes drawn from our own experience, that illustrate the presence, utility and power of a social pedagogical orientation towards CBHE. But first, we take a step back to focus on some of the roots of social pedagogy that have informed our thinking on CBHE.

Breath of Life theory

Maslow's Hierarchy of Needs (1943) has been a significant presence in education and care courses, and many will be familiar with this theory; the concept that humans are driven by self-actualisation, the motivation for individuals to reach full potential. What is less well known, however, is the initial source of this theory. Maslow cultivated his theory whilst travelling and visiting the Blackfoot people, the First Nation in south Alberta, Canada (Bray, 2019), and adapting their model, the *Breath of Life* (BoL) theory (Blackstock, 2011, 2019) in the development of his own. Maslow's theory differs from the principles of BoL in one key aspect, however: the concept of collectivism. Rather than focus upon an innate drive based on *individual* needs, as Maslow does, the Blackfoot people argue the presence of an instinctive and inherent necessity to bond with the *community*. In the BoL theory, self-actualisation forms the basis of existence, leading to cultural *Haltung*, and finally cultural perpetuity, the fundamental purpose of which is to protect and transfer teachings (and, as a result of them, wellbeing) to descendants (Figure 10.1).

Using the social pedagogical concept of *Haltung*, the BoL perspective can be acknowledged alongside Western epistemologies of individualism via reciprocated respect and acknowledgement, within an organisation based upon social pedagogical values. Within such institutions knowledge is not approached in a hierarchical way, as such an approach causes individuals to feel marginalised from the collective, or powerless and individually compromised. A theoretical context where unique strengths are valued and individual need is respected is highly pertinent to contemporary CBHE.

A dominant feature of the discourse in CBHE involves widening participation and social justice, whereby colleges provide HE in a manner which is accessible to all (Tucker, Pedder and Martin, 2021). Recent years have seen significant progress in this. In 2021, 24 per cent of UK 18-year-olds from low participation neighbourhoods (POLAR4 quintile 1) were accepted to study a full-time undergraduate degree through UCAS, compared to 14.1 per cent in 2012 (UCAS, 2021). One factor which impacts accessibility in CBHE (and arguably across all sectors) is the flexibility of delivery, to enable students who have childcare and employment commitments to attend. This might lead lecturers in CBHE to ask themselves,

> knowing that these students are pressed for time, as they are having to balance these other commitments, what can I do to ensure I am providing them with equal opportunities compared to their counterparts who attend a university as opposed to a college?.

But it might also raise conundrums, for example: 'If I flag essential reading and specific page numbers for these students, is this supporting them to gain knowledge or is it disempowering and limiting them by discouraging further/wider reading?'.

Whilst issues of supportive inclusion versus the 'dilution' of the HE experience are not restricted to CBHE, with some university courses likewise providing flexible study pathways with widening

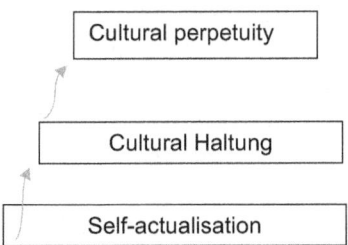

Figure 10.1 Breath of Life model.

participation and social justice also of value for those working in university institutions, the life experiences and knowledge of lecturers working within universities is likely to be different (Keenan, 2021) due to their more ready access to resources, and possibly social capital. Therefore, embracing a social pedagogical approach in CBHE and university partnerships can provide opportunity for such questions to be explored within this merged community. The Haltung relating to both the organisation and the individual can reflect each other and develop in terms of supportiveness and energising function.

Social science theory development in Western society tends to involve a more remote and independent approach, as opposed to a collective and multi-generational methodology, which provides opportunity to focus on the same subject using different outlooks (Blackstock, 2009) through which new possibilities are unlocked and revelations are exposed. As highlighted by Blackstock (2011, 2019), the BoL theory challenges the Western tendency to focus on individual rights, which fragment knowledge using various epistemological approaches, rather than promoting the links and relationships between a range of viewpoints (Lather, 2006). Alternatively, BoL theory values ancestral knowledge which is not fixed to a specific collection of beliefs. Similarly, Cleary (2019, p. 11) argues for a pedagogy which promotes 'a community of others in the formation of self-identity' and a sensitivity towards historical, cultural and biographical narratives. By embracing institutional Haltung, the goal is to prevent, reduce and overcome pain and suffering of all life via the exploration of the 'why' of current and previous actions and consequences. The commitment to shared growth in discovery and understanding, leading to collective accountability and improved wellbeing, is fundamental for maintaining hope when facing adversity (see Bednář et al., 2023).

In order to explore how these theoretical principles can play out in practice, we present narratives based on one of the author's lived experience of CBHE. However, this is more than autobiography; we would frame it as autoethnography in which, 'rather than just writing about yourself, you start to question what happens to you and why it's happening' (de Vries, 2012, p. 355). This fits well with social pedagogy, where we are encouraged to explore our motives and our values. Ethnography is deeply concerned with gaining insight into culture and social process, understanding informal organisations and the meanings people apply to their own experiences (Gilbert, 1994). Such meanings are explored below.

Avoiding individualism and embracing the strength of a collective group in CBHE – two practitioner narratives

(a) An experienced CBHE tutor reflecting on her six years in partnership with a university.
When I was told that the HE course I was leading on was changing to a course running in collaboration with a university, I felt fear resulting from an instinct to protect myself in another demanding but less familiar environment. I was concerned that I would not fit in with the partnership culture due to not having the same expertise as others and felt intimidated by the many accolades, research experience and publications of members of the university group. I was fearful that the students and I would be entering a game in which we did not know the rules.
My first interaction with university staff was at a partnership cross-moderation day. We moderated the required percentage of scripts, discussing and agreeing upon grades. I avoided putting across any alternative ideas and thoughts, considering my knowledge and experience

Why college-based higher education needs social pedagogy

as inferior. I observed university colleagues question each other's assessment decisions in a curious and supportive manner, encouraging the partner CBHE lecturers to join in with these discussions. I was surprised to hear university lecturers say "I had not thought about it like that. Thank you, that's a useful perspective".

I had the opportunity to engage in partnership activities, I went back to the FE campus feeling positive, my confidence boosted. These events initiated a renewed drive to develop my practice. Through this and further interactions in the partnership I not only gained understanding through sharing knowledge and experience but have also stopped feeling isolated when facing challenges and difficulties. Within the relationships formed I feel safe to be open about any doubts, and the partnership has encouraged a growing self-belief through a nurturing environment. My interactions with the CBHE students were positively impacted due to my experiences in this partnership.

(b) A CBHE tutor's account of a conference for students and tutors held at the partnership university.

The first time I went to the conference it felt like such a treat – sitting in workshops led by experts in the field, listening to their research findings and interesting concepts that were new to me. The students said they enjoyed it too, going home with notebooks full of ideas and books bought on special offer from a stall featuring some of the speakers and lecturers in the partnership.

CBHE students often doubt the value of their contributions in HE, however, I saw how they thrived both during and after attending this conference. CBHE students have a wealth of knowledge from their diverse experiences and a commitment to learn and take this back to the communities that they work within. Events like this provide CBHE students with valuable cultural and linguistic social capital by exposing them to unfamiliar concepts. Subsequently they feel legitimised and communicate their practice-based wisdom with growing confidence. When it came to marking their assignments, most students had used concepts from the conference to develop their critical thinking. I was thrilled to see original, creative interpretations and applications of the learning gained from the conference shared at the next partnership away day (a staff training day for members of the partnership).

The university lecturers were delighted to hear about the impact the day had had and asked if examples of the CBHE student's work could be shared with their students. The CBHE students were more than happy to share their work, and when talking to them about this, it was clear that a sense of belonging and purposefulness was felt by not only me, but them too. The CBHE students and I were subsequently invited, and took part in, research conducted by the lecturers at the university. The conference created opportunities and empowering conditions to enable the CBHE teachers and students to set personal and professional targets, and to work towards these with agency and a sense of possibility. I recognise, reflecting on this, the significance of social pedagogy's ethical orientation, as referred to by Eichsteller and Holthoff (2011, p. 176), which promotes a 'profound respect of people's human dignity and their otherness'. Approaching everyone's 'otherness' with unconditional positive regard felt key, in other words it was essential that we felt accepted and supported regardless of our backgrounds and different journeys into the HE environment.

Reflection point

Considering the two narratives above, think about the ways that you could nurture qualities of connectedness, a vital quality in social pedagogy and the *Breath of Life* theory, within your professional collective group/s. What would be the benefits of developing respectful collaborations such as those evidenced in the examples above?

The Three Ps – a tutor's exploration of mental health in CBHE

The *Three Ps* proposes that our selves can be characterised by three spheres: professional, personal and private (Thempra, 2024). The professional sphere includes what we have learned from research and practice to help us to work with people in a professional capacity. The personal sphere is shared in a reflective way with specific audiences to build relationships of trust and to show that we, too, have our own experiences and challenges. The private sphere is what we will only share with those close to us, trusting that it will not be shared any further. Work-based learning, as a significant component of CBHE, exemplifies the bringing together of each of these spheres and is often protected with learning contracts that specify the opportunities and limitations for moving between spheres, enabling and reinforcing a safe learning space for everyone (Gibbs, 2009).

During my time as a CBHE tutor I experienced situations which threatened my health and well-being. Although I wanted to be effective in supporting the teaching and learning of the students, at times I found the pressure and workload overwhelming. I started one CBHE course that I taught (a module based upon their practice experience) by setting out an agreement for confidentiality with the students. This stressed that what we discussed within the module was not shared elsewhere. The module is designed to encourage students to examine work-related dilemmas and reflect on skills, values and knowledge. Through it, students focus on issues relating to compassion fatigue, boundaries, safeguarding and work/life balance, as well as many others. When I gathered feedback from the students on the module, it was unanimously positive. The group activities and discussions with tutors and peers were particularly appreciated, the strength of the module clearly came from the relationships formed.

However, when reflecting on the teaching and learning in this module with other CBHE tutors on the course, I realised I was not practising what I was preaching. Despite being non-judgemental and considerate of the mental health issues of the students, I found myself self-stigmatising and not practising self-care. Over time, myself and a fellow CBHE colleague, with whom I had developed a close, trusting relationship, shared details of what we were experiencing in our private lives that affected us at work: grief, relationship breakdowns and sickness. Feeling comfortable to share my own difficulties improved my wellbeing, enabling me to be kinder to myself. Reflecting the 'positive relationships' aspect of the *Diamond Model* (discussed in previous chapters), it was important that I, too, received unconditional positive regard from someone that I trusted, as this strengthened my ability to demonstrate care and compassion towards my colleagues' and students' problems. As is discussed in Chapter 9, we must show self-care if we are to empathise and support others without experiencing emotional 'burnout'.

My interactions and relationships with CBHE colleagues and students, spanning both the professional and personal spheres, prevented me from feeling isolated. Using the *Three Ps* to reflect and make decisions about when to move between the spheres, meant that I restricted the full openness of my private self to my close relationships. Through this frank sharing of challenges with a trusted colleague I gained insight and confidence in recognising what experiences, and aspects of my private self, needed to be filtered from my professional practice. This meant that I could feel acknowledged and understood, whilst reducing the likelihood of experiencing guilt, embarrassment, worry or regret for oversharing within the professional relationship that I had with my students. As human beings we are social animals, our relationships energise us. The *Three Ps* help us to consider what those relationships should 'look' like in the different contexts of our life.

These types of reflectively analytical discussions are common in student group work in CBHE, often linked to scenario-based learning applied to fictional and non-fictional work settings. When discussing a fictional situation this can act as a *Common Third* activity (we go on to discuss this further in the following section, and it is also discussed in depth in Chapter 5) whereby, the tutor and student hierarchy is flattened, and we problem solve together. The advantage of these discussion spaces which focus upon a fictional scenario is that although personal successes and challenges might be brought into the discussion they can be disguised, in the guise of information shared in relation to 'the case'.

There is no imperative for students and tutors to reveal personal aspects of themselves within their studying relationship, but in my experience CBHE creates close, respectful and professional relationships, which can provide support and strength in a demanding environment. A central tenet of SP is working and learning *alongside* others (Charfe and Gardner, 2019). Through this approach hierarchies between educator and learner are reduced and strong bonds of trust created through openness and authenticity.

> **Reflection point**
>
> How do the reflections above illustrate the Three Ps, and how and what does this 'look like' in your own practice?

The Common Third

The Common Third is an activity used to further collaboration and partnership, key elements of CBHE as it has developed in English Post-Compulsory Education. CBHE acknowledges the value of the learning process as much as the product. The learning object becomes a symbol of the cooperation and collaboration between learners and their tutors, and between learners themselves. Learning through experience, shared learning, peer group assessment, collaborative projects – are all core practice in CBHE at its best, emerging from the learner centred practice so commonly found in FE colleges. The Social Pedagogy Professional Association explains, 'the Common Third creates future possibilities through serendipity and the incidental elements that arise in the course of activities. The 'Third' is an activity that is external to a problem or issue' (Hadi and Johansen, 2023, no page). In CBHE, the tutor views themselves in a relationship with the learner, creating a shared space through activity that values their contribution as equals. Hence, CBHE is frequently regarded as a more democratic form of HE, in contrast with more traditional hierarchical structures commonly found in the university system. This idea is strongly echoed in Kendall and Mitchell's (2020) idea of the 'third space' in CBHE.

The reflective placement portfolio is a feature of many CBHE courses, and as an important formal document relating to the qualification, it opens a dialogue between the student and tutor. A frequent theme is the balancing of numerous roles and responsibilities. Students in CBHE often navigate pressures of employment, work placement and study, whilst maintaining a work-life balance. Having tutors who share strategies they have utilised, whether they have been successful or unsuccessful, is an asset in CBHE. Finding a shared point of connection and understanding through discussing similar experiences reflects key elements of a *Common Third* activity. Discussing the dilemmas faced by both students and tutors reduces power hierarchies and builds trusting relationships. Knowing that others, especially tutors who are viewed as far more knowledgeable, have made similar mistakes and overcome similar challenges, can be empowering and reassuring for the student. However, as has already been mentioned, a psychologically safe and non-judgemental environment is vital to enable this to happen.

Life World Orientation – reflecting on the social and cultural aspects of the actions of a CBHE tutor

Life World Orientation is a social pedagogical principle that underpins all the above. It recognises that everyone has a distinct social, cultural and personal biography that has shaped and continues to shape them, and through which shared meanings are constructed. In CBHE tutors recognise these elements are unique to each student. They appreciate that these will only be shared through innovative learning and teaching structures that are accessible to all learners, embracing and celebrating diversity and fostering inclusion (Feather, 2010). As such the institutional values of CBHE reflect, and are in tune with, core understandings of social pedagogy.

Cultural misunderstandings

As a CBHE tutor I still feel defensive when I hear comments such as "I'll keep that course in mind for one of my students, although she may get the grades to do a proper degree", or "Do you think this Foundation Degree might give them the UCAS points to get into university?" or even "Once they have achieved the Foundation Degree they then could apply for a BSc or BA degree". At such moments I would take a deep breath and try to calmly explain that they were currently doing precisely this on their Foundation Degree, and that students could build on this qualification to obtain a CBHE bachelor's degree or enter various university courses' second or third year. If there was time, I would also share how I would love them to see some of the students' work, as the level of critical, original and creative thinking never ceased to impress me, year on year. I would feel frustrated by the misconceptions concerning our courses and our students, and pained by the fight to protect the student, my colleagues, and my self-esteem as being part of the CBHE community.

Somewhat ironically, comments such as those outlined above were from FE colleagues who were also passionate about supporting students' progression, they just did not really understand CBHE. Eichsteller and Holthoff (2011) state how individuals are experts in their own lives and possess inherent knowledge and strengths that can be drawn on to overcome challenges. I did just that as I gently explained the premise of CBHE to those who were unfamiliar with it. When I was able to explain, they were usually pleasantly surprised and keen to know more. Conversations with fellow CBHE colleagues, who had similar experiences to me were my tonic. These moments of reflection and sharing the many positive outcomes of the CBHE learners would keep me going. For example, the student who missed schooling due to their ill health entering the HE field through CBHE and achieving a Higher National Diploma, enabling them to 'top up' to a bachelor degree; the working mother who believed she had missed her chance to engage in HE; the young carer who was able to complete her Foundation Degree, work part time and continue to care for her loved one ... I could go on.

Cultural constraints and dilemmas

Whilst working in CBHE I was not always able to go to university partnership events and engage with research, despite my wish to, due to teaching commitments. I could empathise, however, with my line manager, who had to consider the wellbeing of students on all courses in the college, as well as the wellbeing of staff who would have to cover my absence. I also felt a pressure to prioritise teaching and learning outputs as opposed to research activities that might result in written publications (in contrast to those on Standard Academic Contracts at universities, where research outputs are a formal expectation of their professional job role and responsibilities). However, I was also aware that modelling enthusiasm for research and continuing to develop professional skills would have a positive impact on the learning and achievements of my students. Nevertheless, opportunities for research activities are limited in CBHE, when teaching contact time sometimes exceeds 24 hours a week.

By expressing concerns about the dilemmas that arose as a result of my attendance at partnership meetings, I felt supported in negotiating my CBHE activity and could reduce the unhelpful self-questioning I engaged in. Drawing on trusting relationships with colleagues who knew of my workload and sharing my feelings with them prevented me from fixating on the difficulties and from viewing my actions (and myself) in a negative way. For instance, a conversation with a colleague enabled me to accept that my options were dependent on context and the impact they would have on numerous individuals. Experiencing uncertainty and doubting my decision due to worries of being seen as selfish for not prioritising my FE colleagues' workloads (as they would have to cover) was replaced by an appreciation that everyone's needs, including students' and my own, must be valued in a culture that promotes everyone's wellbeing.

Partnership community research collaborations enabled colleagues from CBHE and HE to come together and listen to other one another's experiences, learning from the strategies others had employed to overcome potential challenges and problems. We shared this *Common Third* experience as we worked together, although our daily working contexts were very different. Through openly and authentically sharing thoughts and concerns within a secure professional relationship with colleagues, I could avoid damaging my relationships with line managers, and felt less likely to 'burn out' or feel devalued, as I could justify striving for a healthy work-life balance. Following discussions with fellow CBHE colleagues, I was able to explain to my FE line manager that research is a core component on Foundation Degrees and that research activities linked directly to teaching and learning outputs. This led to positive and practical support from my line manager, who authorised such activities as part of my Continual Professional Development (CPD) obligations.

Conclusion

CBHE partnerships can enable students to taste university culture and develop confidence in their academic capabilities, a confidence which is often lacking in those undertaking CBHE courses, compared to traditional HE students (see Brubacher and Sillinder, 2021). Working alongside and enabling engagement is not diluting the quality of education, on the contrary, a more collective approach supports the development and evolution of learning communities through the drawing together of a multiplicity of knowledge and experience. At the individual level (the base of the BoL theory), the drive to self-actualise is not diminished but is fundamental in attaining cultural perpetuity. Consequently, any concerns of such a paradigm lowering individuals' motivation, goals, self-expectations and progression are negated. The aim is to create a culture which supports a sense of purposefulness and respect for all as resourceful agents.

By embracing a life world orientation the CBHE student and tutor's life history is acknowledged and explored. It becomes part of the learning experience. CBHE is not a fairy godmother enabling Cinderella to go to the ball (like Daley et al., 2015, we consider this metaphor devalues the strength and autonomy of FE), but instead illuminates an alternative pathway. CBHE provides a supportive and practical journey to make HE learning accessible and achievable alongside other life demands, and also creates opportunities for lecturers working in FE who have a desire to enter HE teaching. CBHE provides supportive and unconditional positive regard for real life experiences and brings students and tutors together as they work toward a common goal of cultural perpetuity. As social pedagogues we are driven to become our best selves, however, positively impacting on those in our community, and knowing that when we are gone our efforts have helped others to flourish, is, arguably, the ultimate reward.

Summary points

- CBHE provides an alternative route to a HE degree by meeting the needs of non-traditional students, for example, mature students, first time in HE students and those affected by disadvantage and/or disability.
- CBHE prioritises the needs of students in their life world. HE courses are delivered in Further Education (FE) colleges. These settings are supportive and familiar to students and meet local employment needs.
- CBHE offers opportunities for college tutors to work in partnership with local universities.
- The importance social pedagogy places on tackling social inequalities and injustices are congruent with of those of CBHE, particularly the concept of a collective *Haltung*.
- *Breath of Life* theory is also congruent with social pedagogy and the principles underpinning CBHE, as it aims to prevent marginalisation and exclusionary hierarchies.
- CBHE tutors must walk a fine line between empowering students to achieve academic success and limiting their growth by being overly directive.
- CBHE and university partnerships offer opportunities to reflect on these ethical dilemmas by drawing on their collective *Haltung*.
- The benefits (for both tutor and student) of working in a respectful and supportive partnership with a local university are considered in a reflection by a CBHE tutor.
- The *Three Ps* can frame appropriate, trusting relationships when working with colleagues and students and can be empowering, helping to prevent isolation and associated mental health issues.
- CBHE often utilises strategies where students and tutors can participate in *Common Third* activities, which help reduce power hierarchies and build trusting relationships.
- CBHE adopts teaching strategies that take account of students' life world, to ensure learning is accessible to all.
- Tutor's *Life World Orientation* should, similarly, be considered, balancing individual professional needs and a culture of wellbeing.

Recommended reading

Blackstock, C. (2019) Revisiting the breath of life theory. *British Journal of Social Work*, 49, pp. 854–859.
Charfe, L. and Gardner, A. (2020) 'Does my Haltung look big in this?' The use of social pedagogical theory for the development of ethical and value-led practice. *International Journal of Social Pedagogy*, 9(1), pp. 1–10. https://doi.org/10.14324/111.444.ijsp.2020.v9.x.011
Tucker, C., Pedder, S. and Martin, G. (2021) 'The CBHE Lecturer Experience.' In Kadi-Hanifi, K. and Keenan, J. (Eds) *College Based Higher Education and Its Identities*, pp. 89–102. Cham, Switzerland: Palgrave MacMillan.

References

Association of Colleges (2022) Key facts. Available at www.aoc.co.uk/about/college-key-facts (Accessed February 2025).
Bednář, P., Danko, L. and Smékalová, L. (2023) Coworking spaces and creative communities: Making resilient coworking spaces through knowledge sharing and collective learning. *European Planning Studies*, 31(3), pp. 490–507.
Bettinson, E., Young, K., Haven-Tang, C., Cavanagh, J., Fisher, R. and Francis, M. (2023) Employers' conceptions of quality and value in higher education. *Higher Education*, 6 online only on date of accessing. Available at: https://link.springer.com/article/10.1007/s10734-023-01069-x (Accessed February 2025).
Blackstock, C. (2009) First Nations children count: Enveloping quantitative research in an Indigenous envelope. *First Peoples Child and Family Review*, 4(2), pp. 135–144.
Blackstock, C. (2011) The emergence of the breath of life theory. *Journal of Social Work Values and Ethics*, 8(1), pp. 1–16.
Blackstock, C. (2019) Revisiting the breath of life theory. *British Journal of Social Work*, 49(4), pp. 854–859.
Bray, B. (2019). Maslow's hierarchy of needs and Blackfoot (Siksika) Nation beliefs. Available at: https://barbarabray.net/2019/03/10/maslows-hierarchy-of-needs-and-blackfoot-nation-beliefs/ (Accessed 5 July 2023).
Brubacher, M. R. and Silinda, F. T. (2021) First-generation students in distance education program: Family resources and academic outcome. *International Review of Research in Open and Distributed Learning*, 22(1), pp. 135–147.
Charfe, L. and Gardner, A. (2019) *Social Pedagogy and Social Work*. London: Sage.
Cleary, B. (2019) Reinterpreting bildung in social pedagogy. *International Journal of Social Pedagogy*, 8(1): 3, pp. 1–12. https://doi.org/10.14324/111.444.ijsp.2019.v8.1.003
Daley, M., Orr, K. and Petrie, J. (2015) *Further Education and the Twelve Dancing Princess*. London: Trentham.
de Vries, P. (2012) 'Autoethnography'. In Delamont, S. (Ed.) *Handbook of Qualitative Research in Education*, pp. 136–152. Cheltenham, England: Edward Elgar.
Department for Education (2023) Crackdown on rip-off university degrees. Available at: www.gov.uk/government/news/crackdown-on-rip-off-university-degrees (Accessed February 2025).
Eichsteller, G. and Holthoff, S. (2011) Social pedagogy as an ethical orientation towards working with people – historical perspectives. *Children Australia*, 36(4), pp. 176–186. https://doi.org/10.1375/jcas.36.4.176
Eichsteller, G. and Holthoff, S. (2012) The art of being a social pedagogue: Developing cultural change in children's homes in Essex. *International Journal of Social Pedagogy*, 1(1), 4, pp. 30–46.
Elliott, G. (2017) Challenging assumptions about values, interests and power in further and higher education partnerships. *Journal of Further and Higher Education*, 41(2), pp. 143–154.
Elliott, G. (2021) 'College Based Higher Education: Provenance and Prospects.' In Kadi-Hanifi, K. and J. Keenan (Eds.) *College Based Higher Education and Its Identities*, pp. 1–22. Cham, Switzerland: Palgrave Macmillan.
Feather (2010) A whisper of academic identity: An HE in FE perspective. *Research in Post-Compulsory Education*, 15(2), pp.189–204.
Gibbs, P. (2009) Learning agreements and work-based higher education. *Research in Post-Compulsory Education* 14(1), pp.31–41.
Gilbert, N. (Ed.) (1994) *Researching Social Life*. London: Sage.
Gray, C. (2016) Implementing English further/higher education partnerships. *Higher Education Quarterly*, 70(1), pp. 43–58.
Hadi, J. and Johansen, T. (2023) The common third: A kindred spirit to youth work? Online article for the Social Pedagogy Association. Available at: https://sppa-uk.org/the-common-third/ (Accessed February 2025).
Hale, S. (2023) Fees cuts will undermine the foundations of opportunity. WonkHE. Available at: https://wonkhe.com/blogs/fees-cut-will-undermine-the-foundations-of-opportunity/ (Accessed February 2025).

Institute for Fiscal Studies (2023) Widening participation in higher education. Available at: https://ifs.org.uk/articles/widening-participation-higher-education (Accessed February 2025).

Kadi-Hanifi, K. and Elliott, G. (2016) Appraising and reconfiguring HE in FE through research and critical perspectives. *Research in Post-Compulsory Education*, 21(1–2), pp. 1–8.

Keenan, J. (2021) 'The CBHE Lecturer and Student.' In Kadi-Hanifi, K. and Keenan, J. (Eds) *College Based Higher Education and Its Identities*, pp. 23–41. Cham, Switzerland: Palgrave MacMillan.

Kendall, A. and Mitchell, S. (2020) 'Learning Teaching and Assessment in CBHE.' In Kadi-Hanifi, K. and Keenan, J. (Eds) *College Based Higher Education and its Identities*, pp. 43–67. Cham, Switzerland: Palgrave Macmillan.

Lather, P. (2006) Paradigm proliferation as a good thing to think with: Teaching research in education as a wild profusion. *International Journal of Qualitative Studies in Education*, 19(1), 535–557.

Maslow, A. H. (1943) A theory of human motivation. *Psychological Review*, 50(4): pp. 370–396.

Quality Assurance Agency for Higher Education (QAA). (2020) Characteristics statement: Foundation degree. Available at: www.qaa.ac.uk/docs/qaa/quality-code/foundation-degree-characteristics-statement-2020.pdf (Accessed 16 January 2023).

Thempra (2024) The 3 Ps: The professional, personal, and private self of the social pedagogue. Available at: www.thempra.org.uk/social-pedagogy/key-concepts-in-social-pedagogy/the-3-ps/ (Accessed 19 August 2024).

Tucker, C., Pedder, S. and Martin, G. (2021) 'The CBHE Lecturer Experience.' In Kadi-Hanifi, K. and Keenan, J. (Eds) *College Based Higher Education and its Identities*, pp. 89–101. Cham, Switzerland: Palgrave MacMillan.

Tummons, J. (2019) *Professionalism in Post-Compulsory Education and Training*. Abingdon: Routledge.

Universities and Colleges Admissions Service (2021) Undergraduate sector-level end of cycle data resources). Available at: www.ucas.com/data-and-analysis/undergraduate-statistics-and-reports/ucas-undergraduate-sector-level-end-cycle-data-resources-2021 (Accessed February 2025).

Universities UK (2023) Why student number caps will hurt everyone, not just universities. Available at: www.universitiesuk.ac.uk/latest/insights-and-analysis/why-student-number-caps-will-hurt (Accessed February 2025).

11 A social pedagogical approach to tackling social-class bias in higher education

Raquel Labella Jara

Introduction

In the last 50 years, global higher education (HE) has experienced a major expansion (Marginson, 2016, 2018). In the UK the number of higher education institutions (HEI) has increased five-fold (Whitty et al., 2015). This expansion originates with governments in response to changing global economies and their wish to achieve a competitive advantage (Boden and Nedeva, 2010; Gale and Hodge, 2014). This new HE scenario requires not only the participation of traditional students (high and mid socio-economic status (SES) backgrounds), but also of non-traditional, working-class individuals (Gale and Hodge, 2014). As a result, different UK governments have sponsored widening participation (WP) policies to increase the number of non-traditional students attending HEIs. And as a policy instrument WP has problematised the low participation of people from disadvantaged backgrounds as a 'low aspirations' issue, which feeds into a deficit discourse (Sellar and Gale, 2011).

The expansion of HE in the UK has meant that more working-class students are now going to university, but a high proportion of these attend less prestigious institutions than their more affluent peers (Marginson, 2016). Academics posit that this is the result of working-class students lacking the knowledge to make the right choice of institution, that is, the one that will bring more returns (Southgate et al., 2018; Woodward, 2020). The problem this assumption poses is that it suggests that (a) some HEIs are better by default and (b) students attending new universities are not as good academically and lack the ability to make the right choices.

There is another important issue. Traditionally the working classes have underachieved educationally (Reay, 2017). Working-class children's educational outcomes are lower than their more affluent peers. This is the case in all stages of education, but it progressively worsens as children move through the system. Their progression to HE rates are lower than middle-class children, and even those entering HE with higher grades are more likely to drop out or graduate with a lower degree classification than their more affluent peers (Bloodworth, 2016; Ricketts et al., 2022).

The question one could ask is whether the deficit discourse, inherent within WP policies, academic literature and even popular culture, is so ingrained in academia that it actually impacts upon academic practice. If there is a bias inherent in our institutions which is impacting upon opportunities for working-class students, then it must be identified and tackled. Later in this chapter I contend that lecturers should maximise their agency and guide their professional practice with the underlying principles of the social pedagogical approach to education, and in doing so fulfil the original purpose of university education.

DOI: 10.4324/9781003533276-11

> **Reflection point**
>
> Have you been in contexts where there is an implicit assumption that class and academic ability are related?

Higher education and widening participation: aspirations vs expectations

As has already been stated, UK HE has experienced a remarkable expansion in the last five decades, an expansion motivated by market forces and the need for governments to achieve competitive advantage in a new global knowledge economy. Up until the end of 1950s, access to HE in Britan was enjoyed by less than five per cent of young people, this small number attended traditional universities. There were two periods of expansion that followed, the 1960s and the first half of the 1990. In the 1960s the expansion coincided with the Government's introduction of a separate type of HE institution, the 'polytechnic', representing the beginning of the 'binary phase' of higher education. These institutions operated alongside traditional universities and were responsible for two-thirds of the HE participation increase in that decade; however, they occupied a second (lower) tier (Boliver, 2011).

After a period of stagnation in the 1970s and 1980s a new phase of HE expansion started in the 1990s, with a series of political reforms (the Education Reform Act of 1988 and the Further and Higher Education Act of 1992) that culminated with the upgrade of polytechnics to university status. This new phase witnessed a rapid growth in university enrolments (they more than doubled in just six years) and, although meant to represent the end of the 'binary system', this did not occur 'in practice'. Decades later an unofficial stratified system of universities still persists, with the old, traditional institutions (including those comprising the 'Russell Group') enjoying higher reputation and prestige than the new, post-92 universities (Boliver, 2011).

Widening participation (WP) was the policy instrument created by the New Labour Government (1997–2010) in order to respond to economic demands whilst also addressing social inclusion issues (Watts, 2006; Archer, 2007). Despite the existence of a social justice rationale the main policy driver was economic, and even diversity was framed in business terms – that working-class talent would improve economic competitiveness (Archer, 2007; Baxter et al., 2007). WP was underpinned by a heavy neoliberal ideology. Knowledge creation is central in neoliberal states, as it fosters economic growth, therefore mechanisms or governance tools to control the sites of knowledge production (i.e. universities) are put in place (Boden and Nedeva, 2010). WP policy is one of these neoliberal mechanisms through which the government controls HE admissions, demanding that universities commit to the recruitment of non-traditional students (declared in an 'Access Agreement') by limiting public funding and imposing a limit to the fees universities can charge (Leach, 2013).

WP, as a policy instrument, has fed into a deficit discourse, as it places the cause of the low participation of disadvantaged individuals on their lack of aspirations, whilst tending to ignore structural and social explanations (Watts, 2006; Sellar and Gale, 2011). Research has challenged the deficit conception of working-class students by demonstrating these students' high academic commitment and skills (McKay and Devlin, 2016). In fact, there are many other causes, such as prior attainment or social and structural inequalities, rather than low aspirations, which prevent progression onto HE (Chowdry et al., 2013; McCowan, 2016).

Whitty et al. (2015) argue that the idea of low aspirations as a cause of lower HE participation is not sustainable. They conclude that at an early age, all children, regardless of their class background, have very high aspirations. The difference relates to how the expectations others have on them modify these as they mature. In fact, research even suggests that lower teacher expectations (as a result of deficit thinking) could affect their teaching practice (Smit, 2012), conveying implicit messages to children and young people.

According to Harrison and Waller (2018), expectation provides an alternative explanation to HE decision making. For these authors young people's expectations are underpinned by elements of achievability that are strongly influenced by the adults in their lives, such as parents and teachers. Thus, as they explain, low teacher expectations contribute to a low expectation in the student themselves.

> **Reflection point**
>
> Can you think of a time when your ambitions, and your confidence, were inhibited by the views of adults in your life?

Two-tier system – who goes where. A matter of expectations?

The expansion of HE in the UK has not, however, been accompanied by a more equal social access to elite institutions: prestigious institutions are more likely to be attended by those from higher SES and so the low SES students are more inclined to attend post-92 (lower tariff) institutions (Marginson, 2016). Various reasons have been used to explain this difference in choice:

- Financial reasons: working-class students may decide to study locally whilst living at home in order to reduce expenses; besides, working-class students who had part-time jobs during secondary school might have received lower grades as a result of having less time to revise and this might have also limited their choice (Whitty et al., 2015).
- Snobbery: it contributes to constrain people's prospects and so those who feel stigmatised prefer to be away from individuals who 'look down on them' (Pickett and Wilkinson, 2010, p. 168). According to several studies working-class students feel more comfortable at new universities (for example Finnegan and Merrill, 2017; Bathmaker, 2021).
- Classist admissions policies and attitudes at old universities: In their study of admissions staff at selective institutions in England, Jones et al. (2019) highlighted that a discourse of lower attainment students not being able to cope with academic pressures was common. They also pointed at classist admissions policies that disadvantaged less affluent students (for example, volunteering at the theatre gave more points than working at a supermarket).
- Impact of deficit thinking and low expectations: As mentioned earlier, young people's expectations are greatly influenced by the expectations that adults in their lives have of them. Thus, low teacher expectations contribute to a low expectation of the self, so attending a high tariff HEI is seen as out of reach (Harrison and Waller, 2018).

There is another element to consider, and it is the value attributed to social class in academia. It is very interesting to see that one of the variables that Vikki Boliver (2015) used in her classification of HE Institutions was social class. As she states, a variable that 'undoubtedly contributes to different estimations of university prestige, is the socioeconomic mix of the students attending different universities' (Boliver, 2015, p. 614). In other words, the higher the social status of its students, the higher the prestige of the institution. This statement conveys a clear message: being working class is less than being middle or upper class and therefore perpetuates a deficit image. This deficit perspective then contributes to stereotyping, making generalisations which further stigmatise and label non-traditional students (Smit, 2012).

Regardless of their choice of institution, all students should enjoy the benefits of a university education and the opportunity to grow as part of the process, irrespective of their social background. However, the discourses ingrained in the HE two-tier system, university admissions and even a policy which aims to improve HE inclusion such as WP, reinforce deficit thinking and contribute to stereotyping. It is, therefore, useful to consider what effect this deficit thinking may have upon progression and attainment.

Student progression and attainment. Also a matter of expectations?

Data suggest that disadvantage has an impact on student progression and attainment (HEFCE, 2013, 2014, cited in Mountford-Zimdars et al., 2015). According to Mountford-Zimdars et al. (2015), disadvantaged students do worse in relation to employment, attainment and progression to further study than their more advantaged peers, even after controlling for variables like type of institution attended. Among the causes that impact on the student experience identified by these authors, are the relationships among students and between students and staff, and the expectations that lecturers have about students and that students have about themselves. Expectations that might be shaped by unconscious bias.

With regard to relationships that support student experience, it has been found that developing a positive student-lecturer relationship is essential for the academic and social integration of some university students (Cureton and Gravestock, 2018). Having been the traditional domain of the upper and middle classes, universities could represent an intimidating environment for working-class students, potentially hindering their ability to perform academically (Thomas and Heath, 2014). This sense of 'not belonging' that working-class students may feel could also make them reticent to develop a relationship with academic staff, as their lack of confidence and insecurities may prevent them from asking questions and participating in class (Read et al., 2003).

Mallman (2017) suggests that lecturers' unconscious expectations can also limit students' learning and progression. He explains that many working-class students arrive at university carrying negative emotional resources (for example anxiety, insecurity, inadequacy and illegitimacy) and then attribute their difficulties during university transition not to financial or symbolic disadvantages but to inherent inadequacy. Therefore, if lecturers do not intervene to modify this perceived inherited fault, then they participate in its persistence by default. If universities and their lecturers assume that working-class difficulties are a result of diminished ability and do nothing to change this, the students' poor confidence will not improve, and their own perception of self as inadequate will not change, further perpetuating inequalities (Mallman, 2017). If lecturers' expectations are a key element in student success, and there is a deficit thinking ingrained in policy and in university classification, one needs to ask whether that deficit thinking is also present in university pedagogy.

Unconscious bias

Unconscious (or implicit) biases are an automatic association process that operates outside our consciousness: these biases are triggered by different features that we identify in others, such as demographic characteristics, and they influence how we perceive, assess and interact with those individuals (Sie and van Vorst, 2016; Staats, 2016). Across literature, the key characteristics of unconscious bias are presented as such:

- Carrying a negative connotation that can be as damaging as open discrimination.
- Affecting everyone and leading to attitudes of which individuals are not necessarily aware.
- Not being understood as a character flaw.
- The reason that individuals who endorse inclusive values can contribute to the persistence of systemic inequalities.
- A shortcut for the brain to process data, and as such they rely on a combination of stereotypes and prejudices.

(Based on Moule, 2009; Sie and van Vorst, 2016; Staats, 2016; Safir, 2017; Applebaum, 2019; Reinsch et al., 2020)

A stereotype 'is a simplistic image or distorted truth about a person or group based on prejudgment of habits, traits, abilities or expectations' (Weinstein and Mellen, cited in Moule, 2009, p. 321). For a stereotype to persist it must be used repeatedly by many people (Sie and van Voorst, 2016). Repetition is key.

One could argue that if there is a strong correlation between one class (working-class) and their academic ability (low ability) in someone's mind, due to that link being part of a repeated discourse, that association will be automatically assumed and enacted when making decisions or acting upon someone identified as a member of that class. If unconscious biases (and the stereotypes and prejudices that shape them) affect how we perceive and interact with others, they also shape our expectations. In fact, studies indicate that teachers' attitudes towards working-class children are different and detrimental to those children (Weale, 2023).

Biases can be identified, acknowledged and managed. Nevertheless, a focus on the effect or harm caused by the action, rather than the intent or the cause of the action could be a better way to correct behaviours (Applebaum, 2019).

Reflection point

In their study of classism in a US college, Langhout et al. (2007) used a scale with six categories, one of them being interpersonal classism via separation, which measured behaviours that aimed to protect a person from lower SES from being confronted with other's wealth ('I do not invite my underprivileged friend to a party with my wealthy friends as I don't want her to feel bad about not having money'). We could argue that the individual displaying such

> behaviour has good intent, however these authors identify the effects of such behaviour as excluding and harmful. Do you think it possible that the 'classism via separation', used here in reference to wealth, might be also found in relation to academic ability?

Pedagogical stratification

The concept of pedagogical stratification refers to 'how different pedagogical approaches might be enabled or constrained by institutional type' (Burke et al., 2015, p. 30). So, for example, pedagogical relations at high prestigious universities are based on *the assumption* that both staff and students are high performers and really committed (Stevenson et al., 2014). Stevenson et al.'s (2014) investigation into pedagogical practice in teaching-led universities explored the effect of WP students on teaching approaches. Their research indicated that some practice seemed to be increasing pedagogical stratification: some lecturers disclosed that in order to adapt to students with lower entry qualifications they had to 'dumb down' their teaching and change some course content and assessment to ensure those students 'remained satisfied customers' (Stevenson et al., 2014, pp. 34–35). Lower expectations meant a change to teaching approach.

A similar conclusion was reached by Tokarczyk (2004), who analysed the impact of social class in US HE and concluded that in under resourced, 'working-class' institutions students were not helped to adapt to college expectations, instead some faculty oversimplified their courses. This unintentionally perpetuated class-based education, as: 'working class students are taught the basics and given information to absorb, while middle- and upper-class students are taught critical thinking' (p. 163).

> ### Reflection point
>
> Before you continue reading, consider this: What do you think the purpose of a university education is?

What is the purpose of higher education?

What makes universities different from other training institutions and is university education compatible with social pedagogy? According to Hämäläinen (2015, p. 1035), social pedagogy is concerned with 'people's social integration, participation and active citizenship, as well as to alleviate social exclusion through education'. Therefore, education is a process of emancipation and social integration, highlighting the importance of community in personal development. For Collini (2012) what makes university education different is that, among other purposes, universities pursue open-ended enquiries without following utilitarian motivations, but with the aim to develop human understanding and broaden minds. For this author, the *development of understanding* (to include the capacity to challenge information) is the essential purpose of the university, which should be achieved through teaching and research. As social pedagogy stresses, empowerment is central to development (Eichsteller and Holthoff, 2011) and empowerment comes through the confidence to question and to challenge.

According to Zgaga (2009) universities should meet four main purposes, which are linked to the four 'archetypal models' of university developed in the nineteenth and twentieth centuries:

- Universities should be able to train students for *professional* careers (Napoleonic model)
- Universities should produce knowledge and foster *research and innovation* (Humboldtian model)
- Universities must prioritise the *personal (intellectual) development* of students. Professional development, although not discarded, is secondary (Newmanian model)
- Universities should *serve the community* and prepare students for life in a democratic society by developing them as citizens (Deweyan model).

For Zgaga (2009) modern universities should reflect these four models; therefore, the economic purposes represented by the first two models should be accompanied by the 'soft purposes' sought by the two latter models (which represent social pedagogical values of personal development, critical thinking, social cohesion values and so on). If universities meet *all* the above purposes they contribute to citizenship. We could argue that universities pursue a social pedagogical goal, in the development of 'self' they emancipate individuals from isolation, providing the skills and the opportunities for students to achieve social integration to maximise their individual potential.

Nevertheless, a market dominated ideology is now embedded within university education and the principal aims pursued by universities most closely reflect the first two models – that is, training students for professional careers and developing knowledge. In other words, universities are displaying utilitarian vocationalism and are prioritising their economic purposes over the development of critical and independent thinking (Evans, 2004; Zgaga, 2009). According to Gibbs (2019) one of the consequences of a market dominated ideology is that the power relations between lecturers and students have changed and that the core duty of lecturers to tell the truth, even if this is unpopular, has also been diminished. Authenticity, a social pedagogical quality key to all of the pedagogues in Chapter 2 has been removed from a lecturer's job description. And this may contribute to deception, for example, by lecturers allowing grade inflation to improve student evaluations instead of stretching their capabilities.

Walker (2008, p. 277) affirms that for universities to be considered the spaces where important and difficult questions are asked, where 'all students are educated to be critical and active participants in democratic life', they also need to promote social justice values and a more just distribution of knowledge. In social pedagogical terms all students should be met with the same 'unconditional positive regard' (a phrase coined by Carl Rogers in 1956 as one of the necessary conditions for positive development in an individual), all should be recognised as having their own, unique, potential. As Walker (*ibid*) argues, policies encouraging HE participation such as WP should have been conceptualised as widening capability, not profits.

> **Reflection point**
>
> In your work, or your interactions with others, do you demonstrate unconditional positive regard? What does that look like?

Conclusion

Disadvantaged students have traditionally failed in education. Despite the increase in university attendance, disadvantage still affects their university progression and attainment. As a result of my ongoing research I contend that the deficit discourse ingrained in inclusive policies such as WP, admissions regulations and university classification is strengthening a stereotype which shapes individuals' bias. These biases contribute to lower academic expectations which can then impact academic practice.

It is crucial that HEIs and their academic staff reflect upon the messages that they implicitly and explicitly convey to their communities regarding social class. Social pedagogy can assist with this. The concept of *Haltung*, a person's 'moral compass', central to social pedagogy and based on empathic understanding and regard, can offer lecturers a framework to reflect on their ethics and values, and how these impact on their interaction with others and therefore on their professional practice (Charfe and Gardner, 2020). As Charfe and Gardner (2020) explain, an individual's *Haltung* is subjective and influenced by constructed social values. It is then necessary that lecturers critically question the societal values attributed to working-class students which could affect their *Haltung*, shape their expectations and impact on their own practice.

University lecturers should help students achieve the four purposes of university education to the full, they have the duty of telling the truth and having difficult conversations without being influenced by social background or pressures such as student evaluation results. Lecturers also need to share knowledge with, and support all of their students in equal measure. Most of all, lecturers need to challenge their own expectations and biases. The two elements underpinning one's *Haltung*, empathic understanding and regard, can guide lecturers in their quest to appreciate the 'other' (non-traditional students), their circumstances and life experiences, to give them the regard that any human being deserves, and to help them succeed at university. A social pedagogical approach could assist lecturers 'to strive towards understanding people, being respectful and recognising the unconditional value of human beings' (Kasha and Ladbroke, cited in Charfe and Gardner, 2020, p. 4). By doing so they will meet their professional and social pedagogical duty.

Summary points

- Unconscious biases (and the stereotypes and prejudices that shape them) affect how we perceive and interact with others, and also shape our expectations.
- Government policy, institutional classification, university admissions and even research contribute to perpetuate a working-class stereotype which may shape lecturers' biases and expectations.
- Lower lecturer expectations hidden behind a deficit thinking could affect teaching practice.
- Lecturers should guide their professional practice applying a social pedagogical approach which comprises the four purposes of university education in equal measures and remembering their duty of telling the truth.
- Avoid academic '*classism via separation*' and think about the effect or harm caused by the action: if teaching practice is 'adapted' based on academic expectations, are these students getting the most of their university experience? Are there any future opportunities being limited as a result?

- Remember unconscious biases affect everyone and even individuals who endorse inclusive values can contribute to the persistence of systemic inequalities.
- Viewing students with the unconditional positive regard and positive potential advocated in social pedagogical practice can go some way to tackling this.
- Think about WP and inclusion as 'widening capability'.

Recommended reading

Bourdieu, P. (1979) *The Inheritors. French Students and Their Relation to Culture.* Chicago: University of Chicago Press.

Hockings, C. (2010) *Inclusive Learning and Teaching in Higher Education: A Synthesis of Research.* York: Higher Education Academy. Available at www.advance-he.ac.uk/knowledge-hub/inclusive-learning-and-teaching-higher-education-synthesis-research (Accessed 7 February 2025).

References

Applebaum, B. (2019) Remediating campus climate: Implicit bias training is not enough. *Studies in Philosophy and Education*, 38, 129–141.

Archer, L. (2007) Diversity, equality and higher education: A critical reflection on the ab/uses of equity discourse within widening participation. *Teaching in Higher Education*, 12(5–6), 635–653.

Bathmaker, A. M. (2021) Social class and mobility: Student narratives of class location in English higher education. *Discourse: Studies in the Cultural Politics of Education*, 42(1), pp. 75–86.

Baxter, A., Tate, J. and Hatt, S. (2007) From policy to practice: Pupils' responses to widening participation initiatives. *Higher Education Quarterly*, 61(3), pp. 266–283.

Bloodworth, J. (2016) *The Myth of Meritocracy: Why Working-Class Kids Still Get Working-Class Jobs* (Provocations Series). Hull: Biteback Publishing.

Boden, R. and Nedeva, M. (2010) Employing discourse: Universities and graduate 'employability.' *Journal of Education Policy*, 25(1), pp. 37–54.

Boliver, V. (2011) Expansion, differentiation, and the persistence of social class inequalities in British higher education. *Higher Education*, 61, pp. 229–242.

Boliver, V. (2015) Are there distinctive clusters of higher and lower status universities in the UK? *Oxford Review of Education*, 41(5), pp. 608–627. doi:10.1080/03054985.2015.1082905

Burke, P. J., Stevenson, J. and Whelan, P. (2015) Teaching 'excellence' and pedagogic stratification in higher education. *International Studies in Widening Participation*, 2(2), pp. 29–43.

Charfe, L. and Gardner, A. (2020) 'Does my *Haltung* look big in this?': The use of social pedagogical theory for the development of ethical and value-led practice. *International Journal of Social Pedagogy*, 9(1), pp. 1–10.

Chowdry, H., Crawford, C., Dearden, L., Goodman, A. and Vignoles, A. (2013). Widening participation in higher education: analysis using linked administrative data. *Journal of the Royal Statistical Society: Series A (Statistics in Society)*, 176 (2), 431–457.

Collini, S. (2012) *What Are Universities For?* London: Penguin.

Cureton, D. and Gravestock, P. (2018) Supporting Students' Learning: The Power of the Student-Teacher Relationship. In M. Shah and J. McKay (Eds) *Achieving Equity and Quality in Higher Education: Global Perspectives in an Era of Widening Participation.* Cham: Palgrave Macmillan, pp. 51–71.

Eichsteller, G. and Holthoff, S. (2011) Conceptual Foundations of Social Pedagogy: A Transnational Perspective from Germany. In C. Cameron and P. Moss (Eds) *Social Pedagogy and Working with Children.* London: Jessica Kingsley Publishers, pp. 33–52.

Evans, M. (2004) *Killing Thinking. The Death of the Universities.* London: Continuum.

Finnegan, F. and Merrill, B. (2017) 'We're as good as anybody else': A comparative study of working-class university students' experiences in England and Ireland. *British Journal of Sociology of Education*, 38(3), pp. 307–324.

Gale, T. and Hodge, S. (2014) Just Imaginary: delimiting social inclusion in higher education. *British Journal of Sociology*, 35(5), pp. 688–709.

Gibbs, P. (2019) Why academics should have a duty of truth telling in an epoch of post-truth? *Higher Education*, 78, pp. 501–510.

Hämäläinen, J. (2015). Defining social pedagogy: Historical, theoretical and practical considerations. *The British Journal of Social Work*, 45(3), pp. 1022–1038.

Harrison, N. and Waller, R. (2018) Challenging discourses of aspiration: The role of expectations and attainment in access to higher education. *British Educational Research Journal*, 44(5), pp. 914–938.

Jones, S., Hall, D. and Bragg, J. (2019) 'If they've had a middle-class upbringing that's not their fault': The professional practices and personal identities of admissions staff at selective universities in England. *Higher Education: The International Journal of Higher Education Research*, 77(5), pp. 931–947.

Langhout, R.D., Rosselli, F. and Feinstein, J. (2007). Assessing classism in academic settings. *Review of Higher Education*, 30(2), pp. 145–184.

Leach, L. (2013) Participation and equity in higher education: Are we going back to the future? *Oxford Review of Education*, 39 (2), pp. 267–286.

Mallman, M. (2017) The perceived inherent vice of working-class university students. *The Sociological Review*, 65(2), pp. 235–250.

Marginson, M. (2016) The worldwide trend to high participation higher education: Dynamics of social stratification in inclusive systems. *Higher Education*, 72, pp. 413–434.

Marginson, M. (2018) World Higher Education under conditions of national/global disequilibria, Working paper 42, Centre for Global Higher Education. London: UCL Institute of Education.

McCowan, T. (2016) Three Dimensions of Equity of Access to Higher Education. *Compare: A Journal of Comparative and International Education*, 46(4), pp. 645–665.

Mckay, J. and Devlin, M. (2016) 'Low income doesn't mean stupid and destined for failure': Challenging the deficit discourse around students from low SES backgrounds in higher education. *International Journal of Inclusive Education*, 20 (4), pp. 347–363.

Moule, J. (2009) Understanding unconscious bias and unintentional racism. *Phi Delta Kappan*, 90 (5), pp. 321–326.

Mountford-Zimdars, A., Sabri, D., Moore, J., Sanders, J., Jones, S. and Higham, L. (2015). *Causes of Differences in Student Outcomes (HEFCE)*. Manchester: Manchester Institute of Education.

Pickett, K. and Wilkinson, R. (2010) *The Spirit Level: Why Equality Is Better for Everyone*. London: Penguin Books.

Read, B., Archer, L. and Leathwood, C. (2003) Challenging Cultures? Student Conceptions of 'Belonging' and 'Isolation' at a Post-1992 University. *Studies in Higher Education*, 28(3), pp. 261–277.

Reay, D. (2017) *Miseducation: Inequality, Education and the Working Classes*. Bristol: Policy Press.

Reinsch, R. W., Goltz, S. M. and Hietapelto, A.B. (2020). Student evaluations and the problem of implicit bias. *JC and UL*, 45, 114.

Rickett, B., Easterbrook, M., Sheehy-Skeffington, J., Reavey, P. and Woolhouse, M. (2022) *Psychology of social class-based inequalities: Policy implications for a revised (2010) UK Equality Act*. The British Psychological Society. Available at www.bps.org.uk/tackling-social-class-inequalities. (Accessed 7 February 2025).

Rogers, C. (Originally 1956, reprinted 1992) The necessary and sufficient conditions of therapeutic personality change. *Journal of Consulting and Clinical Psychology*, 60(6), pp. 827–832.

Safir, S. (2017) *The listening leader: Creating the conditions for equitable school transformation*. San Francisco: Jossey-Bass.

Sellar, S. and Gale, T. (2011) Mobility, aspiration, voice: A new structure of feeling for student equity in higher education, *Critical Studies in Education*, 52(2), pp. 115–134.

Sie, M. and Vader-Bours, N. (2016). Stereotypes and Prejudices: Whose Responsibility? Indirect Personal Responsibility for Implicit Biases. In M. Brownstein and J. M. Saul, (Eds) *Implicit Bias and Philosophy. Volume 2, Moral Responsibility, Structural Injustice, and Ethics*. Oxford: Oxford University Press, pp. 90–114.

Smit, R. (2012) Towards a clearer understanding of student disadvantage in higher education: problematising deficit thinking. *Higher Education Research and Development*, 31(3), pp. 369–380.

Southgate, E., Grimes, S. and Cox, J. (2018) High Status Professions, Their Related Degrees and the Social Construction of 'Quality. In M. Shah and J. McKay (Eds) *Achieving Equity and Quality in Higher Education: Global Perspectives in an Era of Widening Participation*. Cham: Palgrave Macmillan, pp. 287–306.

Staats, C. (2016) Understanding implicit bias: What educators should know. *American Educator*, 39(4), p. 29.

Stevenson, J., Burke, P. J. and Whelan, P. (2014) *Pedagogic Stratification and the Shifting Landscape of Higher Education*. Project Report. York: Higher Education Academy.

Thomas, L. and Heath, J. (2014) Institutional wide implementation of key advice for socially inclusive teaching in higher education. A practice report. *The International Journal of the First Year in Higher Education*, 5(1), pp. 125–133.

Tokarczyk, M. M. (2004) Promises to Keep. Working Class Students and Higher Education. In M. Zweig (Ed.) *What's Class Got to Do with It? American Society in the Twenty-First Century*. Ithaca, NY: ILR Press, pp. 161–167.

Walker, M. (2008) Widening participation; widening capability. *London Review of Education*, 6(3), pp. 267–279.

Watts, M. (2006) Disproportionate Sacrifices: Ricoeur's theories of justice and the widening participation agenda for higher education in the U. *Journal of Philosophy of Education*, 40(3), pp. 302–311.

Weale, S. (2023) Warning over unconscious bias against working-class pupils in English schools, *The Guardian*, 1 October 2023.

Whitty, G., Hayton, A. and Tang, S. (2015) Who you know, what you know and knowing the ropes: a review of evidence about access to higher education institutions in England. *Review of Education*, 3(1), pp. 27–67.

Woodward, P. (2020) Higher Education and Social Inclusion: Continuing inequalities in Access to Higher Education in England. In R. Papa (Ed.) *Handbook on Promoting Social Justice in Education*. Cham: Springer, pp. 1229–1251.

Zgaga, P. (2009) Higher education and citizenship: 'The full range of purposes'. *European Education Research Journal*, 8(2), pp. 175–188.

12 Building relationships within blended learning

Samantha Sutton-Tsang

Introduction

First it is useful to note that although the terms 'student' and 'tutor' have been used throughout the chapter, the following discussion relates to any learning online that involves a facilitator and participants and is not restricted to an education context in the formal sense. It explores characteristics of effective online pedagogy that could be transferred to any context, as it considers how a values-based, relationship-centred approach can be developed and maintained in the context of distance and online education. The student reflections that are included are based upon experience of a flexible and distributed learning (FDL) approach to undergraduate study at higher education. The course that is referred to combined monthly face-to-face sessions with weekly, asynchronous (meaning completed independently, in their own time) online learning tasks.

The definition of blended learning varies depending on such factors as the extent of a student's in-person or online attendance, the completion of online learning tasks (whether done synchronously, together with the rest of the group, or asynchronously), and the overall course format (Heilporn *et al.*, 2021; Serrano *et al.*, 2019). Benson *et al.* (2011) contend that blended education extends beyond simply merging traditional and online teaching together. It entails a complete redesign of conventional courses to integrate technology for online communication, activities, and delivery (Kyei-Blankson *et al.*, 2014, p. 244). For this chapter, I adopt the term 'blended learning' as a combination of independent online learning activities and 'face-to-face' sessions, led by a tutor, which can occur either in person or synchronously online.

As contemporary life becomes more complex, many adults and young people seek alternative educational delivery modes that accommodate their busy schedules. Given the current economic climate, rising living costs and technological advances (Heilporn *et al.*, 2021), distance learning and online degrees, whilst not novel concepts, (the Open University initiated its first distance learning course in 1969, and the earliest online courses emerged in the 1980s), have increased significantly in popularity (Serrano *et al.*, 2019; Zhu *et al.*, 2020). These online and blended learning formats attract a growing number of non-traditional students, addressing their diverse needs and removing barriers related to time, location, and individual circumstances, whilst facilitating high-quality interactions and a flexible study option (Serrano *et al.*, 2019).

Empowering individuals to study flexibly

Below, Amy explains her rationale for choosing the flexible and distributed learning (FDL) route for her BA (Hons) Top up degree:

> I chose FDL so that I could continue to work whilst studying for my degree. Having a family and full-time job, the FDL route enabled me to further my career whilst still being able to fulfil these commitments. Although studying alongside work was challenging, the benefit of being able to apply theory to practice daily really helped me to embed my learning. Despite having to travel 200 miles for the monthly face-to-face sessions, the FDL route enabled me to consider universities outside my local area and gave me the opportunity to study a subject that was not available locally.

Online options can offer a solution for balancing educational, professional, and familial responsibilities in addition to narrowing the learning gap for students who require more time to digest information as they can re-watch recorded lectures at their own pace (Serrano et al., 2019). They can also increase choice by removing distance as a barrier to accessing a course.

Amy's choice of a FDL route enabled her to pursue her educational ambitions by taking control of her study methods. She was able to effectively balance her personal and professional responsibilities with course requirements, enabling her to foster her independence and autonomy. The interactive lessons, online and face-to-face discussions, integration of various teaching methods, as well as reflection on practice, all supported her holistic learning, enabling her to succeed beyond the basic module requirements. Additionally, her learning experience provided experiential learning opportunities that bridged the gap between theoretical knowledge and practical application, for example by engaging in simulations through case study work. By choosing a more personally sustainable approach to study, Amy's wellbeing and happiness needs were also met, thus contributing to a positive experience of learning.

The diamond model and online delivery

Social Pedagogy's Diamond Model (Eichsteller and Holthoff, 2011) illustrates how empowerment, relationships, holistic learning and wellbeing and happiness are all necessary for positive education experiences which can support students to flourish and reach their full potential (Figure 12.1).

Charfe and Gardner (2019, p. 49) highlight that social pedagogical approaches to education seek to balance independence and interdependence, and in doing so establish long-term, sustainable developments for all learners. Likewise, FDL routes can offer an adaptive approach to education, suitable for each unique learner, rather than taking an approach that assumes that 'one size fits all'.

> **Reflection point**
>
> What are some of the ways that flexible learning options might empower individuals to more easily balance education with their personal and professional responsibilities?

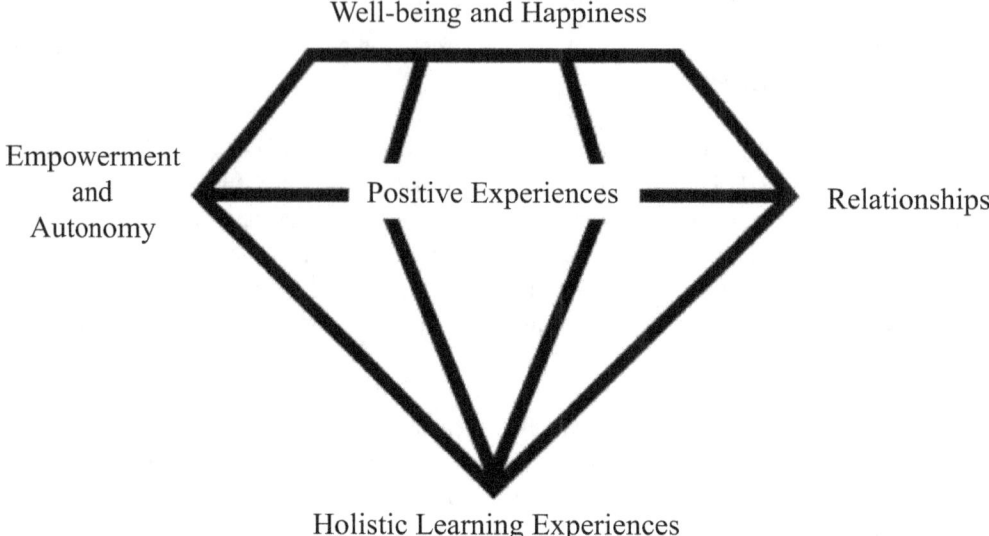

Figure 12.1 Aims of social pedagogy by Eichsteller and Holthoff (2012) based upon the diamond model.

A relationship-centred approach to online learning

Although some students may intentionally select online courses to maintain a degree of separation from others, the tutor is responsible for encouraging their engagement with the course material, so there will always be some degree of relationship building required. Despite the advantages of blended and online study, it can pose certain challenges for some. Studying at a distance can create a sense of isolation (Kaufmann and Vallade, 2020), even when students are engaging online synchronously. The lack of clear social cues that are more evident in a face-to-face environment may be missed in a virtual classroom, and this becomes even more difficult when cameras are switched off. Setting clear expectations of online learning, and creating connections to support student engagement, relies on the tutor's ability to foster relationships through genuine, respectful, and professional interactions (Archambault et al., 2022). This approach acknowledges power imbalances and fosters shared experiences and common goals (Thempra, no date a). Tutors need to 'consider and facilitate social presence, communication, and interaction' to minimise students' isolation. (Liu et al., 2009, cited by Kaufmann and Vallade, 2020). This may be approached by the tutor sharing a tutorial availability calendar, replying with timely responses to emails or discussion threads, or having regular check points with students throughout an online session and over the duration of a course.

Social connection is part of human nature and having a sense of wellbeing and belonging increases engagement, collaboration and commitment to a task (Baumeister and Leary, 1995), therefore, to create the 'positive experiences' at the core of the *Diamond Model*, relationships are vital. Collaborative activities provide opportunity for students to build their social presence within the learning community, and in doing so to enhance their own learning opportunities, as well as those of others. Simulations, for example, a case conference or workshop activity in smaller breakout rooms online, or in groups in person, or the examination of case studies from practice, can be used to support this. It is important that tutors facilitate meaningful discussions which challenge previous understanding, help students to self-regulate their learning and provide multiple opportunities to become active participants in the online community (Archambault et al., 2022).

Below, Amy reflects on her experiences of building learning relationships in the virtual classroom:

> The online lectures highlighted a difference in IT ability across my peer group and sometimes this felt frustrating. Many were reluctant to use cameras so you would only see a couple of faces, including the lecturer. At first this made me feel self-conscious, but I became more confident, and as the year wore on, so did others.
>
> Breakout rooms sometimes presented a new challenge especially if you were in a room with people that were less confident to talk on screen. It sometimes felt awkward, and I would talk just to fill the silence. Again, this was something that improved as we grew in confidence and began to form relationships. Looking back, I think having your camera on was essential to building peer relationships.

The time taken to enable students to feel confident enough to 'have their cameras on' here, illustrates the importance of developing trusting relationships for successful learning. In a similar vein, Charfe and Gardner (2019, p. 12) highlight that to build positive relationships, people need to feel supported 'to learn, grow and feel good about themselves'. This requires individuals to develop the interpersonal skills needed in practice. Even something as simple as an individual switching on their camera in a virtual classroom can be daunting at first, it involves an element of 'allowing strangers into your home', if only in a virtual sense, yet, as Amy reflects, it became the norm as relationships, and trust, developed between peers over time.

For effective online learning it is important that tutors endeavour to quickly create a warm, welcoming environment; introducing themselves, but also encouraging students to introduce themselves. As a tentative start this may be participants putting something about themselves in the chat. This works most effectively when a Common Third approach is taken, providing an opportunity for all to engage as equals. So, the tutor may start the chat, for example, by stating where they are from and what their favourite take-away treat is, and asking participants to follow suit. This most basic initiation helps with building relationships through sharing and discovering common ground, but is also the start of establishing an online presence. This is the first step in students feeling comfortable enough to interact and engage with content.

Reflection point

Reflect on your own experiences with online learning. What relationship-building strategies have you seen used to foster connection between participants? Which did you find most effective?

Learning communities

Both informal (social) and more formal (collaborative working) relationships are important in blended learning environments (Heilporn et al., 2022). According to Jacob and Radhai (2016) students enrolled on this type of course need 'additional motivation, organisation, and self-discipline' to succeed (cited in Dumford and Miller, 2018, p. 454). Online courses typically attract a more diverse student cohort, differing in gender, age, academic discipline, and prior education compared to those studying traditional education programs (Dumford and Miller, 2018). Academic behaviours and strategies for self-regulated learning are dependent on what each individual brings, both in terms of study skills and personal attributes, but all can be nurtured through authentic communication and quality collaboration with tutors and peers (Dumford and Miller, 2018). One way is through consistent feedback between tutor and student. It is important to note, however, that this is not the same as the tutor 'marking tasks', but is, instead, a learning dialogue. Within this dialogue it is important that the tutor models learning 'from and with', by using phrases such as 'that's a really interesting idea, I must do some research and find out more about that', or 'I'm not sure, I wonder if someone else in the group knows about that'. In this way a community of openness, mutual interdependence and trust is created. Relationships can also be nurtured through the careful management of online discussion forums within 'breakout rooms', where the students focus together on a specific task.

Where students lack self-regulation abilities, they may require support to engage in learning online, both from the tutor and their community. Borup *et al.* (2020) emphasise the significance of both 'personal' and 'course' communities. This highlights the crucial role of a student's personal community, those students that they choose to collaborate with for knowledge exchange and support. Borup *et al.* (2020) discuss how individuals within a student's course community can gradually become part of a personal community, and this is reflected in the following reflection from Beccy:

> I knew that as part of the course curriculum there would be a focus on collaboration to develop pedagogy and practice. However, the relationships that were developed between myself and my fellow students have far surpassed the necessity of group projects.
>
> The bond that developed over our shared drive to improve, evolved into the group that was turned to when things in our lives separate from university needed celebration; turned to when life was hard, and we needed somebody to lean on. Peer support helped with deadline reminders, or when that tricky reference was needed, and no amount of searching would uncover it!
>
> It was so important to have people who understood what was happening in my life and could empathise with the highs and lows. This familiarity was a boon to my university life and, even with 90 miles separating the furthest of us, I knew that these people will be at the other end of the phone whenever they were needed, as I am for them, even now.

Beccy's reflection illustrates how she safely integrated her personal self within her professional interactions with peers on the same course, even though this was predominantly done via technology, and in doing so strengthened the happiness and wellbeing aspects of the *Diamond Model* (Charfe and Gardner, 2019). Through this relationship-based approach that began with shared activities such as collaborative tasks (for example, presentation work and online discussions), Beccy and her peers cultivated a culture of 'unconditional positive regard', a phrase coined by Carl Rogers in 1956 as a necessary condition for positive change. It also illustrates how individuals' personal and professional selves can overlap as they grow to trust their peers over time (Jappe, 2010, cited in Jacaranda, 2015).

Online and blended learning can be an isolating place when students are unable to make connections with their peers or receive meaningful feedback from tutors. Borup et al. (2020, p. 820) emphasise the importance of the tutor themselves establishing a social presence to strengthen these online relationships. Kauffman and Vallade (2020, p. 1803) explain that tutors need to be 'approachable, supportive, respectful, engaging and understanding and responsive' to foster a sense of belonging within the learning community. This correlates with Steph's reflection of her experiences during her studies but, Steph also raises the issue of parameters in online study:

> The tutors make themselves available one evening per week for online meetings, which is a great security blanket. And they are always at the end of an email too. However, they can only reply during their working hours, so if you are feeling panicky over an assignment on a Friday night and have a deadline looming, you will not get a reply till the next working day, which can be a bit stressful.
>
> In the first few months of the course, I started to 'spin out' due this need to have a response ASAP and knowing it was not going to happen. You just have to breathe and do what you can, knowing you will receive a response at some point. I think this is where time management and self-discipline come in. You must plan ahead to give yourself time to contact the tutor with any questions so that you can get feedback in time.

Here Steph illustrates how she needed to manage her emotions to prevent herself from 'spinning' into a panic as she transitioned into a new way of learning. It also demonstrates how important it is for clear parameters and expectations of tutor and student to be established, in an environment where expectations could stretch, and potentially intrude into a tutor's personal life. This aligns with the 'self-care' aspect of the *Diamond Model*. Although the wellbeing of students is a priority, this should not be at the cost of the tutor's own. As is discussed in Chapter 9, only someone who looks after their own wellbeing will be able to effectively care for others, and that includes having clear times 'on' or 'offline', at work and with friends and family.

Below Steph reflects on wellbeing and happiness when studying at a distance, the support she received, and how this was enhanced by the relationships that were created through the course:

> Being aware of your mental health and how to manage it is a crucial skill. The tutors were brilliant, signposting me to a counselling service that was offered by the university when I experienced some major disruptions in my personal life including the impact of COVID-19 and additional responsibilities at work. I managed to bounce back independently but was really glad the resource was there. Fellow students were also a great support. But the most valuable aspect was coming together for the face-to-face sessions, seeing everyone, real people, and chatting about work, listening to their experiences.

Steph's comments highlight the value of in-person sessions, which, for her served as the essential 'glue' that maintained student relationships during weeks of online-only interaction. These face-to-face meet-ups provided opportunity for fostering supportive connections between students, as they shared their personal experiences of practice with an interested audience, who could empathise with their challenges and triumphs. These challenges, in both practice and study, were a *Common Third* for a group of once disparate individuals. They provided a point of connection and commonality. These experiences of positive support then fed back into the other important elements of the *Diamond Model*, relationships, wellbeing, holistic learning and empowerment. Each aspect of the model leads to, and is reliant upon, the others.

> **Reflection point**
>
> Reflect on the role of both formal and informal learning communities in your educational experiences. How might these communities have influenced your motivation, organisation, and self-discipline in online or blended learning environments?

Encouraging collaboration

Vygotsky (1978, p. 86) describes the 'Zone of Proximal Development' (ZPD) as:

> The distance between the actual developmental levels as determined by independent problem solving and the level of potential development as determined through problem solving under adult guidance or in collaboration with more capable peers.

Within this theory the importance of collaboration for an individual to achieve their full potential or higher outcomes is emphasised. Effective online pedagogy supports students in reshaping, or developing, their existing understanding as they learn not only from the tutor but from the experiences and the knowledge of their peers. Dyer *et al.* (2018) and others (for example Borup *et al.*, 2020; Heilporn *et al.*, 2021) discuss establishing a Community of Inquiry (CoI) as a teaching strategy to support online pedagogy between the students themselves and not just tutor and student. The CoI model depends significantly on the quality of student interactions, and can thrive in situations where students are encouraged to provide constructive feedback to one another to scaffold their own and others' professional practice, and where they supportively challenge each other though discussion and group work.

Integration into a community enables learners to engage in critical discourse (Tucker, 2012) and this can happen in various ways. For example, through sharing perspectives and practice experiences on discussion boards, by enabling peer feedback on one another's work, or by creating virtual study groups that might, for example, collaborate on virtual learning tools such as shared documents, 'resulting in community-constructed knowledge' (Borup *et al.*, 2020, p. 808). It cannot be assumed that students will know online etiquette and therefore the tutor must model active participation, for example in online discussions, to encourage even the shyest of students to engage and build positive relationships. An implicit assumption of the Diamond Model is that everyone can make a positive contribution if they are enabled to do so in an accessible way (Thempra, no date b). It is the tutor's responsibility to notice where more help may be needed with that.

Charfe and Gardner (2019) emphasise that building positive relationships is based upon individuals feeling supported in their learning, growth, and self-esteem. The level of sensitivity needed demands that practitioners reflect on their own interpersonal skills, not just those of their students. Eichsteller and Holthoff (2011, as cited by Charfe and Gardner, 2019) assert that relationships are central to social pedagogical practice and that they must be founded on kindness, compassion, open-heartedness, and generosity. Stephens (2013) describes 'Caritas' as going beyond kindness and compassion, focusing on working with others to support and provide opportunities for them to build their skills, confidence, and self-efficacy, thereby helping them to feel empowered to take make control and manage their own lives. Therefore, as online educators, we need to carefully consider the approaches that we take, and how they might embody kindness and care whilst still encouraging our students' autonomy.

Based on insights from Charfe and Gardner (2019), Eichsteller and Holthoff (2011), and Stephens (2013), tutors might take the following actions to create positive experiences for online learning:

1. **Create a Supportive Environment**. Ensure students feel supported in their learning, growth, and self-esteem. This involves being attentive to their needs and providing encouragement (either written or verbally) in feedback and acknowledging contributions in the virtual classroom.
2. **Develop Interpersonal Skills**. Continuously work on and reflect upon interpersonal skills to build authentic and genuine relationships through active listening and responses. This includes being kind, compassionate, open-hearted, and generous, as well as being open to feedback yourself.
3. **Foster Engagement**. Actively engage with students to help them establish their social presence, whether in online or classroom settings. This might require additional time and being more 'present' for some students.
4. **Promote what Stephens (2013) refers to as Sympathetic Expansiveness.** Encourage a sense of connection and empathy among students, linking their experiences and emotions to those of others.
5. **Practice 'Caritas'** by going beyond kindness and compassion, and working collaboratively with students to support their skills development, confidence, and self-efficacy. Encourage students to take control of their own learning and life management, focusing on enabling rather than directing.

By implementing these practices, tutors can more consciously build positive, supportive relationships that enhance the learning experience and personal growth of students, facilitating holistic learning.

Self-regulated learning

To more effectively support students, tutors must consider the students' perspective and learning behaviours. According to Thempra (no date b), self-regulated learning refers to an individual's self-initiated behaviours towards achieving positive learning outcomes. Zhu et al. (2020, p. 1490) explain that this involves three aspects: 'learners' cognitively processing learning materials, metacognitive strategies [understanding the way that they learn and approaches that will be helpful for them], and determination'. Zhu et al. (ibid) propose that when students show determination and a positive attitude to their learning, they are more likely to persist and achieve positive outcomes.

Amy reflects on her experience of self-regulating her learning to enable her to maximise her learning experience:

Being at home whilst attending lectures required some adjustment. Online learning required me to be self-disciplined to ensure I committed to lectures and carve out protected time for study. Although the lectures were recorded and could be accessed later if needed, I preferred to attend them live. This way any questions I had could be answered and I could join in the discussions. That being said, having the lectures recorded was helpful as I could revisit them if necessary.

Cohen (2021, p. 16) makes clear that effective online learning should be designed using resources that are 'organized, scaffolded, and clustered'. In doing so learners can navigate independently without needing a tutor's presence, promoting an autonomous learning experience and encouraging active participation. Shearer et al. (2019, p. 322) suggest that online 'learners are highly autonomous and have control of their own learning process. They are motivated, self-controlled, and self-monitored', learning through engagement with deep discussions and interactions with their peers and instructors. Instructors should act as facilitators, negotiators, and guides to enable this; therefore, the most critical factor for success is the student's readiness and motivation to learn. Expectations concerning these aspects should be made clear from the moment of induction.

Steph's reflection, below, highlights the importance of student readiness for online learning, including developing empowerment and self-efficacy (an individual's belief in their ability to complete a task or achieve a goal), technology usage, and time management skills (Heo et al., 2020).

Navigating the university's online interface was different to anything I had used before. I had some laptop/internet experience through work and homelife, however learning how to use new online platforms took a bit of effort. I found that I just had to open up my inner child and play for a while, clicking on everything to see what happened. There were a few sessions in summer school days to introduce us to these apps and some brilliant videos, but when you are at home miles away from campus on a weekend, which is your learning time but everyone else's out of hours' time, and you can't quite remember how to do that thing, and where was that video again? There were a few eek moments! So, you have to click and find out the answer yourself.

> **Reflection point**
>
> Reflect on your own self-regulated learning habits in online learning. How could you support students to manage their own time and resources?

Bao (2020) highlights that effective online learning depends more on students' attitude to self-directed learning than their proficiency with technological devices. Although students must demonstrate self-regulated learning, it is the tutor's responsibility to check in with their students, offering support and signposting to resources and/or services where and when necessary. Strategies that tutors can use to support online learning are mentioned in Steph's reflection:

Having downloadable resources was great as I love to print off paper versions because I can get a little lost online. The tutors provide PowerPoints of online activities and face to face sessions, which was helpful again for reference and assessment support. Embedded within these documents were links created by the tutors to websites so that you can't lose these websites in the ether, which is so helpful. Having an online reading list with the library was invaluable, especially when working on assessments.

Both Amy and Steph's reflections align with the Diamond Model, as they explain how they felt empowered to learn at their own pace, take ownership of their learning and development, access necessary resources and make connections with peers and tutors.

Maussumbayev et al. (2022) discuss how knowledge construction can occur through self-directed and personalised learning experiences, which are supported by digital technologies and innovative teaching strategies. These technologies facilitate social interaction, foster collaborative learning, enhance flexibility to learn, enable personalisation, and support a student-centred educational approach. Nevertheless, Huang (2019) identifies that prompt and effective feedback from tutors is required to support student retention. As previously mentioned, effective feedback, including its frequency, is crucial for engaging students in online learning. Personalised feedback is especially important for fostering students' sense of connection to the course and their peers, as well as enhancing student satisfaction (Heo et al., 2020). When students develop a meaningful relationship with their tutor and peers, they are more likely to share information and engage in conversation and critical discourse.

Maddix (2012) emphasises the crucial role of high-quality interactions and discussions online, noting that student success relies heavily on the effectiveness and quality of course discussions. Properly conducted online discussions foster student engagement, enabling them to build relationships with their peers that create a sense of proximity even when studying at a distance. Consequently, this can result in more meaningful interactions and advanced learning, as students broaden their understanding by reflecting on the knowledge and experiences shared by their peers and the tutor (Serano et al., 2019). Ellis et al. (2004) found that online discussions facilitated deeper reflections on learning objectives and issues. Supported by the tutor, social interaction online can facilitate open communication, foster meaningful relationships, and promote group cohesion as a Community of Practice (CoP) (Lave and Wenger, 1991). Students can develop a sense of proximity to their peers, improving their wellbeing and providing an opportunity to be part of an 'information exchange' process leading to 'knowledge creation' (Alonso et al., 2015). These do not have to take place during synchronous activities, asynchronous discussions online can provide students with the thinking time needed by some to make meaningful contributions and share their perspectives.

Conclusion

The reflections from Amy, Beccy, and Steph have highlighted how they themselves evolved into social pedagogues through their online and flexible learning experiences and continue to 'walk beside' each other even after the course has ended. Online learning can offer unique opportunities and is likely to be most successful when focusing on the core elements of the *Diamond Model*: empowerment, student wellbeing and happiness, relationships, and holistic learning. These elements can be developed into positive experiences through flexible delivery and engaging online interactions that motivate learners. By adopting a relationship-based approach, tutors can support students' wellbeing and happiness, foster a peer network to enhance interconnectedness through maintained, regular communication with students and careful programme design, supporting students from induction to course completion and beyond.

Summary points

- Online and blended learning approaches offer advantages but can also present challenges.
- The *Diamond Model* (Eichsteller and Holthoff, 2011) proposes four aspects that need to be included in the development of all positive learning experiences. These are: wellbeing and happiness, supportive relationships, empowerment and holistic learning.
- Effective online pedagogy relies on tutors facilitating learning, supporting student empowerment by helping them understand their needs and motivations.
- Tutors can foster autonomy and empowerment through regular and personalised feedback to encourage students' self-directed learning.
- Tutors can encourage a sense of community online by modelling the exchange of ideas and learning 'with and from' one another, as well as by the careful orchestration of groupwork on shared activities.

Acknowledgements

The author would like to thank Amy Bowles, Rebecca Martindale and Stephanie Jempson for contributing reflections to support this chapter.

Recommended reading

Find out more about the Diamond Model:

Eichsteller, G. and Holthoff, S. (2011) Conceptual Foundations of Social Pedagogy: A Transnational Perspective from Germany. In C. Cameron and P. Moss, P. (Eds) *Social Pedagogy and Working with Children and Young People*. London: Jessica Kingsley, pp. 33–52.

Thempra (no date) ThemPra's Diamond Model. Available at www.thempra.org.uk/social-pedagogy/key-concepts-in-social-pedagogy/thempras-diamond-model/ (Accessed 12 July 2024).

Find out more about Academic Communities of Engagement:

Borup, J., Graham, C.R., West, R.E., Archambault, L. and Spring, K.J. (2020) Academic communities of engagement: An expansive lens for examining support structures in blended and online learning. *Education Technology Research Development*, 68, pp. 807–832. https://doi.org/10.1007/s11423-020-09744-x

References

Alonso, F., Manrique, D., Martinez, L. and Vines, J.M. (2015) Study of the influence of social relationships among students on knowledge building using a moderately constructivist learning model. *Journal of Educational Computing Research*, 51(4), pp. 417–239. https://doi.org/10.2190/EC.51.4.c

Archambault, L., Leary, H. and Rice, K. (2022) Pillars of online pedagogy: A framework for teaching in online learning environments. *Educational Psychologist*, 57(3), pp. 178–191. https://doi.org/10.1080/00461520.2022.2051513

Bao, W. (2020) COVID-19 and online teaching in higher education: A case study of Peking University. *Human Behavior and Emerging Technologies*, 2(2), pp. 113–115.

Baumeister, R. F. and Leary, M. R. (1995) The need to belong: Desire for interpersonal attachments as a fundamental human motivation. *Psychological Bulletin*, 117(3), pp. 497–529.

Benson, V., Anderson, D. and Ooms, A. (2011) Educator's perceptions, attitudes and practices: blended learning in business and management education. *Research in Learning Technology*, 19(2), pp. 143–154.

Borup, J., Graham, C. R., West, R. E., Archambault, L. and Spring, K. J. (2020) Academic communities of engagement: An expansive lens for examining support structures in blended and online learning. *Education Technology Research Development*, 68, pp. 807–832.

Charfe, L. and Gardner, A. (2019) *Social Pedagogy and Social Work*. London: Sage Publications.

Cohen, J. A. (2021) A fit for purpose pedagogy: Online learning designing and teaching. *Development and Learning in Organisations: An International Journal*, 35(4), pp. 15–17. https://doi.org/10.1108/DLO-08-2020-0174

Dumford, A. D. and Miller, A. L. (2018) Online learning in higher education: Exploring advantages and disadvantages for engagement. *Journal Computing in Higher Education*, 30, pp. 452–465.

Dyer, T., Aroz, J., and Larson, E. (2018) Proximity in the online classroom: Engagement, relationships, and personalization. *Journal of Instructional Research*, 7, pp. 108–118.

Eichsteller, G. and Holthoff, S. (2011) Conceptual foundations of social pedagogy: A transnational perspective from Germany. In C. Cameron and P. Moss (Eds) *Social Pedagogy and Working with Children and Young People*. London: Jessica Kingsley, pp. 33–52.

Ellis, R., Calvo, R.A., Levy, D. and Tan. K. (2004) Learning through discussions. *Higher Education Research and Development*, 23(1), pp. 73–93. https://doi.org/10.1080/15512169.2011.539913

Heilporn, G., Lakhal, S. and Belisle, M. (2021) An examination of teachers' strategies to foster student engagement in blended learning in higher education. *International Journal of Educational Technology in Higher Education*, 18(25), pp. 1–25.

Heilporn, G., Lakhal, S. and Belisle, M. (2022) Examining effects of instructional strategies on student engagement in blended online courses. *Journal of Computer Assisted Learning*, 38, pp. 1657–1673. https://doi.org/10.1111/jcal.12701

Heo, H., Bonk, C.J. and Doo, M.Y. (2020) Enhancing learning engagement during COVID-19 pandemic: Self-efficacy in time management, technology use, and online learning environments. *Journal of Computer Assisted Learning*, 37(6), pp. 1640–1652. https://doi.org/10.1111/jcal.12603

Huang, Q. (2019) Comparing teacher's roles of f2f learning and online learning in a blended English course. *Computer Assisted Language Learning*, 32(3), pp. 190–209.

Jacaranda (2015) *Social Pedagogy, an Invitation*. London. Jacaranda Development.

Kaufmann, R. and Vallade, J. I. (2020). Exploring connections in the online learning environment: student perceptions of rapport, climate, and loneliness. *Interactive Learning Environments*, 30(10), 1794–1808. https://doi-org.apollo.worc.ac.uk/10.1080/10494820.2020.1749670

Kyei-Blankson, L., Godwyll, F. and Nur-Awaleh, M.A. (2014) Innovative blended delivery and learning: Exploring student choice, experience, and level of satisfaction in a hyflex course. *International Journal of Innovation and Learning*, 16(3), pp. 243–252.

Lave, J. and Wenger, E. (1991) *Situated Practice: Legitimate Peripheral Participation*. Cambridge: Cambridge University Press.

Maddix, M. A. (2012) Generating and facilitating effective online learning through discussion. *Christian Education Journal*, 9(2), pp. 372–385. https://doi.org/10.1177/073989131200900209

Maussumbayev, R., Toleubekova, R., Kasiyev, K., Baibaktina, A. and Bekbauova, A. (2022) Development of research capacity of a future social pedagogue in the face of digital technologies. *Education and Information Technologies*, 27(5), pp. 6947–6966. https://doi.org/10.1007/s10639-022-10901-3

Rogers, C. (Originally 1956, reprinted 1992) The necessary and sufficient conditions of therapeutic personality change. *Journal of Consulting and Clinical Psychology*, 60(6), pp. 827–832.

Serrano, D.R., Dea-Ayuela, M., Gonzales-Burgos, E., Serrano-Gil, A. and Lalatsa, A. (2019) Technology-enhanced learning in higher education: How to enhance student engagement through blended learning. *European Journal of Education*, 54(2), pp. 273–286. https://doi.org/10.1111/ejed.12330

Shearer, R. L., Aldemir, T., Hitchcock, J., Resig, J., Driver, J. and Kohler, M. (2019) What students want: A vision of a future online learning experience grounded in distance education theory. *American Journal of Distance Education*, 34(1), pp. 36–52.

Stephens, P. (2013) *Social Pedagogy: Heart and Head. Studies in Comparative Social Pedagogies and International Social Work and Social Policy, Vol XXIV*. Bremen: Europaischer Hochschulverlag.

Thempra (no date a) *The Common Third*. Available at www.thempra.org.uk/social-pedagogy/key-concepts-in-social-pedagogy/the-common-third/ (Accessed 24 January 2025).

Thempra (no date b) *ThemPra's Diamond Model*. Available at www.thempra.org.uk/social-pedagogy/key-concepts-in-social-pedagogy/thempras-diamond-model/ (Accessed 12 July 2024).

Tucker, S. Y. (2012) Promoting socialization in distance education. *Turkish Online Journal of Distance Education*, 16 (3), pp. 131–150. https://doi.org/10.1207/S15389286AJDE1603_2

Vygotsky, L. (1978) *Mind in Society: The Development of Higher Psychological Processes*. Cambridge, MA: Harvard University Press.

Zhu, Y., Zhang, J. H., Au, W. and Yates, G. (2020) University students' online learning attitudes and continuous intention to undertake online courses: A self-regulated learning perspective. *Education Technology Research Development*, 68(3), pp. 1485–1519. https://doi.org/10.1007/s11423-020-09753-w

13 A head, heart and hands approach to collaborative mentoring

Yvonne Cashmore and Margaret Tildesley

Introduction: what is collaborative mentoring?

Collaborative mentoring in settings is a reciprocal relationship between mentor (experienced professional) and mentee (trainee professional) where the common goal is shared responsibility and construction of knowledge by both parties (Clutterbuck, 2005). Historically, mentoring in education, specifically within a UK context has been fraught with tension between performance management agendas linked to competency procedures and genuine opportunities for professional development (Lofthouse, Leat and Towler, 2017; Knight and van Nieuwerburgh, 2012). Unlike traditional mentoring where the knowledge is transferred from the mentor to the mentee, collaborative mentoring is an approach where both the mentor and mentee share their experiences, ideas, reflections and feedback, which helps both parties to engage in continuous development.

In a traditional mentoring relationship, there is a hierarchical structure, where the mentor is often more senior in the organisation to the mentee (expert-novice). However, in collaborative mentoring there is a more reciprocal relationship, where both mentor and mentee actively contribute to the mentoring process by creating a psychologically safe environment where both parties exchange feedback, share and reflect on experiences to enable improvement and development (Ghosh, 2013, p. 163). While it is still necessary to identify roles and responsibilities, the mentor is considered a leader, not an authority (Gazibara, 2013, p. 80). It is important to have a shared commitment to success where both parties agree to organising regular meetings and taking an active role in communication. There also needs to be opportunity for mentors and mentees to adapt to meet the needs of the other. This is particularly important as each grows and develops their skills, so a commitment to enhancing the mentoring experience over time sustains the collaborative mentoring.

The hierarchical power dynamic present in the novice expert relationship, can be mitigated by creating opportunities to value each other's strengths, insights and experiences. The collaborative mentoring relationship is characterised by a holistic relational approach, which draws upon Pestalozzi's philosophy that education 'should not *put things into* a person, but develop something within…and *bring it out*, namely full humanity' (Brühlmeier, 2010, p. 18). Their relationship provides development opportunities for both the mentor and mentee. As explored in the research by Rubbi Nunan et al. (2023) a relationship built on trust is imperative for success in collaborative mentoring, where boundaries are set to enable each to respect the others' opinions and thoughts so that both parties feel safe to share ideas and that their experiences can be explored in a productive way to generate development.

DOI: 10.4324/9781003533276-13

The collaborative approach to mentoring enables co-construction of knowledge as the mentor and mentee work together to support each other with overcoming challenges and developing strategies for successful and productive ways of working. Mentors support mentees to build their independence in taking initiative to tackle new projects and challenges and to take responsibility for their learning. Määttä and Uusiautti (2013, p. 34) stress that 'Pedagogical love speaks to interdependence – the recognition and acceptance that we need others'.

In settings, collaborative mentoring can have many advantages to the organisation and to the individuals involved. One of the benefits is the sharing of practice and reflecting on experiences which aids a greater range of solutions to be considered and explored, supporting innovation and new ideas. Setting mentors often comment on how the research-informed strategies that trainee practitioners apply to classroom practice can refresh their knowledge. Strengthening relationships through a collaborative approach supports mentors and mentees to be engaged and motivated through their shared discussions. Määttä and Uusiautti (2013, p. 37) comment that 'Teachers have to believe in their work and endeavour to build a nurturing environment and a more humane world' and this is not restricted to teacher/pupil relationships.

> **Reflection point**
>
> In your context, what does collaborative mentoring mean to you and what might be the benefits of collaborative mentoring?

Theoretical knowledge held in the head

What do you need to know to engage in collaborative mentoring within a social pedagogy context? In this segment we signpost to the theoretical knowledge that underpins the collaborative approaches introduced in this chapter and some integral models for mentoring. We are just dipping our toe into a sea of ideas, and while we do not have time to go into depth, we aim to guide you in the right direction. Additionally, any mentor/mentee will need to reflect upon and feed in the substantive and disciplinary knowledge that is the requirement of their specific area of expertise, for example the facts and methods that underpin your specialism.

A *head, heart and hands* approach to collaborative mentoring is not a prescriptive one-size-fits-all scheme. It is a series of approaches that combine to create a holistic philosophical model that can be applied to practice. The approach is flexible and can be personalised to meet the needs of each individual and community of learners. The key idea that underpins this approach is a social-constructivist theory of learning: that learners make their own meaning through experience and interaction with others (Bruner, 1960; Vygotsky, 1980; Littleton and Mercer, 2013). We consider mentoring to be an effective method of social-constructivist learning, where the roles of educator and learner/mentor and mentee are not rigid but overlap and interweave. In this segment the terms educator and learner / mentor and mentee are used interchangeably.

Lev Vygotsky was a Russian psychologist whose research into collaborative learning is highly influential in the field of education. One of his key concepts introduced in this chapter is the zone of proximal development (ZPD) (Vygotsky, 1980), which is the place where development can occur with the help of a more knowledgeable other. Educators need to know a learner's current level of development and their potential and carefully guide them to make progress. Educators need to pitch the learning at just the right level so that there is a manageable amount of challenge with enough support to enable a process of transformation to occur.

Academic Neil Mercer's research into how we use language to think together 'interthinking' (Littleton and Mercer, 2013) builds on the concept of ZPD and proposes that dialogical learning is perhaps key to humankind's survival because it 'enables humans to combine their intellects into a mega-brain, a problem-solving device whose power can be greater than that of its individual components' (Mercer, 2001, p. 648). Dialogic learning: learning that occurs through dialogue, is also a key theme for Brazilian educator Paulo Freire (2017).

Paulo Freire (1970) advocated for critical pedagogy in the pursuit of social justice. Freire's pedagogical approach sought to reveal oppressive hierarchical structures in education and support more democratic relationships. Critical pedagogy relies upon critical reflection and action. Later in this chapter, we will explore Schön's (1983) Reflective Model, what it means to be a reflective practitioner and why this is an essential characteristic of collaborative mentoring.

American psychologist Jerome Bruner's concept of 'scaffolding' (Bruner, 1960) is also an important concept for understanding how a mentor can successfully coach a mentee to acquire new levels of expert performance. 'Scaffolding' is a metaphor for how educators support a learner's progress and development by reducing the complexity of a task. By enabling the learner to focus on the acquisition of a specific skill, the educator can manage the cognitive load (the amount of information the working memory can process at any given time). After a complex task is broken down into smaller chunks, it can be mastered step-by-step.

To bring scaffolding to life let us look at it through a public health lens and consider the National Health Service's (NHS) 'Couch to 5K' (Get running with Couch to 5K, 2022). The challenge of running five kilometres (3.1 miles) is broken down into manageable chunks over nine weeks. The level of challenge gradually increases and mentors such as Sarah Millican and Sanjeev Kohli (popular celebrities in the UK) coach novice runners towards their goal of running 5 kilometres in its entirety. Communities of practice such as Parkrun (Parkrun | our story, *no date*) have sprung up around it and support people to begin and stay active (Relph et al., 2023). Communities of practice (Wenger, 1999) is another significant idea in this chapter. We consider how knowledge is produced and used in practice in collaborative communities of learners such as the teaching profession.

Collaborative mentoring is a broad field with a variety of models, theories, frameworks and narratives. Clutterbuck (2023, p. 64) states that 'Mentoring is an interaction between two partners, with the outcomes highly dependent on the motivation of both'. A successful partnership has seven key principles: equality, choice, voice, dialogue, reflection, praxis (we will discuss this later) and reciprocity (Knight and van Nieuwerburgh, 2012). Collaborative learning is not easy. It requires a commitment to continuous improvement through a cycle of indentifying goals, learning strategies and making improvements (Knight, 2018). To make improvements and develop expertise a certain type of practice is most effective: Deliberate Practice (Ericsson and Pool, 2016). When engaging in Deliberate Practice, the mentor will encourage the mentee to get outside their comfort zone and into the Zone of Proximal Dvelopment (Vygotsky, 1980). To traverse the challenging terrain of practice, the mentor/mentee partnership requires an ONSIDE aproach: Off-line; Non-evaluative; Supportive; Individualised; Developmental and Empowering (Hobson, 2016). Collaborative mentoring could be conceptualised as collaborative action research (Lofthouse and Thomas, 2017) whereby communities of practice co-construct new knowledge and journey to utopia, which is always slightly out of reach.

> **Reflection point**
>
> What is the key factual and practical knowledge that you require for your specialism and how can you keep up to date with new developments? Which mentoring frameworks do you most relate to and how could you apply these to your context?

Relationship between the mentors and mentees

At the heart of collaborative mentoring lies the relationship between mentors and mentees. The dynamic between the two parties is important to enable the building of trust that is required to ensure a successful two-way relationship. One of the key features of the relationship is the partnership approach, with both the mentor and mentee valuing the strengths and characteristics of the other as they work together to share experiences and reflections, supporting the other to develop and grow. When the mentor and mentee work with each other, arguably, a *Common Third* is created, which is the external activity or shared interest that is the focal point for the interaction. The *Common Third* helps to balance the possible power dynamic between the mentor and the mentee as the shared focus enables both parties to contribute equally and share in the others learning process. For example, where an experienced professional and a novice professional are working together to develop specific teaching skills such as questioning, and together they explore questioning strategies to use in the classroom this becomes the focal area for both parties to focus on, and aids the mentor and mentee to build rapport and trust naturally. In the case of the mentee who is a novice, they will, according to Noel Burch's Learning Stages Model (Adams, *no date*), be unconsciously incompetent in questioning strategies at the start of their career. In contrast, the mentor, as the experienced teacher, may automatically use questioning in their approach and so have not thought about questioning strategies for some time. This enables the shared focus of questioning strategies to bring the mentor to more conscious competence, and therefore enables them to consider, explore and refine their own strategies as they are intentional in their work with the mentee. Effective collaboration in modelling the questioning strategy by the experienced mentor, followed by the mentee planning and rehearsing the strategy before putting it into practice in the classroom, enables a shared focus for both parties to grow from.

In this case, the Common Third gives a practical focus for applying and developing new skills and the collaborative engagement by both the mentor and mentee means that they can reflect on their experiences, gain insights from the other and develop a higher level of competency in the skill or strategy being developed (Kolb, 1984). The shared activity of modelling, planning, rehearsing and delivering the questioning techniques enables opportunity to arise for reflection, questions and discussion and supports a deeper and trusting collaborative mentoring environment. Working together towards a shared goal enables a process of open communication, vulnerability as new techniques are tried out and encouragement as the techniques are refined.

Collaborative mentoring has a developmental focus, which allows both the mentor and the mentee to grow professionally and personally. As they work together towards a common goal the exchange of knowledge, skills and experiences enable the reciprocal interaction of learning from each other and supporting each other to learn. In the trusting environment, ideas can be explored, and critical reflection undertaken, resulting in development for both parties. Collaborative mentoring works well when the mentor and mentee appreciate the individual values of the other (Islam, 2022) giving an emotionally safe space in the relationship to speak from the heart and for their words and ideas to be valued.

Sipos et al. (2008) discuss the heart and the emotions necessary to establish beliefs and ideals, which then translate to action. When the mentor and mentee share beliefs and ideals they can work together to organise and internalise these values. When the mentee receives information and feedback from the mentor, they are able to respond in a way that is aligned to their shared values. An important part of collaborative mentoring is to identify the challenges faced and to work together to co-construct solutions through setting achievable targets to work towards overcoming them. By setting a goal there is a vision to inspire the direction of the work and the development for both parties.

By co-constructing targets, there is a shared responsibility and commitment to working towards the common goal. Both the mentor and mentee need to listen, and respond, to feedback and reflect on the shared discussions and experiences. A successful collaboration requires both commitment and active participation where both parties are accountable to each other for the progress against agreed targets and for each other's development.

Further to the developmental focus, Ghosh, Reio and Haynes (2012) discuss how mutual reciprocal support can motivate mentees to seek and participate in further collaboration opportunities with other trusted colleagues in the organisation. Further collaboration could build stronger relationships within, and commitment to, the organisation, which in turn leads to improving productivity and effectiveness and supporting strengthened relationships.

> **Reflection point**
>
> How might a mentee feel when they have a positive and productive relationship with their mentor? What might motivate a mentor to work with a mentee?

Practice-able hands-on strategies

hWhat is more important in your field, knowing or doing? What if the distinction between the two is somewhat arbitrary? Consider how you learned to ride a bike or drive a car: this is a type of knowing founded in doing. It is useful to consider what aspects of your work involve a synthesis of theory and practice. In a *ead, heart and hands* approach to collaborative mentoring, the mentor plays a critical role in enabling the mentee to bridge the knowing-doing gap through practice-able, hands-on strategies.

Collaborative mentoring is a cycle of continuous personal/professional development for the purpose of transformation. Transformation, or any process of change is challenging. It requires a commitment to practice. But it is useful to consider what kind of practice is most effective in bringing about the desired change, as well as how a mentor and mentee can create a climate that is conducive to change. We discuss this below.

Reflective practice

A hands-on approach to mentoring involves focused activity on professional 'practice'. A process of knowing through doing. American educator and philosopher Donald Schön (1983) observed professional practice in a range of different fields from architecture to psychotherapy, to explore the nature of professional practice or 'artistry' as he described it. He explored the difference between knowledge presented in academic literature and the 'intellectual rigor in professional practice' (Schön, 1983, p. viii). Schön identified the problem of tacit knowledge: that often experts knew more than they could say. He developed processes of 'reflection-in-action' and 'reflection-on-action' (reflection during the activity and reflection after the activity) that enable experts in any field to identify, deconstruct and analyse their practice. The reflective practitioner can then create a shared language of professional practice leading to Communities of Practice (Lave and Wenger, 1991). Schön recognised the significance of 'interpersonal and institutional contexts' (Schön, 1983, p. ix) which we will return to later. Engagement in critical reflection is a commitment to improving practice and therefore also a commitment to being accountable to the communities that each profession serves. The reflective practitioner is therefore also an ethical practitioner as they are committed to improving shared practice for the benefit of society, a key principle of social pedagogy.

Transformational praxis

Brazilian educator and philosopher Paulo Freire explored how processes of action, reflection and theory could democratise education and transform society, 'Liberation is a praxis: the action and reflection of men and women upon their world in order to transform it' (Freire, 2017, pp. 52–53). The concept of 'praxis' as a method of thinking and doing, is presented as a dynamic, collaborative process rooted in dialogue and critical reflection where the boundaries between teacher and learner, or in this context mentor and mentee, become blurred. The goal is to work in partnership to pose problems and explore shared solutions on a small and large scale. Freire recognised that learning cannot be separated from historical, social, or political contexts and that an individual's experiences shape the way they interpret the world. Therefore, the process of learning needs to be culturally responsive, and a dialogical approach is required to nurture shared understanding and reciprocal trust. Shared action is also key to this learning theory, as it is only through acting upon the world that we can transform it.

Deliberate practice

Cognitive psychologist Anders Ericsson extensively researched how expertise is developed. His research reveals the adaptability of the brain and *body* and highlights that 'learning isn't a way of reaching one's potential but rather a way of developing it' (Ericsson and Pool, 2016, p. 26). Ericsson explores the potential of mentoring as a method of guiding individuals to develop expertise. In this model, everyone has the potential to improve and if you are not improving, you are not practising the correct way (Ericsson and Pool, 2016). Ericsson identifies a special type of practice that is most developmental: Deliberate Practice. But what distinguishes Deliberate Practice from other types of practice? Deliberate Practice focuses on improving performance by:

- being purposeful and informed
- using well-defined goals
- involving effective mental representations
- building upon and modifying previously acquired skills
- reflection, feedback and modification to reach defined goals.

Mentors use skills that other people have already developed in order to practically coach the mentee. The process of engaging in the practice should push the mentee outside their comfort zone and beyond their current capabilities, leading to expert performance. This links to Lev Vygotsky's (1980) theory of the zone of proximal development (ZPD) – the distance between what a learner can do with help and without help (Vygotsky, 1980).

There are three commonly held myths obstruct Deliberate Practice:

1. FALSE: Abilities are limited by genetically prescribed characteristics.
2. FALSE: If you do something for long enough, you're bound to be better at it.
3. FALSE: All it takes to improve is effort (Ericsson and Pool, 2016, p. 284).

Talent or innate ability do not define expertise. There is no quick fix to developing expertise and it certainly requires effort, but effort alone will not suffice: ten thousand hours is not the magic number of hours required for 'greatness' (Gladwell, 2009), it is another myth. A lifelong commitment to continuous improvement, dedication to Deliberate Practice, and an effective mentor can help everyone improve their performance.

Ericsson and Pool's (2016) research indicated that expert performers from a range of professions had similar strategies including forming mental representations of what success looks like, and revising their performance based on reflection in action. For example, they might compare a procedure with a mental representation, a medical operation, perhaps, or imagine the sound of a symphony; if there was disparity, something was wrong (Ericsson and Pool, 2016). Highly skilled mentors can then coach others to develop their skills. The focus here is on the development of the skill as opposed to the talent of the individual.

Deans for Impact (2023, p. 3) applied the framework of Deliberate Practice to the science of teacher expertise, and they identified five key principles:

1. Push beyond one's comfort zone
2. Work toward well-defined specific goals
3. Focus intently on practice activities
4. Receive and respond to high-quality feedback
5. Develop a mental model of expertise.

Let us zoom-in on principle three: Focus intently on practice activities. Deans for Impact (2023) identify two ways to focus: decomposition and approximation. Decomposition involves isolating a specific element of practice and critically analysing how to do this well: building a mental representation of the skill. Approximation then occurs after decomposition and concerns the rehearsal of the skill in relation to the mental representation involving feedback and adjustments to develop expertise. It is important that the rehearsal of the isolated skill takes place outside of a busy setting so that the mentee can focus intensely on this one aspect. By rehearsing in a quiet space and focusing on one very specific skill for which a mental representation and/or checklist has been created, with the support of an expert mentor, the trainee is much more likely to 'get better faster' (Bambrick-Santoyo, 2016).

There is something very democratising about the partnership that mentor and mentee engage in where Deliberate Practice is involved: it is a genuine desire to practically work together to find better solutions to problems for the common good. Both parties need to be committed, both will need to dare to be vulnerable and, critically, both parties need to be of the mindset that personal, professional and social change is possible.

In summary, practice-able hands-on strategies combine the theory and practice of what works in your field, based on the best available evidence. The mentor and mentee use mental representations of best-practice and processes of critical reflection to identify gaps in current practice to isolate the skill that requires rehearsal. The mentor will coach the mentee focusing intently on the skill they wish to develop. The coaching will push the mentee outside their comfort zone, but with expert help, plenty of practice, dedication, dialogue and reflection anyone can improve.

> **Reflection point**
>
> What practice techniques will improve the specific skills you want to develop? Who can help you? What level of commitment is required? What mindset will enable success?

Conclusion

A *head, heart and hands* approach to collaborative mentoring encompasses the theoretical knowledge of mentoring held in the head, the emotional heart of the mentor mentee relationship and the hands-on practice-able strategies to bridge the knowing-doing gap.

The core of collaborative mentoring is the reciprocal relationship where both the mentor and mentee have an equal relationship and actively contribute to the mentoring process by creating an environment of empowerment where both parties meet regularly to exchange feedback and reflect on experiences, to enable improvement and development (Ghosh, 2013, p. 163). The collaborative approach enables the co-construction of knowledge by sharing ideas, feedback and reflecting on experiences.

Underpinned by a social-constructivist theory of learning, the concept of the zone of proximal development (Vygotsky, 1980) suggests that development can occur with the help of a more knowledgeable other, and Freire's (1970) dialogic learning advocates democratic relationships, which are at the heart of collaborative mentoring. In addition, the concept of scaffolding (Bruner, 1960) is used with learners to reduce the complexity of a task, enabling them to focus on acquiring the skill, managing the cognitive load before increasing the level of challenge. The theoretical underpinning of how people learn influences the two-way, non-hierarchical relationship between the mentor and the mentee. A collaborative mentoring relationship is one where the strengths and experiences of the other are listened to and valued, with shared beliefs and focus through target setting and accountability to support each other to meet goals. As a shared focus the Common Third gives a practical focus for the mentor and mentee that helps to balance the possible power dynamic and enables both parties to contribute equally and share in the other's learning process.

The Common Third as a focus shared by mentors and mentees can provide a way for the mentee to bridge the knowing-doing gap through practice-able hands-on strategies. With a belief that everyone has the potential to improve through Deliberate Practice, the mentor and mentee can identify areas for improvement, set small goals, develop excellence models, practice strategies and adjust based on feedback. The practical rehearsal of strategies is crucial in a supportive reflective partnership that fosters growth and expertise.

Summary points

- Collaborative mentoring is a reciprocal relationship where both the mentor and mentee play an equal role in building trust and valuing the other's skills and understanding.
- Theoretical knowledge consists of the facts and methods that underpin your specialism.
- Collaborative mentoring is about co-construction of knowledge and a continuous quest for enlightenment.
- Building a collaborative mentoring relationship rooted in trust is critical to the success of the partnership. At the heart of the relationship the *Common Third* can provide the focal area for both parties to explore and contribute equally toward the learning process.
- Practice-able hands-on strategies for mentoring succeed within a non-judgemental partnership rooted in a commitment to cycles of continuous improvement.
- Deliberate Practice, which is the most effective kind, is situated in critical reflection and a supportive partnership which nurtures personal growth and professional expertise.

Recommended reading

Clutterbuck, D. (2023) *Coaching and mentoring: A journey through the models, theories, frameworks and narratives of David Clutterbuck.* Abingdon: Routledge.
Ericsson, A. and Pool, R. (2016) *Peak: Secrets from the new science of expertise.* London: The Bodley Head.
Growth Coaching International (2022) *Impact cycle overview.* Available at: www.youtube.com/watc+h?v=NGF7 4cytoAU (Accessed 17 July 2024).

References

Adams, I. (no date) *Learning+ a new skill is easier said than done.* Available at: www.gordontraining.com/free-workplace-articles/learning-a-new-skill-is-easier-said-than-done/ (Accessed 16 July 2024).
Bambrick-Santoyo, P. (2016) *Get better faster.* Oxford: John Wiley and Sons Inc.
Brühlmeier, A. and World, P. (2010) *Head, heart and hand: Education in the spirit of Pestalozzi.* Cambridge: Sophia Books in association with Pestalozzi World.
Bruner, J. S. (1960) *The process of education.* Cambridge, MA: Harvard University Press.
Clutterbuck, D. (2005) Establishing and maintaining mentoring relationships. An overview of mentor and mentee competencies. *SA Journal of Human Resource Management*, 3(3): pp. 2–9.
Clutterbuck, D. (2023) *Coaching and mentoring: A journey through the models, theories, frameworks and narratives of David Clutterbuck.* Abingdon and New York, NY: Routledge.
Deans for Impact (2023) *Practice with purpose: The emerging science of teacher expertise.* Available at: www.deansforimpact.org/files/assets/practice-with-purpose.pdf (Accessed 15 July 2024).
Ericsson, A. and Pool, R. (2016) *Peak: Secrets from the new science of expertise.* London: The Bodley Head.
Freire, P. (2017) *Pedagogy of the oppressed.* Penguin Classics; 13th edition (first published 1970, 1993). Harmondsworth: Penguin Random House.
Gazibara, S. (2013) 'Head, heart and hands learning' – A challenge for contemporary education. *The Journal of Education, Culture, and Society*, 4(1): pp. 71–82.
Get running with Couch to 5K (2022) nhs.uk. Available at: www.nhs.uk/live-well/exercise/get-running-with-couch-to-5k/ (Accessed: 15 July 2024).
Ghosh, R. (2013) Mentors providing challenge and support: Integrating concepts from teacher mentoring in education and organizational mentoring in business. *Human Resource development Review*, 12(2): pp. 144–176.
Ghosh, R., Reio Jr, T. G. and Haynes, R. K. (2012) Mentoring and organizational citizenship behavior: Estimating the mediating effects of organization-based self-esteem and affective commitment. *Human Resource Development Quarterly*, 23(1): pp. 41–63.
Gladwell, M. (2009) *Outliers: The story of success.* London: Penguin.

Hobson, A. J. (2016) Judgementoring and how to avert it: Introducing ONSIDE Mentoring for beginning teachers. *International Journal o Mentoring and Coaching in Education*, 5(2): pp. 87–110.

Islam, M. A., Mat Said, S., Umarlebbe, J. H., Sobhani, F. A. and Afrin, S. (2022) Conceptualization of head-heart-hands model for developing an effective 21st century teacher. *Frontiers in Psychology*, 13: pp. 968723–968723.

Knight, J. (2018) *The impact cycle: What instructional coaches should do to foster powerful improvements in teaching.* Thousand Oaks, CA: Corwin.

Knight, J. and van Nieuwerburgh, C. (2012) Instructional coaching: A focus on practice. *Coaching: An International Journal of Theory, Research and Practice*, 5(2): pp. 100–112.

Kolb, D. A. (1984) *Experiential learning: Experience as the source of learning and development.* London and Englewood Cliffs: Prentice-Hall.

Lave, J. and Wenger, E. (1991) *Situated learning: Legitimate peripheral participation.* Cambridge: Cambridge University Press.

Littleton, K. and Mercer, N. (2013) *Interthinking: Putting talk to work.* Abingdon: Routledge.

Lofthouse, R. and Thomas, U. (2017) Concerning collaboration: Teachers' perspectives on working in partnerships to develop teaching practices. *Professional Development in Education*, 43(1): pp. 36–56.

Määttä, K. and Uusiautti, S. (2013) Pedagogical love and good teacherhood. In K. Määttä and S. Uusiautti (Eds) *Many faces of love.* Rotterdam: Sense Publishers, pp. 93–101.

Mercer, N. (2001) *The psychologist*, 14(12): pp. 648–649.

Parkrun | our story (no date). Available at: www.parkrun.com/about/our-story/ (Accessed 15 July 2024).

Relph, N., Owen, M. Moinuddin, M., Noonan, R., Dey, P., Bullas, A., Quirk, A. and Haake, S. (2023) How can UK public health initiatives support each other to improve the maintenance of physical activity? Evidence from a cross-sectional survey of runners who move from *Couch-to-5k* to *parkrun*. *Health Promotion International*, 38(5): p. daad108. Available at: https://doi.org/10.1093/heapro/daad108 (Accessed 7 February 2025).

Rubbi Nunan, J. L., Ebrahim, A. B. and Stander, M. W. (2023) Mentoring in the workplace: Exploring the experiences of mentor–mentee relations. *SA Journal of Industrial Psychology*, 49(1), pp. e1–e11.

Schön, D. A. (1983) *The reflective practitioner: How professionals think in action.* Farnham: Arena, Ashgate Publishing Limited.

Sipos, Y., Battisti, B. and Grimm, K. (2008) Achieving transformative sustainability learning: engaging head, hands and heart. *International Journal of Sustainability in Higher Education*, 9(1): pp. 68–86.

Vygotsky, L. S. (1980) *Mind in society: Development of higher psychological processes.* Cambridge, MA: Harvard University Press.

Wenger, E. (1999) *Communities of practice: Learning, meaning, and identity.* Cambridge: Cambridge University Press.

14 Leadership

Not a role but a way of being

Shaun McInerney and Emma Laurence

Introduction

At its heart, social pedagogy is a 'belief that you can decisively influence social circumstances through education' (Hämäläinen, 2003, p. 71) and in doing so, create a more equal, just and sustainable society. For colleagues working with children and young people, social pedagogy offers a lens through which they can become more intentional about how relationships can help others to learn, grow and develop, and to invest in these from a deep sense of purpose. For practitioners working in education and care, social pedagogy also offers the tantalising possibility of systems grounded in relational practice, systems that are more responsive to the emerging needs of young people.

We recognise that this is an urgent imperative, but also a complex one, as it is enmeshed within wider systemic challenges. Therefore, this chapter is a 'call to action' for us to widen our perspective and deepen our practice. Our times call for us to evolve our approach to leadership so that we can all recognise ourselves as leaders – not over others, but in the shared mission of preparing ourselves and young people to meet the needs of a changing planet, one that is undergoing unprecedented technological and social change.

In this chapter, we apply a social pedagogical lens to reframe leadership to focus on those capabilities that help us grow into our own awareness as social pedagogues and develop the capacities and conditions to bring 'who we are' into 'what we do' in service of this wider vision. To support this, we offer some emerging leadership principles, approaches and practices that can support those who are willing to embark on their own social pedagogical leadership journey.

The historical leadership landscape: where are we, and how did we get here?

The notion of leadership can be traced back as far as ancient Egypt and China. It is a concept which permeates our storybooks, our academic literature, our societal structures and the sense we make of the world. Whilst much of the earlier, heroic, ideas of leadership are largely now refuted, often our 'gut level grasp' (Northouse, 2021) better aligns with these ideas than more up-to-date research on the topic. Therefore, it is useful to understand how perspectives of leadership have evolved in order to better understand the legacy these concepts have left within the hearts and minds of the people we work with.

Early concepts of leadership in the 1800s align with the 'great man theory' (Day and Antonakis, 2012) whereby leadership was considered an innate capacity that few people hold, based upon superior intellect, strength, heroism or divine inspiration. Within this construct, leadership was considered primarily in terms of control and domination. Over time, more nuanced ideas of influence developed such as persuasion and coercion (Rost, 1991). Around the 1930s, leadership was starting to be considered as made up of personality traits (Stodghill, 1948) or behaviours. This meant that ideas of leadership were changing from something you *are*, toward something you *do*. An explosion of interest in the leadership field through the last half a century brought with it a melting pot of contradictory definitions. Despite the many contradictions, several more consistent themes emerged during this time. For example, there was a movement toward understanding leadership as a transformational rather than transactional process (Burns, 1978). The former considered to encourage, inspire and motivate followers, rather than the latter which is reliant on authority, threat and reward for motivation.

Throughout the 1960s and 1970s, the notion of reciprocity within the leadership process was also being introduced (Burns, 1978) and much of the literature shifted focus, exploring the role of followers within the leadership dynamic (Uhl-Bein et al., 2014). With this came a more relational understanding of leadership. Literature also began to identify the contextualised nature of leadership. That is, what makes for good leadership depends upon the circumstances and what the situation requires. By the turn of the twenty-first century, the value-laden nature of leadership was recognised, so that moral and ethical dimensions of the concept took a new focus within literature (Brown and Trevino, 2006).

Leadership continues to be understood as inherently relational, normative and complex. Despite the persistence of hierarchical organisational models, leadership is understood to be embedded within a complex web of relationships and environmental factors and is imbued with moral visions of what 'good' is. Leadership has a strongly ethical dimension. It is important to emphasise that social pedagogy cannot offer a new definition of leadership, or prescriptive methods for its enactment. Instead, it provides an overarching conceptual framework which helps leaders and organisations to manage human complexity 'while anchoring them to their moral purpose' (Charfe, 2023, p. 11).

> **Reflection point**
>
> Consider this brief timeline which illustrates some of the theories of leadership outlined above. Do you recognise any of these constructs in your own practice or in your workplace?
>
>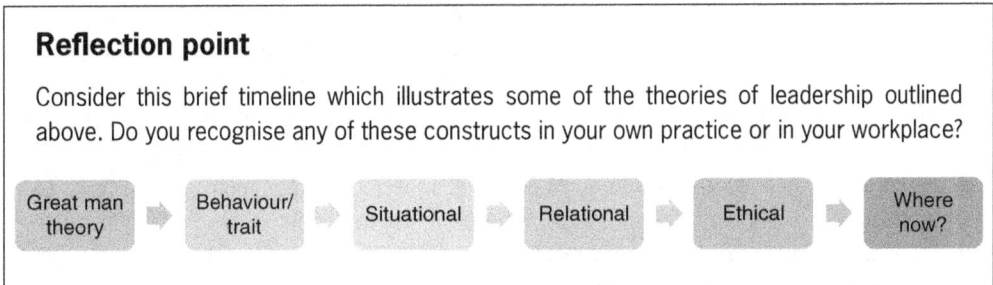

Why we need to reframe leadership through a social pedagogy lens

Leadership styles tend to fit around policy priorities. For example, over the last 20 years, the English education system has been increasingly focused on improving student outcomes. As a result, instructional leadership has reinforced a single-minded focus on improving teaching, learning and assessment. Despite a brief policy window between 2004 and 2010 when the *Every Child Matters* (HM Government, 2003) agenda encouraged more integrated and child-centred working across public services, the relationship-centred principles of social pedagogy have remained largely invisible in the professional learning and care discourse in England. As a result of this, many children and young people (CYP) are not receiving the support that they desperately need.

The focus upon product and not people was also seen in the policy response to COVID-19 in England. Rather than considering more human-centred approaches following the extreme challenges of the pandemic and the trauma that resulted, education policy-makers chose to continue to set a narrow, performance related agenda for schools, thus preventing leaders from responding to the human needs of their students and staff. The result of this is evidenced in record numbers of withdrawals from the school system to homeschooling and poor pupil attendance. This 'opting out' of state systems is particularly prevalent in families of children with SEND, who are increasingly finding schools unable to meet their children's care needs within strictures of rigid 'high stakes' accountability frameworks (Connolly *et al.*, 2023).

According to Young Minds, in 2021 one in three adolescents in the UK were diagnosed with a mental health condition, with one in six children aged five to 16 showing signs of mental health problems – a 30 per cent increase from 2017. If ever there were a time for a more sensitive approach to education and care (from here referred to as 'educare'), one that attends to the underlying causes of problems rather than their symptoms, it is now.

A similar deterioration has been seen within the teaching profession, as teachers leave the profession in record numbers (Long *et al.*, 2022). Burrow *et al.* (2020) argue that 40 years of neoliberal reform to the UK education system has stripped teachers of time and the freedom to operate and innovate. Similarly, Skinner *et al.* (2019) attribute the erosion of teachers' mental health and wellbeing to an increase in tasks that remove their autonomy and erode their professional identify. In contrast the essential concerns of social pedagogy are wellbeing, learning and growth through positive relationships (ThemPra, 2017); hence it is offering a path to renewal of the educare professions by recognising and maximising the use of, the positive human potential that lies at its core.

The third reason that the time is right for considering social pedagogical approaches to leadership is that we are entering a period of unprecedented and inestimable change both from the adoption of AI technology and the next phases of the climate emergency. In a time of intense instability, the best chance we have to maintain social cohesion and community wellbeing through this transition is to lean into, and on, the educare systems, to accentuate the relational qualities that make us human, and to intentionally privilege the development of these. Adnan (2021) tells us that we all need to 'wake up' to the changing circumstances that are emerging. The process that makes this possible is becoming more intentional about who we are and more discerning about our own sense of purpose. Only then can we understand our values and learn to enact them through the roles we have as parents, practitioners, and children and young people (CYP).

Social pedagogy foregrounds this way of being in the world. It uses the term *Haltung* which describes how we integrate our inner world and our outer actions. It is about *being*, as well as *doing*. *Haltung* invites us to metaphorically take off the 'jacket' that represents the professional and technical aspects of our roles and step into our own skin, encouraging us to enact our roles as our authentic selves (Eichsteller, 2010 in Charfe and Gardner, 2020, p. 3). Through the choices we make and the relationships we forge, we can become agents of personal growth, as well as organisational and community change.

> **Reflection point**
>
> Where do you see the key strains of the current education and care systems? Post-pandemic, why do you think a focus upon holistic wellbeing is needed?

What might a social pedagogical approach to leadership look like?

Leaders have a unique opportunity to embed social pedagogical perspectives within their roles in order to contribute meaningfully to social change. Leaders cannot be understood in isolation from the volatility, uncertainty, complexity and ambiguity that surround them and those they lead. Leadership is relational, contextualised and complex. Charfe and Gardner (2019, p. 33) explain how the principles of social pedagogy and educare align when they state that 'by placing relationships at the heart of all engagements, social pedagogues seek to facilitate individuals being included and contributing to the wider society'. But Charfe (2023, p. 2) also adds that 'ethical leadership, from a social pedagogical viewpoint, is situated in the everyday practice of *all* practitioners and is not reliant on authority, job title or managerial position within organisations' (*our emphasis*). Leadership, Charfe argues, does not reside in just one person within an organisation but is emergent from any interaction of influence between people in any position within the organisation.

The fabric of leadership interactions is made up of existing relationships and results in the continued shaping of future ones. Within organisations, the web of relationships which impact upon leadership is multi-faceted and multi-directional. However, despite system complexity being recognised within leadership literature (for example see Lichtenstein *et al.*, 2006 or Uhl-Bien and Arena, 2018), a preoccupation with valorised images of leader agency persists. These heroic conceptualisations of leadership suggest that complexity is intrinsic only to the system and does not also reside within each of the individuals therein. Instead, leaders continue to be positioned as the 'vanguard of solutions to effect continuous improvement and change' (Morrison *and* Ecclestone, 2011, p. 199). Throughout both academic and political discourse there persists an image of the leader 'as an all-powerful actor who is primarily responsible, by dint of their own particular super-abilities' (Morrison and Ecclestone, 2011, p. 199) to energise others in the direction of system improvement. However, such superhuman expectations perpetuate a functionalist perspective of leaders as being devoid of any human dimension (Orchard, 2002).

Much like dominant business perspectives of leadership, educational and care leadership across the western world has, likewise, come to separate logic from emotion (Blackmore, 2011; Bolton and English, 2010) as though they are at odds with one another, and for effective decision making to take place, logic must prevail. Recent research conducted with primary school headteachers in the Midlands of England identified the potential for this discourse to be internalised by school leaders, resulting in feelings of inadequacy. The data demonstrated that participants subconsciously considered feelings of stress and anxiety to be indicators of their incompetence within their role (Laurence, 2025). The existing paradigm of leadership as 'more than human' and therefore emotionless mitigates against more holistic understandings of leaders as people.

From a social pedagogical perspective, leadership is ultimately considered a human endeavour, underpinned by human values, ethics and visions of 'good'. It is rooted in a concern for human flourishing through supporting the human potential within a system. Leadership interactions happen in the spaces between people whereby leader identities are continuously socially constructed and negotiated based on their relationships with those around them. It is important, therefore, to recognise the organic nature of organisations and consider complexity to not only exist within these environments, but also within the people who occupy these spaces as both leaders and followers.

> **Reflection point**
>
> Do you consider yourself a leader within your work context? On what basis do you make that decision?

How might we integrate social pedagogy as leaders?

There is not a simple answer to the question 'how do we become social pedagogical leaders?' Social pedagogy is not a prescriptive set of methods or rules and, as such, 'it's not something you either do or don't do' (Thempra, 2024, no page). However, it is possible for leadership to be more or less aligned with the values of social pedagogy and journeying towards this requires a compass rather than a map, in that there is no end destination, and the terrain is always changing. However, there are guiding principles and navigation points, or way markers, which can support individuals in orientating themselves and their practice.

People who occupy the role of leader in an organisation are simultaneously acting as their personal self: a human being who holds a high profile and often isolating position, and their professional self, embodying the job description of leader/manager and the expectations that this comes with. The separation of emotion from logic within leadership discourse serves to undermine the sense of belonging of many leaders within their role. This can be particularly problematic within educare settings where emotions and personal relationships 'are woven into the fabric of the everyday life' (Crawford, 2007, p. 87) and 'are quite literally at the heart' (Crawford, 2007, p. 88) of work here. The lack of alignment between these opposing identities can impede a sense of belonging within the role. This, in turn, has the potential to impact upon authenticity within relationships as leaders experience incongruence between who they are and how they are expected to act. However, social pedagogues would argue that it is not possible to be professional without also being personal, we *must* be both.

With that said, social pedagogues do not argue for a lack of professional boundaries. Instead, they make the distinction between the professional, the personal and the private. For leaders, like many professionals, this distinction has the potential to support a more integrative professional identity that legitimises emotion in leaders and mitigates the barriers to collaboration posed by hierarchical power structures. Through leaders feeling comfortable to be their whole selves – including aspects they may consider a weakness – the people they work with are encouraged to be their authentic selves and not to feel inferior because of their own shortcomings (Thempra, 2024). This supports a culture of psychological safety where empathy affords mutual understanding, which improves collaboration (Edmondson, 2018). The development of an integrative sense of self as a social pedagogue is a crucial aspect of the authentic and reciprocal relationships which are to follow: relationships which form the core of the social pedagogue's work.

Social pedagogy leadership: an invitation to all practitioners

In recent years, within the education system in England, there has been an emphasis on instructional leadership (Schleicher, 2012) and transformational leadership (Daniels et al., 2019) both of which reinforce 'strong leader' archetypes and emphasise the positional power of the leader. This has shaped priorities and limited the scope and impact of leadership development. Just one example, Normore and Issa Lahera's (2018) survey of education leadership programmes, points to an over emphasis on administration and management, poor recruitment processes, inadequate pedagogy, a lack of rigour, inadequate attention to social justice issues, insufficient opportunities to generate new knowledge, and insufficient impact on student outcomes.

The neglect of person-centred leadership development that prioritises the individual needs, values and personal growth of leaders is illustrated in England by the National Professional Qualifications (NPQs) for school leaders. These programmes focus on knowledge content ('learn that…') and implementation ('learn how to…') (Department for Education, 2021). We need to extend the framing of this 'learning' so leaders can reflect on their emerging identity, their evolving role and the contribution they make as leaders in their settings. This is important because the leadership models driven by the standards agenda do not sufficiently prepare leaders for the complexity of the human challenges they face (Robinson and Hallgarten, 2024).

In recent years there has been a growing population of system leaders who recognise that if we are to have a more relevant, responsive and resilient education system, we need to embrace more holistic approaches to developing leaders (Rethinking Leadership, 2024). This calls for a reconsideration of the potential of leadership to ignite the efficacy, agency and motivation of educare leaders wanting to find their purpose through what they do. It re-introduces values to the heart of education and does not rely upon role. It recognises policy can be influenced from within the classroom, workshop or community centre. In this sense, all practitioners who integrate social pedagogical values into their practice and their professional identities are leaders – their empathy and care for the children and young people that they work with means that they create conditions and influence others as a means of doing their best for them. They act to bring about change.

Social pedagogy leadership at the levels of self, setting and system

There are three ways in which we might conceptualise social pedagogical leadership. Underlying each of these is the principle that 'every person has inherent potential, is valuable, resourceful and can make a meaningful contribution to the wider community if we find ways of including them' (ThemPra, 2017, in Charfe and Gardner, 2020, p. 6). At the level of **self**, leaders of social pedagogy apply a social pedagogy lens to their practice and create 'space' for themselves to do this by growing their internal, or social and emotional, strengths. This authentic leadership approach allows them to 'bring all of who they are to the party' (Watkins, 2016, p. 7).

Secondly, leadership *for* social pedagogy might be concerned with advocating for and creating conditions that help colleagues enact social pedagogy through their roles at a **setting** level. This may be building relationships or establishing a formal or informal community of social pedagogical practice.

Thirdly, from a **system** perspective, leadership *in* social pedagogy might be considered as building the field for the adoption and spread of social pedagogy practice through the wider system. This might include getting involved in national bodies such as the Social Pedagogy Professional Association.

This conception of **self, setting and system** opens up for consideration the different domains that leaders operate in and brings into focus the integration of these (McInerney and Kewalramani, 2023). This vertical of **self, setting and system** emphasises a shift that we need to see more of in leadership development. A move from the horizontal – getting better at what we are already doing – towards vertical leadership development that is characterised by holistic personal development and growth. This is an important shift because social pedagogical practice needs supportive organisational conditions that recognise the whole self. By thinking in an integrated way about how we are developing ourselves, our practice, our organisations and the wider system, we are creating conditions for alignment that are essential for social pedagogy practice to flourish. Moreover, we are contributing to the evolution of a values base for a new educare paradigm built on essence, limitless, dignity, and wholeness (Fullan *et al.*, 2021).

Reflection point

What does 'wholeness' mean to you? What conditions might enable wholeness, for you, and for others, in your setting?

Practice like this is rare and often remains largely hidden within the educare systems. In one programme with primary school headteachers which was investigated by a chapter author, a non-directive coaching approach was used within cluster groups of school leaders over the course of several years. This approach combined emotional support and co-constructed learning opportunities to create a holistic and context-sensitive leadership development programme. Participating school leaders experienced this as a psychologically safe space in which they were willing to be vulnerable with others in a similar role due to the high levels of trust developed. They described being uniquely allowed to bring their 'whole self' to this space and considered the success of this practice to contribute to a greater ability to sustain their role despite the challenging landscape they worked within. Many of the headteachers explained that they adopted the same approach within their own settings and found this to have empowered their staff and created improved collaborative working cultures (please see Laurence, 2025, for further details of this research).

Our social pedagogical leadership journey

We know that 'the map is not the territory': we forge our own singular leadership journey through the opportunities and relationships we forge. Social pedagogy is a life-world orientation that becomes part of who we are and stays with us as we enact our professional roles. A self, setting and system framing lends itself to a deeper, more integrated consideration of our own social pedagogical leadership journey. It may also help us organise our thinking about how leaders can support practitioners to enact social pedagogy within their roles.

Considering ourselves as leaders in the three domains of self, setting and system also brings us into contact with three of the key conceptual pillars of social pedagogy: **care, connection** and **community. Care**, or its deeper more active interpretation of *caritas* signals benevolent concern for others (Stephens, 2013) and highlights an ethical orientation in how we respond to others (Noddings, 1984). It is rooted in a deeply humanistic appreciation of who we are as practitioners (Palmer, 2017) and a critical sense of our transformative and liberatory potential impact (hooks, 1994). **Connection** is the action that drives the relational heart of social pedagogy. Meeting others with unconditional positive regard (Rogers, 1951) and holding an aspiration for them as integrated, whole and fulfilled beings, brings a developmental quality to the interactions we have as social pedagogues, driving our individual and collective wellbeing. Seeing ourselves as social beings allows us to recognise that leadership is always relational and holistic (Giles, 2019).

Social pedagogy has a regenerative role at a **community** level that can shape a more equitable and sustainable society. This is essentially developmental as we need to grow into our own sense of agency – extending our own intention to act from a place of deeper awareness and purpose. This impetus is not just developing ourselves, but helping others to grow into their potential (Kegan and Lahey, 2016). Modelling our 'becoming' as social pedagogical leaders, we can create the conditions for learning at an organisational and systems level. The deeper sense of authenticity and purpose driving this stems from our desire to contribute reciprocally within the systems we inhabit (Sanford, 2020) and intervene strategically to shape these (Meadows, 1999).

Whether an educator, nurse or social worker, we are sensing our way through the signifiers of our social pedagogical practice and emerging leadership. The question that remains is 'how might we develop ourselves and others as leaders *as, for* and *in* social pedagogical leadership?' Below we offer some reading that relates to helpful leadership approaches that can help us integrate social pedagogical principles into our thinking and practice as social pedagogical leaders (Table 14.1).

Table 14.1 Readings to support our social pedagogical leadership journey

Capability domains	Leadership…	Social pedagogical leadership principles	Helpful leadership approaches and capabilities
Self 'becoming'	'as' social pedagogy	Care	Ethical leadership (Noddings, 1984) Critical thinking, praxis, reflexivity (hooks, 1994; Palmer, 2017)
Organisation 'creating conditions'	'for' social pedagogy	Connection	Relational leadership (Giles, 2019) Positive leadership (Cameron, 2012) Appreciative inquiry (Cooperrider and Whitney, 2005)
System 'building a field'	'in' social pedagogy	Community	Developmental leadership (Kegan and Lahey, 2016), Systems leadership (Fullan et al., 2021; Senge, 1990). Regenerative leadership (Sanford, 2020) Systems change (Meadows, 1999)

> **Reflection point**
>
> In which domain is your leadership most evident: in your own practice, supporting others across your organisation, or in the wider system? How might social pedagogical approaches help you to become more courageous? What might be possible, for you, if you were to do this?

What emerging leadership development practice can we draw on?

This section outlines some emerging practice of the School Effectiveness Team at University of Worcester which is based on Ashoka's *Togetherness Practice* (www.togethernesspractice.org) framework. Ashoka is an international NGO whose work is to help people foster 'changemaker' mindsets that allow us to move towards a more equitable and sustainable world. Changemaking is the practice of imagining a new reality, taking action and collaborating to bring that new reality into being for the good of others (Ashoka, 2024). Changemaking is grounded in empathy and agency, recognising that addressing systemic challenges needs us to work in new ways that unlock the potential of all, particularly young people.

Changemaking leadership resonates strongly with the social justice ethic of social pedagogy. Changemaking is grounded in four changemaker capabilities: conscious empathy necessary for relational practice; fluid teamwork where people collaborate by creating shared understanding and purpose across 'teams of teams'; changemaking leadership that seeks opportunities for others to lead; and practising changemaking through social innovation that emphasise the relational, collaborative and socially impactful purposeful leadership. The *Togetherness Practice* was designed to support changemakers unlock potential in self and others. It can easily be mapped to the social pedagogy *Diamond Model* developed by Eichstellar and Holthoff (2011) (Figure 14.1). In doing so it proposes four shifts from established leadership development practice towards new approaches that can serve us as social pedagogical leaders.

The *Diamond Model* of social pedagogy has been mentioned in most chapters of this book, and it can be seen as a heuristic for social pedagogical practice. The holistic, relational, empowering sensibilities of the diamond are evident in the capacities, conditions and practices of the *Togetherness Practice* framework. We understand leadership as being socially constructed, intertwined within our own identity as a leader and embedded within the relationships and empathy we have with and for others (De Rue and Ashford, 2010). People cannot thrive in isolation, we become who we are in, and through, relationship with others.

We can create conditions for our development by engaging in practices such as '*pausing, patterning, trusting and enacting*' that are unpacked in the Togetherness Practice. This is the route to deepening our learning and developing capacities that we need to lead change in complexity such as *awareness, meaning-making, self-permission and responsibility*. There is a vulnerability to engaging in these practices and learning in this way; it requires conducive cultural conditions such as *receptivity, reflection, belonging and emergence*. The symbiotic relationship between internal capacities and external conditions is similar to the role of wellbeing in the *Diamond Model*, our own wellbeing cultivates the inner conditions that enable outer change.

Leadership: not a role but a way of being 149

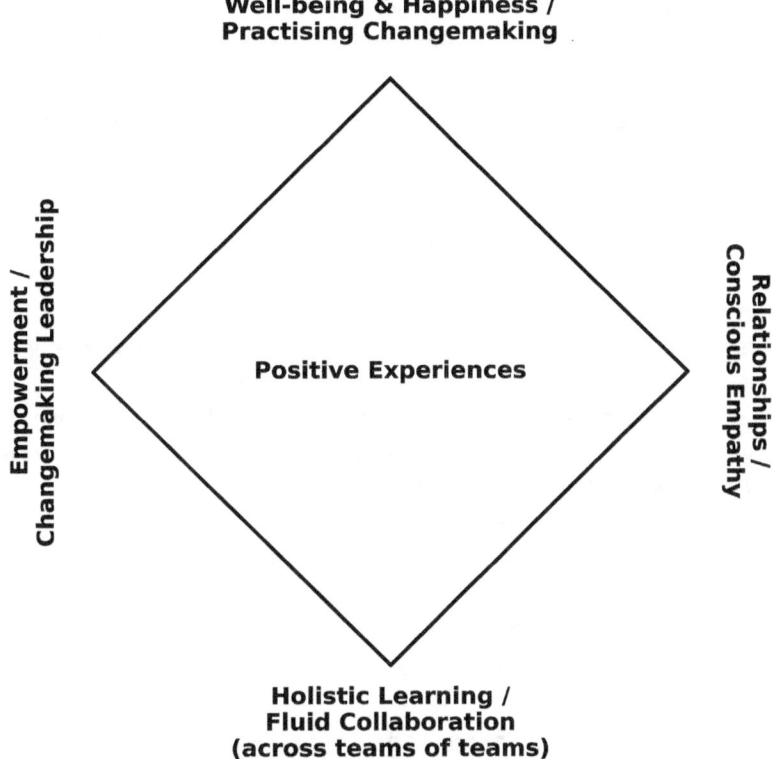

Figure 14.1 Changemaker capabilities mapped to the *Diamond Model* of Social Pedagogy based upon Eichstellar and Holthoff (2011).

> **Reflection point**
>
> Visit www.togethernesspractice.org and reflect on the capacities and conditions in the framework. Which come naturally to you? Which might you need to work on? Reflect on the conditions in your own setting. How might they help you develop your internal capacities?

Four shifts in leadership development

Shift 1: From technical, role-based leadership development to embodied learning for systems leadership

Pestalozzi's 'head, heart and hand' model (Gazibara, 2020) has inspired social pedagogy since its inception, and this is enjoying renewed attention in England as more school leaders challenge normative approaches to learning. Our practice of social pedagogy and leadership is embodied: we bring who we are into what we do. Therefore, to get better at what we do, we need to be better at being who we are. This suggests leadership development that goes beyond 'task roles' into more holistic and integrated ways of knowing and being. In short, this is a shift from developing leaders 'to do' their jobs towards developing leaders 'who do' their roles. Creating opportunities for leaders to develop greater awareness of themselves and of others, and a deeper, more nuanced, understanding of the wider system within which they play a part, can help them develop a connection to their deeper purpose, to others and the contribution they want to make.

Shift 2: From empowering others to self-empowerment through others

Leaders often talk of empowering others. Social pedagogical leadership emphasises our responsibility to empower ourselves and to create opportunities for others to do the same. The subtle difference is in creating relationships of equal human beings where power is used not as a form of control but as a responsibility (Eichsteller *and* Holthoff, 2011). An aspect of this responsibility is to create opportunities for critical thinking that encourage others, or leaders in this case, not to wilfully accept the existing social order, but to critique it, and act from a place of knowledge and awareness of their own position within the power relationships they create and inhabit.

Reflexivity and praxis (Cunliffe, 2016) become core concepts underlying social pedagogical leadership development as a result of the shifts outlined above. If social pedagogues can create space to reflect on who they are in relation to what they value (reflexivity), they can use their role to create conditions of connection, and caring relationships that engender community wellbeing (praxis). For Sandford (2020), allowing leaders opportunities to connect with their deepest purpose by engaging a range of intelligences (including social and emotional) brings a sense of renewal and opens up possibilities for organisational and systemic transformation. The *Togetherness Practice* can be seen as an instrument for these moments of empathic relationship, engagement and reflexive action.

Shift 3: From deficit to asset-based leadership development

We often feel compelled to try to create order and certainty in a rapidly changing world. We seek to return systems to stability even when, as is the case with education, they are inherently complex (Lent, 2022). For public services, the unintended consequence of this is a tendency towards narrow targets and accountability measures that encourage deficit-based thinking. Looking for quick fixes to problems produces patterns of activity that dissipate energy, as well as creating cultures of high-stakes accountability and mistrust. It pulls strategic thinking in the direction of remediation and away from the organisational learning and development that is needed to meet the complex needs of young people in a rapidly changing world.

In contrast, positive leadership approaches (Cameron, 2012) and the purposeful cultivation of acceptance can help us negotiate uncertainty, lead change and create conditions for wellbeing and efficacy as social pedagogical leaders. This application of positive psychology to organisational and leadership development through practices such as appreciative inquiry (Cooperrider and Witney, 2005) help to locate social pedagogical leadership development within an emerging evidence base of asset-based and systems informed approaches that encourage integrated thinking and allow for more responsiveness to the needs of service users through innovation (Laloux, 2014).

> **Reflection point**
>
> Would you say that your current setting is asset-focused or deficit-based? What evidence would you base that upon?

Shift 4: From transactional to relational leadership development

As leadership is inherently a relational activity, Giles' (2019) model for relational leadership may be helpful in conceptualising social pedagogical leadership development.

- Live orientated towards a deep moral and ethical commitment to critical, humane and interconnected relationships
- Live in a way that authentically models and embodies *care-full* relationships
- Attune to the subtleties of the context through refined relational sensibilities
- Use these to enact a 'phronesis', or practical wisdom that is context specific.

The *Togetherness Practice* instrument intentionally builds a relational field. It encourages us to intentionally engage with a 'space in-between' that is a '*we*' space, through which we can deepen our self-awareness by intentionally recognising our own responses to challenging situations and people. This process leverages what is *in* the way, *as* the way, that is the route to greater learning and maturity. *Togetherness Practices* of 'pausing, patterning, trusting and enacting' can help us structure experiences and opportunities for reflection that develop our individual capacities and create conducive cultural conditions to unlock potential, and in doing so: 'make [...] it possible for us as collectives of whole people to reconnect with our caring, illuminate new pathways, and realize transformation' (Thekk et al., 2023, no page).

Conclusion

Once you believe in the potential of social pedagogy to better serve children and young people, the challenge becomes one of leadership, or more specifically, how we might enable our own social pedagogy practice to flourish and amplify conditions for others to do the same. To fulfil this goal, social pedagogy reframes leadership to be more inclusive and holistic, recognising that leadership starts but does not end with the leader. Social pedagogical leadership is integrative: it invites us to think of our own development, the conditions we are creating in our organisations, and encourages us to locate ourselves in wider systems as we lead learning and change that improves the life chances and wellbeing of children and young people in our care.

In our current education landscape, there is a need for social pedagogical principles to elevate the place of relational practice, proposing a new educational paradigm that will help us contend with a challenging future, one that is AI enabled, resource constrained, and potentially economically and socially disruptive. In the face of all of this, policy is a blunt instrument. Even if there were a will and a way, the conditions for real change lie in changemaking, building our empathy and unlocking our individual and collective agency to lead in ways that drive our own and each other's evolution and growth. Harnessing social pedagogical leadership in service of this, we can support our transition towards a more aware, sensitive, appreciative and humanistic response to the challenges that are shaping our futures, together.

Summary points

- Leadership is framed as a way of being rather than a formal role, encouraging all individuals to see themselves as leaders capable of creating change.

- Social pedagogical leadership centres on care, connection, and community, emphasising relational, ethical, and human-centred leadership as essential to social change.
- Leadership is explored across three interconnected domains – self (personal capacities), setting (organisational culture), and system (wider societal change) – highlighting the interdependence of these levels.
- Leaders are encouraged to align their inner values with their outer actions, fostering authenticity, relational trust, and psychological safety within teams and communities. This is referred to as *Haltung* and authenticity.
- Leadership is understood as a dynamic process that emerges within relationships, supported by changemaking capabilities such as empathy, shared purpose, and systems thinking.
- Leaders are invited to act; to adopt a social pedagogical stance, leading with care, connection, and collective responsibility to meet the challenges of a rapidly changing world.

Recommended reading

Cameron, K. S. (2012) *Positive leadership: Strategies for extraordinary performance*. San Francisco, CA, Berrett-Koehler Publishers.
Scharmer, O. (2018) *Theory U: Leading from the future as it emerges: The social technology of presencing*. London: McGraw-Hill.
The Togetherness Practice is available at: www.togethernesspractice.org/ (Accessed 7 February 2025).

References

Adnan, I. (2021) *The politics of waking up*. London: Perspective Press.
Ashoka U. (2024) *Definitions and Frameworks | Ashoka U*. [online] Available at: https://ashokau.org/definitions. (Accessed 7 February 2025).
Blackmore, J. (2011) Lost in translation? Emotional intelligence, affective economies, leadership and organizational change. *Journal of Educational Administration and History*, 43(3), pp. 207–225.
Bolton, C. and English, F. (2010) De-constructing the logic/emotion binary in educational leadership and practice. *Journal of Educational Administration*, 48, pp. 561–578.
Brown, M. E. and Treviño, L. K. (2006) Ethical leadership: A review and future directions. *The Leadership Quarterly*, 17(6), pp. 595–616.
Burns, J. M. (1978). *Leadership*. New York: Harper and Row.
Burrow, R., Williams, R. and Thomas, D. (2020). Stressed, depressed and exhausted: Six years as a teacher in UK State education. *Work, Employment and Society*, [online] 34(5), p. 095001702090304. https://doi.org/10.1177/0950017020903040.
Cameron, K. S. (2012) *Positive leadership: Strategies for extraordinary performance*. San Francisco, CA: Berrett-Koehler Publishers.
Charfe, L. (2023) Ethical and relational leadership in a complex world: The use of the Human Learning Systems and social pedagogical leadership framework to navigating complexity. *International Journal of Social Pedagogy*, 12(1), p. 16. https://doi.org/10.14324/111.444.ijsp.2023.v12.x.016.
Charfe, L., & Gardner, A. (2019) *Social pedagogy and social work*. London: Sage.
Charfe, L. and Gardner, A. (2020) 'Does my Haltung look big in this?': The use of social pedagogical theory for the development of ethical and value-led practice. *International Journal of Social Pedagogy*, 9(1). https://doi.org/10.14324/111.444.ijsp.2020.v9.x.011
Connolly, S., Constable, H. L. and Mullally, S. L. (2023) School distress and the school attendance crisis: A story dominated by neurodivergence and unmet need. *Frontiers in Psychiatry*, 14. https://doi.org/10.3389/fpsyt.2023.1237052.
Cooperrider, D. and Whitney, D. (2005) *Appreciative inquiry: A positive revolution in change*. San Francisco: Berrett-Koehler.
Crawford, M. (2007) Rationality and emotionality in primary school leadership. An exploration of key themes. *Educational Review*, 59(1), pp. 87–98.

Cunliffe, A. L. (2016) Republication of 'On Becoming a Critically Reflexive Practitioner'. *Journal of Management Education*, 40(6), pp. 747–768.

Daniëls, E., Hondeghem, A. and Dochy, F. (2019) A review on leadership and leadership development in educational settings. *Educational Research Review*, 27(27), pp. 110–125.

Day, D. V. and Antonakis, J. (Eds.) (2012) *The nature of leadership* (2nd ed.). Thousand Oaks: Sage.

Department for Education (2021). *National Professional Qualifications Frameworks: From September 2021*. [online] GOV.UK. Available at: www.gov.uk/government/publications/national-professional-qualifications-frameworks-from-september-2021. (Accessed 7 February 2025).

DeRue, D. S. and Ashford, S. J. (2010) Who will lead and who will follow? A social process of leadership identity construction in organizations. *Academy of Management Review*, 35(4), pp. 627–647.

Edmondson, A. C. (2018) *The fearless organization* London: John Wiley and Sons.

Eichsteller, G. (2010). The notion of 'Haltung' in social pedagogy. Available at https://thetcj.org/in-residence/the-notion-of-haltung-in-social-pedagogy (Accessed 23 March 2025).

Eichsteller, G. and Holthoff, S. (2011) Conceptual foundations of social pedagogy: A transnational perspective from Germany. In C. Cameron and P. Moss (Eds) *Social pedagogy and working with children and young people*. London: Jessica Kingsley, pp. 33–52.

Fullan, M., Mackay, T., Redman, K., Cropley, M. and Miller, A. (2021). *The Right Drivers for Whole System Success CSE LEADING EDUCATION SERIES*. [online] Available at: https://michaelfullan.ca/wp-content/uploads/2021/03/Fullan-CSE-Leading-Education-Series-01-2021R2-compressed.pdf. (Accessed 7 February 2025)

Gazibara, S. (2020). "Head, Heart and Hands Learning" - A challenge for contemporary education. *Journal of Education Culture and Society*, 4(1), pp. 71–82. https://doi.org/10.15503/jecs20131.71.82

Giles, D. L. (2019) *Relational leadership in education: A phenomenon of inquiry and practice*. Abingdon and New York, NY: Routledge.

Hämäläinen, J. (2003) The concept of social pedagogy in the field of social work. *Journal of Social Work*, 3(1), pp. 69–80.

HM Government (2003) *Every Child Matters*. [online] GOV.UK. Available at: https://assets.publishing.service.gov.uk/media/5a7c95a4e5274a0bb7cb806d/5860.pdf. (Accessed 7 February 2025).

hooks, b. (1994) *Teaching to transgress: Education as the practice of freedom*. New York: Routledge.

Kegan, R. and Lahey, L. (2016) *An everyone culture*. Cambridge, MA: Harvard Business Review Press.

Laloux, F. (2014) *Reinventing organizations: A guide to creating organizations inspired by the next stage of human consciousness*. Brussels: Nelson Parker.

Laurence, E. (2025) *People-powered leaders: A case study exploration of how collaborative leadership development programmes can support school leaders emotionally and professionally*. PhD Thesis. University of Worcester.

Lent, J. (2022) *WEB OF MEANING: Integrating science and traditional wisdom to find our place in the universe*. London: Profile Books Ltd.

Lichtenstein, B.B., Uhl-Bien, M., Marion, R., Seers, A., Orton, J.D. and Schreiber, C. (2006) *Complexity leadership theory: An interactive perspective on leading in complex adaptive systems*. Department of Management: Faculty Publications. 8. https://digitalcommons.unl.edu/managementfacpub/8

Long, R., Danechi, S., Maisuria, A. and Roberts, N. (2022) *Teacher Recruitment and Retention in England*. [online] Parliament.uk. Available at: https://researchbriefings.files.parliament.uk/documents/CBP-7222/CBP-7222.pdf. (Accessed 7 February 2025).

McInerney, S. and Kewalramani, R. (2023) *New Capabilities for a New World: Leadership Development for School and System Improvement*. [online] Available at: www.edge.co.uk/documents/425/Edge_New_Capabilities_Report_5.6.23.pdf. (Accessed 7 February 2025).

Meadows, D. (1999) *Leverage Points Places to Intervene in a System*. [online] Available at: www.donellameadows.org/wp-content/userfiles/Leverage_Points.pdf (Accessed 7 February 2025).

Morrison, M. and Ecclestone, K. (2011) Getting emotional: A critical evaluation of recent trends in the development of school leaders. *School Leadership and Management*, 31(3), pp. 199–214.

Noddings, N. (1984) *Caring: A feminine approach to ethics and moral education*. Oakland, CA: University of California Press.

Normore, A. H. and Issa Lahera, A. (2018) The evolution of educational leadership preparation programmes. *Journal of Educational Administration and History*, 51(1), pp. 27–42. https://doi.org/10.1080/00220620.2018.1513914.

Northouse, P. G. (2021) *Leadership: Theory and practice* (Eighth ed). London, Sage.

Orchard, J. (2002) Will the real superhero stand up? A critical review of the national standards for headteachers in England. *International Journal of Children's Spirituality*, 7(2), pp. 159–169.

Palmer, P. J. (2017) *Courage to teach: Exploring the inner landscape of a teacher's life – 20th anniversary edition.* 20th ed. London: Jossey-Bass.

Rethinking Leadership (2024). *Rethinking Leadership.* [online] Available at: https://bigeducation.org/rethinking-leadership/ [Accessed 20 Feb. 2025].

Robinson, L. and Hallgarten, J. (2024). *What else? What next? What if? A report by Big Education and CfEY into the future of leadership development in England.* [online] London: Big Education/Centre for Education and Youth. Available at: https://bigeducation.org/wp-content/uploads/2024/01/Big_Education_Rethinking_Leadership.pdf [Accessed 1 Sep. 2025].

Rogers, C. (1951) *Client-centered therapy: Its current practice, implications and theory.* London: Constable.

Rost, J. C. (1991) *Leadership for the twenty-first century.* New York: Praeger.

Sanford, C. (2020) *The regenerative life.* London and Boston: John Murray Business.

Schleicher, A. (Ed.) (2012) *Preparing teachers and developing school leaders for the 21st century: Lessons from around the world.* Paris: OECD Publishing. https://doi.org/10.1787/9789264174559-en

Senge, P. M. (1990) *The fifth discipline: The art and practice of the learning organization.* New York: Currency Doubleday.

Skinner, B., Leavey, G. and Rothi, D. (2019) Managerialism and teacher professional identity: Impact on well-being among teachers in the UK. *Educational Review*, 73(1), pp. 1–16.

Stephens, P. (2013). *Social pedagogy: Heart and head.* Bremen: Ehv.

Stodghill, R. M. (1948) Personal factors associated with leadership: A survey of literature. *Journal of Personality*, 25, pp. 35–71.

Thekk, V., Yarmuth, L. and McInerney, S. (2023) *The Togetherness Practice.* [online] The Togetherness Practice. Available at: www.togethernesspractice.org (Accessed 7 February 2025).

ThemPra (2017) *Social Pedagogy.* Available at: www.thempra.org.uk/social-pedagogy/ (Accessed 7 February 2025).

ThemPra Social Pedagogy. (2024). *Resources.* [online] Available at: www.thempra.org.uk/resources/ (Accessed 7 February 2025).

Uhl-Bien, M. and Arena, M. (2018) Leadership for organizational adaptability: A theoretical synthesis and integrative framework. *The Leadership Quarterly*, 29(1), pp. 89–104.

Uhl-Bien, M., Riggio, R., Lowe, K. and Carsten, M. (2014) Followership theory: A review and research agenda. *The Leadership quarterly*, 25(1), pp. 83–104.

Watkins, A. (2016) *4D leadership: competitive advantage through vertical leadership development.* London: Kogan Page.

15 Accepting relationships and emotions in research

Carla Solvason

Introduction

Research and education are intrinsically linked. Without research, all education becomes no more than the reproduction of old ideas and outmoded methods. Education is based upon the fact that there is always more to know, always new perspectives to see. As educationalists, we should always be open to new ways of thinking and never presume to know it all, because 'humility is the only lens through which great things can be seen' (Palmer, 1998, p. 108).

> **Reflection point**
>
> Before we go any further consider this: Is a genuine openness to new ideas a part of your professional life? If it is, how does that look? Perhaps one example of that openness is that you are reading this book…

Most of us recognise that education, or at least the education of children, includes the head, heart and hands. We want children to feel excited, to feel awe, to feel pride in their achievements; we accept that emotions, the heart, play a key role in their learning. But many are not so willing to connect emotions with the very grown-up area of research. Research, we tell ourselves, is about objectivity. To allow emotions into research, even social research, would make it invalid, insipid, shallow, fluffy nonsense. In fact, many would argue, to allow emotions means that it is not 'real' research at all. But emotions are there.

When I was bumbling my way through my PhD I remember coming across this:

Entry and departure, distrust and confidence, elation and despondency, commitment and betrayal, friendship and abandonment- are all as fundamental here as dry discussions on the techniques of observation, taking field notes, analysing the data and writing the report.

(Punch, 1994, p. 84)

I was carrying out a longitudinal case study at the time and every word of this rang true. Those that I was researching with had, in fact, become 'work friends', I was invited to their Christmas 'social'. Their barriers were down with me, they openly shared their confidences, criticisms and failures. They forgot I was a researcher, I had become a colleague, and as such they shared information with me that, had I coldly used, could have been damaging for them. They trusted me with their human frailties, we connected as equally flawed human beings.

The years that I spent carrying out that research I had to continually make decisions about what was 'data' that I could use, and what was not. What I should write in my fieldnotes and what I should leave out. Every day required multiple ethical decisions about identifiability, implications, trust and betrayal that no handbook of postgraduate research prepares you for. Social research involves people, and emotions, in all their complexity.

No matter what approach you take to collecting data, the researcher and the researched come together in a relationship, and that relationship is based upon trust. As Costley *et al.* (2010, p. 14) put it when they were exploring work-based research, research is a 'mutual activity with individual consequences'. As respondents we are putting our faith in those that we share our thoughts with that they will use them sensitively and respectfully. The same applies to *all* social research. Research is not only logical decisions and effective question design, it cannot involve people without also involving 'heart'. Therefore, in this chapter, I recommend two things: the first is that we stop claiming objectivity that doesn't exist in social research and accept that people, and so hearts and emotions, are very much a part of it. The second is that we carefully consider our *Haltung*, our beliefs, or our attitude that we bring to research, and how that might impact upon our participants.

The problem with objectivity and social research

Anyone who is involved in social research is interested in people's experiences. Numbers are very good at telling us *what* people do: what they buy, how often they visit their doctor, the support groups that they attend, and so on. What numbers do not tell us is *why*: what it is that influences their decisions, and what their experience is when they engage with said action. To understand this we need their words, their thoughts, and so qualitative data becomes central to social research. And why is knowing individual perceptions important? Well, it is important because as social researchers our ultimate aim should be to improve the experiences of others. Without the aim of *improving* society, social research becomes null and void.

MacNaughton *et al.* (2010) explain that the purpose of research is to challenge accepted approaches and to discover the potential of alternatives. Therefore, it is fair to say that a researcher embarks on research with the expectation that there are better ways that processes can be improved. As McGrath and Coles (2013, p. 91) contend, a researcher chooses to research the things that they believe to have value, therefore 'it is not possible for the researcher to come to the research with an empty mind'; the best they can hope for is 'an open mind'. Subjectivity is part and parcel of social research.

So let us consider why qualitative researchers feel the need to aspire to, or feign, objectivity. This is because, as has already been mentioned, the presumption is that 'real' research is objective, emotionless. As Stenhouse (1979, p. 5) noted some decades ago, there are those that regard 'science' and 'discipline' as words of reverence rather than description. Research is based upon a history of exclusivity. Only 'real' researchers, in their ivory towers, know how to research 'properly'. And 'proper' research involves cold detachment, obfuscating vocabulary, and the researcher, on the rare occasion that they acknowledge their existence, referring to themselves in the third person.

Qualitative research's emergence in the twentieth century, with all its unreliability and bias, was like the 'poor relation' (Silverman, 2000) turning up late (and bottle-less) to the party. And in a vain attempt to be accepted into the exclusive research family, qualitative researchers felt compelled to don many of the characteristics of quantitative research. They employed (and many continue to use) terms such as 'reliability' and 'objectivity' and claimed distance between themselves and those that they were researching. As a result, social researchers have, for decades, been stuck between a rock and a hard place in terms of their researcher positionality. Despite social researchers' predilection to take on projects that might bring about change that they recognise as meaningful, many still feel compelled to claim emotional objectivity.

Qualitative research must acknowledge the hand of the researcher; to attempt to do otherwise would be like trying to push porridge uphill. But it is also worth acknowledging that this can result in data that is 'problematic, and, at times, contradictory' (Fontana and Frey, 1994, p. 372). There is no constant to measure against within qualitative data; we cannot use the phrase 'all things being equal' because they never are (Stenhouse, 1979, p. 5). Every social context is unique and transitory (Winter, 1989). Atkinson and Hammersley (1994, p. 254) propose that 'there is no perfectly transparent or neutral way to represent the natural or social world', but the challenge is for us to see this as a positive. Likewise, Denzin and Lincoln (1994, p. 501) recommend that we unashamedly celebrate the fact that 'the age of a putative value-free social science appears to be over'. Authentic qualitative research will always acknowledge the voice of the researcher, and authentic qualitative data will always hold a meaning that lays just beyond the reach of researcher and reader.

> **Reflection point**
>
> Have you previously carried out qualitative research? To what extent was your voice present in the resulting report?

Social research is not objective, because we are not objective

It is important to recognise that social research involves complex and ever-evolving individuals collecting data from complex and ever-evolving individuals. The researcher will influence the researched and the researched will influence the researcher. And that is a good thing, because therein lies the opportunity for positive change. McNiff (2010, p. 106) stresses that we will always all hold preconceptions about what we are researching, but the trick is to 'always hold your knowledge lightly, and be aware that what you know today may change tomorrow. Always remember that you may, after all, be mistaken'. It is impossible to be unbiased, but it is vital that we recognise that bias and are open to alternative realities.

As an academic, a researcher and a writer certain key phrases have shaped my development: they have become part of the lexicon that guides my decisions, they have significantly shaped my *Haltung*. I'm sure that many of you reading this can bring to mind such sayings that have profoundly influenced your understanding. A key phrase for me came from Maria Luca in 2009, when she discussed the need to accept the *whole self* that researchers bring to their participants during data collection and analysis. She argued that in the meeting of two sets of knowledge, that of researcher and researched, 'understanding becomes illuminated' (Luca, 2009, p. 22). And through this deeper insight potential for change is created. Researcher subjectivity does not have to be a negative.

Charfe and Gardner (2019, p. 34) explain how the German word *Haltung* has no exact equivalent in English, but is most easily comprehended as a 'mindset' or a 'moral compass'. I hope that the significance of this to research becomes clear when we consider their explanation below (*my emphasis*):

> An individual's Haltung is an important and fundamental aspect of their personal being and *shapes the way they think and feel about the world around them*, situations that they face and the relationships they have with other people.

Our own Haltung will influence the way in which we view and understand others.

In 2010 Eichsteller explained how our '*Haltung* is not something we can adopt just for a particular situation': it is an aspect of your being, he stresses, 'a skin and not a jacket' (*no page*). Therefore, our *Haltung* impacts upon how we approach research situations, people and data. How we *feel* about something will impact the decisions that we make about them. That we hold certain mindsets about the topics that we explore is a fundamental fact of social research. To attempt to deny this would be a pointless exercise that would undermine, rather than strengthen, any authenticity in the researcher's claims.

> **Reflection point**
>
> Can you identify three key values that drive your professional decisions in your work with others?

In their 2020 exploration of *Haltung*, Charfe and Gardner discuss Mührel's (2008) concept of the two pillars of *Haltung* – comprehending and regarding. The first is particularly pertinent to research as it relates to understanding the individual experience, how the individual lives and their view of things. These aspects, I'm sure we would all agree, are central to collecting qualitative data. During their discussion of comprehending Charfe and Gardener (2020, p. 4) refer to 'the German term '*Verstehen*', which translates as empathic understanding and being able to see the lifeworld orientation of an individual'; and although no social researcher would debate the aim to understand an individual's drivers, the use of the word 'empathic' here begins to draw in the personal. We move away from a purely intellectual appraisal and further toward an 'emotional connection' (*ibid*). And here is where more conventional researchers begin to feel uncomfortable, because it demands the recognition that social research involves emotions.

> **Reflection point**
>
> How comfortable do you feel about researcher emotions being recognised within research? Why do you think that is?

To aim to comprehend, or to understand another in any genuine way requires a personal connection to them. Mührel's (2008) concept of 'regarding' recognises the role that the positionality of the researcher plays in our perception of the other. Eichsteller (2010, *no page*) explains this term most clearly:

> By 'regarding', Mührel refers to accepting the otherness in people different from ourselves who, as strangers, deserve our profound respect. He argues that we cannot understand the other (only what we recognise of ourselves in others), and accepting their strangeness means that we do not try to reduce them to what we are familiar with, what we know.

If we are to accept the notion of 'regarding' in our dealings with research participants and the data that we collect from them, then we need to accept that we sort all data into two categories, that which is 'like us', and familiar, and that which is 'not like us' and so strange. The key point for all data analysts here, is that we do not then attempt to reconfigure alien aspects of a research subject into terms that are more familiar to us, as this would be to 'reduce' them (Eichsteller, 2010, *no page*). Instead, we should show 'profound respect for their human dignity' and unconditional acceptance of their traits and understandings that fall outside our own realms of experience.

Social research is personal and includes emotions

Emotions are not a tap to be turned on and off, we simply learn to manage them. Extreme self-control is part of becoming an adult in Britain, hence our horror and fascination when we see someone 'lose it'. Yesterday I cried in a coffee shop, despite being acutely aware of the discomfort this would cause to those around me. I just was not able to keep it reined in (as per my public duty). Of course, crying in a coffee shop is not what reserved Brits do, and I felt compelled to apologise as I left. But emotions are always there, laying just below the surface, and that includes during research. Of course, we 'control' them as professionals, but that does not mean that they are not there. If I were to select words or phrases to describe my PhD experience there would not be an 'ology' in sight; instead, the list would be made up of terms like displacement, fear, ineptitude, excitement, relief. And actually, most of those resurface with each research project that I embark on 20 plus years later. Social research is based upon interactions and relationships with *people*, it is deeply personal. As Atkinson and Hammersley (1994) put it 'we cannot study the social world without being part of it' (p.249). Our research practices are no different to any other aspect of our professional lives, in that it is 'not so much about *what* is done, but more about *how* something is done' (Eichsteller and Holthoff, 2011, p. 33). And here we return to our *Haltung* which guides our actions.

The Swiss educationalist reformer Johann Pestalozzi (1746–1827) is often recognised as an early adopter of the concept of holistic education, and also for introducing the phrase 'head, heart and hands' (Laubach and Smith, 2011). The basis of his theorising is that effective learning will not take place without some sort of emotional drive, or yearning, to know more. We use the phrase 'their heart is not in it' when we are referring to underperformance. To complete a task, or a role, convincingly, requires an emotional connection to it. Heart is a part of effective performance, it is also an aspect of effective learning, and that includes learning about others through social research.

Effective research, just like effective teaching, involves emotional connectedness. It involves 'tuning into' our respondents, asking the right questions in the right way. 'But what of research that involves no physical interaction?' I hear you ask: 'What of survey? What of a simple online provocation?' There is a whole field of research, mostly belonging to the fields of marketing and advertising, that would tell you *exactly* the role that emotions play in such scenarios. But if we were to stay within the field of educational research my favourite article on this topic is Hartman and Schachter's (2019) *High School Students 'Talk Back' to the Anonymous Researcher behind the Questionnaire*. These researchers mistakenly left a feedback box on their survey, related to the survey design, which should have been removed following the pilot. Their error resulted in all sorts of comments addressed to them, as survey designers, including 'if you genuinely want to know what I think why don't you just ask me'. Those young people completing the survey still assumed a 'relationship' with the designers, even through this most impersonal approach.

In recognising the role that emotions play in research it is worth a brief discussion about power. Other chapters in this book allude to an educator's reluctance to 'share' their power with a learner, as this upsets the traditional teacher/ pupil hierarchy. The same can be said of research. In social research in particular, where there are so many diverse and fluctuating variables, it is natural as a researcher to want to feel that you are guiding the research in at least a vague direction; it is good to feel at least in some semblance of 'control'. But when does this become leading, or bias? Power is intrinsic to all research. No matter how 'collaborative' an approach has been taken to data collection, the powerful influence of the researcher lurks.

With children, the power dynamic is more apparent. Researchers are most often adults, and, as Gallagher (2008, p. 16) explains, 'even in the absence of coercion, children may rely upon cues from adults whom they trust'. Children do not make decisions, adults make them on their behalf; children will naturally follow an adult's lead. But even in participant-led research with fellow adults, the researcher guides the research direction. Regardless of the levels of collaborative discussion that have gone before, the researcher makes the final decisions about the questions to be asked and the data that will become a key focus in discussions. The researcher decides what is shared externally and what is not. There is no solution to this, even the most collaborative of projects need someone to make a final decision, but it is worth showing awareness of this in your work.

Reflection point

If you have ever led on collaborative research (for example with children, students, members of the public or other professionals) reflect upon the extent to which you steered approaches to data collection, data analysis and dissemination.

If we want positive results, we need to approach the project positively

Bearing concepts of influence in mind, our *Haltung*, the framework of beliefs that form the basis for our research approach, becomes more important than ever. Bloor (2010) stresses that our ultimate aim as social researchers should not be to do 'good research' but that we should strive to 'bring about good' through our research. However, our concept of this 'good' will be influenced by our *Haltung*, our ethical underpinnings, as well as our beliefs about the intrinsic value of human beings (Eichsteller and Holthoff, 2011). These beliefs will influence the way that we interact with others (Petrie, 2007) and how our participants respond to us – they will affect both the data that we collect and how we analyse it.

Several years ago, I researched the work of a formidable individual, whom we referred to as 'Katie' in our outputs (see Lyndon et al., 2024 and Solvason et al., 2024 for more about this). Katie held the role of 'health and wellbeing lead' in a primary school, and in one of our interviews with a parent she was referred to as 'amazing' no less than 24 times. We spoke at length with six families at the school, and for each of these families Katie had become a rock that they could cling to for support through mental health struggles, domestic abuse, the challenges of poverty, child illness, crippling anxiety, the list goes on. These parents overcame their own anxiety to talk openly to us about their interaction with Katie, and they could not praise her highly enough. So, what was her secret? This was clear: she wore unconditional positive regard for these families as a skin, and not a jacket. Katie fiercely protected and supported the families that she worked with, in the unwavering belief that they were all 'good parents' facing crippling challenges. Anyone aware of Carl Rogers' (1956) theories for positive change in individuals will understand the importance of this approach. And our participants shared with us their experiences of personal growth and development as a result of Katie's positive approach.

With the concept of unconditional positive regard in mind, I argue that as social researchers whose aim is 'to make a positive difference' (Munford et al., 2008, p. 64), it is vital that our approach to research is a positive one. Returning to how our *Haltung* impacts our perceptions of others, if I was looking to find fault when embarking upon the research above, then I might have viewed the actions of Katie as 'mollycoddling', emasculating parents, making them more dependent and unable to 'stand on their own two feet'. I would have looked for examples that supported this, and my resulting report would have denigrated roles such as this health and wellbeing lead, as simply reflecting a 'nanny state' where individuals have become overly dependent. Needless to say, I did not. The beliefs that underpinned my approach to this research were that parenting is a difficult job, and that the pressures of modern society make it harder. I also believe that our education system in England is based upon a deficit view of parents that encourages and perpetuates feelings of parent incompetence. Having struggled many times as a parent myself, I understand how the poor mental health of a parent can impact negatively upon a child, and I applaud any attempt to support parents struggling with this. This, *of course*, influenced my approach to the research. The data collected through this research could have been looked at in numerous different ways, and clearly my researcher lens was one of positive appreciation. But an interesting question to consider is whether the *data collected* would have been the same had my *attitude* on approaching the research, and the research participants, been different.

Reflection point

Reflect upon a time when you have interviewed someone, this might be an informal or a formal scenario. Did you take any particular approach to put the other at ease? How might this approach have influenced the data that was collected?

It is important to remember that the 'Katie-related' data we collected from our participants was recorded within the parameters of a hastily established relationship. The interview window was just one hour. Eichsteller (2010) tells us that our *Haltung* 'shines through' in our interactions with others, and that this then 'colours' the way that they respond to us. These parents (selected from a range of parents who had experienced considerable challenges and so had all needed Katie's support at some point) walked into an office with myself and a fellow researcher, and quickly made judgements about our trustworthy-ness, our capability for empathy and our understanding; and these judgements will have influenced the information that they chose to share with us. I led on the interviews, immediately establishing my position as 'often struggling, single mother', which created a connection with the respondents. I also used self-depreciative humour, my go-to to diffuse the tenseness of an uncomfortable situation.

The common third established between the parents and I was a shared understanding that 'parenting is hard' and it is impossible to always get it right. I like to think that this put the parents at ease and enabled them to be open; and it is interesting to consider whether other researcher colleagues whose experience of parenting was very different, or those who had no experience of parenting, would have been able to do this. I was presenting my authentic self. However, in my attempts to encourage openness I must also accept that my own positionality would have steered the respondents' responses in a certain direction. No data is 'untainted' by the researcher, but as social pedagogues we should strive to ensure that our influence is a positive one on those that we research with.

> **Reflection point**
>
> The concept of 'bias' seems all pervading when we consider how our Haltung influences our approach to participants, the questions that we ask and the way that we approach the data. But if we consider these aspects, would it not be just as present in positivist research approaches?

Concluding thoughts

McDermid *et al.* (2019, p. 27), in their exploration of social pedagogy's potentiality within foster care, stressed that:

> Social pedagogy is not a set of techniques of practices that are applied. Rather practitioners are encouraged to adapt and arrive at different conclusions for different circumstances in different contexts.

Each and every research site, and each and every research participant that we deal with, will be unique. Even we, as researchers, will change with each project as we grow and develop as researchers. We will, over time, favour different approaches, different methods. But I believe that as social pedagogues, certain values and beliefs will always underpin our research endeavours. For me, these include:

- There should always be a clear identification of the potential for positive outcomes that could result from the research.
- The personal cannot be 'bracketed out' from research, relationships, and emotions will be involved.

- Only a positive approach to research has the potential to bring about positive change.
- In social research the researcher will impact upon the research respondent (and vice versa) and, as a result, this relationship will impact upon the data collected and the conclusions reached.

I hope that this chapter has challenged you, if only in some small way, to reflect upon how our perceptions of qualitative research have been influenced by traditions of scientific research which are not fit for purpose. I also hope that you have been able to consider your own role as researcher and the beliefs that underpin your values concerning research. Finally, I encourage you to be brave enough to justify your own approach to research, without feeling that only quantitative measures are able to give your research value. Krieger (1991, cited in Denzin and Lincoln (1994, p. 502), sums this up beautifully:

> The challenge lies in what each of us chooses to do when we represent our experiences. Whose rules do we follow? Will we make our own? Do we…have the guts to say, 'You may not like it, but here I am'?

Summary points

- Research is part and parcel of our continual development as educators.
- Research should always have the potential for positive change.
- Relationships, and emotions, are present in research, we cannot 'switch them off'.
- Research includes the head, heart and hands.
- Our beliefs about the purpose of research and the intrinsic value of others (our *Haltung*) will impact how we approach a research project.
- A positive approach is necessary if we are to bring about positive change.
- When carrying out social research, the researcher will inevitably impact upon the research, and that is okay.

Recommended reading

Bloor, M. (2010) The researcher's obligation to bring about good. *Qualitative Social Work*, 9(1), pp. 17–20. https://doi.org/10.1177/1473325009355616

Eichsteller, G. (2010) The Notion of 'Haltung' in Social Pedagogy. Children Webmag. Available at https://thetcj.org/in-residence/the-notion-of-haltung-in-social-pedagogy (Accessed 27 September 2024).

Luca, M. (2009) *Embodied Research and Grounded Theory*. Wales, UK: University of Wales. Available at www.researchgate.net/publication/216188540_Embodied_Research_and_Grounded_Theory (Accessed 27 September 2024).

References

Atkinson, P. and Hammersley, M. (1994) Ethnography and Participant Observation. In N. K. Denzin and Y. S. Lincoln (Eds) *Handbook of Qualitative Research*. Thousand Oaks, CA: Sage, pp. 248–261.

Bloor, M. (2010) The researcher's obligation to bring about good. *Qualitative Social Work*, 9(1), pp. 17–20. https://doi.org/10.1177/1473325009355616

Charfe, L. and Gardner, A. (2019) *Social Pedagogy and Social Work*. London: Sage.

Charfe, L. and Gardner, A. (2020) 'Does my Haltung look big in this?' The use of social pedagogical theory for the development of ethical and value-led practice. *International Journal of Social Pedagogy*, 9(1). https://doi.org/10.14324/111.444.ijsp.2020.v9.x.011

Costley, C., Elliott, G. and Gibbs, P. (2010) *Doing Work-Based Research: Approaches to Enquiry for Insider Researchers*. London: Sage.

Denzin, N. K. and Lincoln, Y. S. (Eds) (1994) *Handbook of Qualitative Research*. Thousand Oaks, CA: Sage.

Eichsteller, G. (2010). The Notion of 'Haltung' in Social Pedagogy. Children Webmag. Available online: https://thetcj.org/in-residence/the-notion-of-haltung-in-social-pedagogy (Accessed 8 February 2025).

Eichsteller, G. and Holthoff, S. (2011) Conceptual Foundations of Social Pedagogy: A Transnational Perspective from Germany. In C. Cameron and P. Moss (Eds.) *Social Pedagogy and Working with Children and Young People*. London: Jessica Kingsley, pp. 33–52.

Fontana, A. and Frey, J. H. (1994) Interviewing. The Art of Science. In N. K. Denzin, and Y. S. Lincoln (Eds) *Handbook of Qualitative Research*. Thousand Oaks, CA: Sage, pp. 361–376.

Gallagher (2008) 'Power is not an Evil': Rethinking power in participatory methods. *Children's Geographies*, 6(2), pp. 137–150.

Hartman, T. and Schachter, E. (2019) High school students 'talk back' to the anonymous researcher behind the questionnaire. *The Journal of Experimental Education*, 89(1) pp. 196–208. https://doi.org/10.1080/00220973.2019.1573795

Laubach, M. and Smith, J. K. (2011) Educating with heart, head, and hands: Pestalozzianism, women seminaries, and the spread of progressive ideas in Indian territory. *American Educational History Journal*, 38(1), pp. 341–356.

Luca, M. (2009) *Embodied Research and Grounded Theory*. Wales, UK: University of Wales. Available at www.researchgate.net/publication/216188540_Embodied_Research_and_Grounded_Theory (Accessed 8 February 2025).

Lyndon, S., Solvason, C. and Webb, R. (2024) 'It's a struggle' – The role of the school health and well-being lead in supporting families in poverty. *Journal of Poverty and Social Justice* (published online ahead of print 2024). Retrieved Apr 20, 2024, from https://doi.org/10.1332/17598273Y2024D000000014

MacNaughton, G., Rolfe, S. A. and Siraj, I. (2010) *Doing Early Childhood Research: International Perspectives on Theory and Practice*. 2nd edition. Maidenhead: McGraw-Hill Open University Press.

McDermid, S., Holmes, L., Ghate, D., Trivedi, H., Blackmore, J. and Baker, C. (2019) *Evaluation of Head, Heart, Hands: Introducing Social Pedagogy into UK Foster Care*. Final Report. Available at: www.thempra.org.uk/wp-content/uploads/2022/03/HHH-evaluation-full-report-FINAL.pdf (Accessed 8 February 2025)

McGrath, J. and Coles, A. (2013) *Your Education Research Companion*. 2nd edition. Hoboken: Taylor and Francis.

McNiff, J. (2010) *Action Research for Professional Development*. Church Stretton: September Books.

Munford, R., Sanders, J., Mirfin, B., Conder, V. and Conder, J. (2008) Ethics and research: Searching for ethical practice in research. *Ethics and Social Welfare*, 2(1), pp. 50–66. https://doi.org/10.1080/17496530801948754

Palmer, P. J. (1998) *The Courage to Teach: Exploring the Inner Landscape of a Teacher's Life*. San Francisco: Jossey-Bass.

Petrie, P. (2007) Foster care: A role for social pedagogy. *Adoption and Fostering*, 3(1), pp. 73–80.

Punch, M. (1994) Politics and Ethics in Qualitative Research. In N. K. Denzin and Y. S. Lincoln (Eds) *Handbook of Qualitative Research*. Thousand Oaks, CA: Sage, pp. 83–95.

Rogers, C. (1956/1992) The necessary and sufficient conditions of therapeutic personality change. *Journal of Consulting and Clinical Psychology*, 60(6), pp. 827–832. https://doi.org/10.1037/0022-006x.60.6.827.

Silverman, D. (2000) *Doing Qualitative Research. A Practical Handbook*. London: Sage.

Solvason, C., Lyndon, S. and Webb, R. (2024) 'Oh … that Mommy needs a bit of help as well': Why every school needs a health and wellbeing lead. *Health Education*, 124(5/6), pp. 255–269.

Stenhouse, L. (1979) Case study in comparative education: Particularity and generalisation. *Comparative Education*, 15(1), pp. 5–10.

Winter, R. (1989) *Learning from Experience: Principles and Practice in Action-Research*. Lewes: Falmer Press.

16 The next chapter

Stuart Gallagher

Introduction

Build it, and they will come. I am not exactly sure who first wrote those words; my search engine is split between the Bible and a feature film starring Kevin Costner. I am pretty sure, though, that they did not have a Social Pedagogy Research Group (or SPRiG as we like to refer to it, as it seems fitting) in mind at the time. Nonetheless, come they did. My abiding memory of our inaugural SPRiG gathering is of the numbers walking through the door. More than once furniture had to be re-arranged to accommodate the growing number of chairs being pulled up to the table. All phases of education were represented round that table, from early childhood through to researchers of higher education.

Most authors of this book's chapters attended that get-together. Why had they, and so many others, come? Answering that question was a missed research opportunity, perhaps. Instead, we might hazard some guesses. Shortly before this meeting, our university work had shifted online due to the pandemic, and on-campus classes and meetings had been slow to resume. Perhaps we underestimated how eager colleagues were to resume in-person collaboration and creative conversations that might shape our new normal, and that had played a part.

As educators, most were unphased by the word pedagogy; it was familiar to us. Some may have been curious, however, about *social* pedagogy rather than *classroom* pedagogy. It is interesting to consider whether it was the concept of education as something *more than* the accumulation of knowledge that raised such interest for the group. The potential of education as a community good, rather than a private possession for individual competitive advantage. Perhaps recent memories of lockdown restrictions, and our experience of the shared responsibility to act collectively to meet the conditions for easing them, had shifted our educational imagination from the individual to the collective. Whatever the reason (and no doubt there were many reasons), there we were, making room for newcomers, shifting up a space or two to accommodate slightly latecomers. And here we are now, with a collection of chapters that tell a story of social pedagogy within an education faculty at an English university. It is a landmark achievement, and it is worth exploring how we got here before considering where we might go next.

Proceed until apprehended

It started when Early Childhood (Professional Practice), an undergraduate degree programme that several of us were involved in, was due to be revalidated. Revalidation is an opportunity to look at our courses with fresh eyes, to re-align a subject or discipline with critical and current issues, without necessarily cutting ties with its philosophical and ethical roots. At that time, these roots included:

- the contradiction between the low status of the Early Years sector relative to other care and education practices, and the high status placed upon future generations in global policy planning, sometimes framed by discourse around intergenerational inequity;
- the tension between Early Years qualifications and the criteria that account for Graduate Employment and Graduate Destinations data;
- the contrast between course requirements for student placements within regulated education settings, and students' own preferences to advocate for young children's best interests in a broader range of placements, within education but also beyond it, too.

Up until this point, the course had been animated by a philosophy of reflective activism (Hanson and Appleby, 2015), in which Early Childhood undergraduates were encouraged to re-imagine children's best interests within a framework of transformed and transformative Early Years education and care. Perhaps it was inevitable that this approach would eventually reach the limits of regulated practice and seek to push beyond them, acknowledging society, more broadly, as a source of nurture for young children. The course revalidation at this time was an opportunity for a new vision, and it was then that we renamed it Early Childhood in Society. The task was to find a framework that might enable an explanatory power for theory and practice that would have even more reach than reflective activism. A framework that would allow the roots of early childhood studies to entangle themselves with the roots of other social interests, theories and practices.

In the process of revalidation, Course Leader Niki Stobbs (author of our Introduction), working with Sue Baylis (author of Chapter Four) proposed social pedagogy as a potential foundation stone. Social pedagogy already enjoyed well-established national and international networks. These included the Centre for the Understanding of Social Pedagogy at the University College London, the Social Pedagogy Professional Association (SPPA) in the UK, the Social Pedagogy Association Asociación de Pedagogía Social (SPA) in the US (currently on hiatus) and Thempra. Their respective resources enabled a rapid evaluation of the philosophical and ethical dimensions of social pedagogy and its suitability for an undergraduate course on Early Childhood in Society. It was possible to learn of its European heritage and analyse its recontextualisation in a UK context. Here, when faced with the kind of socio-political issues that we wanted the new course to address head-on, we were familiar with the retort of, "I'm a teacher not a social worker!", or, indeed, "I'm a social worker, not a teacher!" Rather than being ground down by these well-worn disciplinary divisions, there was a new energy generated by the prospect of introducing students to the multi-disciplinary concepts of Haltung, Bildung, the Three Ps and the Common Third. These ideological approaches would combine teaching approaches with the development of the whole child, as part of their family and as part of their community.

Early Childhood in Society BA (Hons), led at that time by Niki Stobbs, was approved to run from September 2020, the first academic year to follow the first national lockdown during the coronavirus pandemic. That point in time was characterised by a realisation that most of the social inequalities and divisions of the so-called 'old normal' were now further exacerbated and amplified by the 'new normal'. For a society that had become used to social distancing, an education approach based upon close and nurturing relationships was something entirely new. Without any off-the-shelf manual to follow, yet aware of steps previously taken to consider social pedagogy within UK education and care contexts, colleagues began meeting weekly, in-between classes, to consider how social pedagogy and Early Childhood overlapped, stood apart, and could be creatively combined. We reviewed the course's teaching and learning activities as well as the course administration and student placement possibilities in light of Haltung, Bildung and so on – making sense of how these new values might reshape our practice.

Whilst Niki and Sue Baylis (author of Chapter 4) got busy with teaching the course, Carla Solvason galvanised us into writing – another sense-making activity. Along with Geoffrey Elliott, Carla encouraged us to contribute to an edited book on education, ethics and leadership (Solvason and Elliott, 2023), that responded to the moment, charged as it was with schools' responses to 'mutant algorithms', teacher-assessed grades, priority year groups and vulnerable pupil lists. The book provided us with room to articulate how social pedagogy and Early Childhood studies might be combined (specifically in Gallagher 2023, Stobbs, 2023) to prepare our students for such a transformed landscape of education.

Then the time came for some kind of external test of our in-house efforts. We presented some of the work that we had been engaged in at an online conference organised by the SPA and SPPA. Encouraged by the reception received, we submitted our writing to be peer reviewed in the *International Journal of Social Pedagogy* (see Gallagher and Stobbs, 2023; Stobbs et al., 2023), and we are delighted to see this work continuing (see, for example, Cliffe, 2024). Our baby steps toward social pedagogical activism were paying off.

With a view on widening placement opportunities for undergraduates on our course, which spread far beyond the boundaries of educational settings, we were further encouraged by the appetite for social pedagogy within our wider professional networks. A virtual school for looked-after children and a young carers association enthusiastically embraced the potential of social pedagogy to produce practitioners capable of the 'personalisation' of children's and young people's learning in a post-lockdown environment. Such was the response that they not only attended but also contributed to the design and delivery of a Social Pedagogy in Schools continuous professional development (CPD) event.

By this stage, the course's first undergraduates were approaching their graduation. Niki and Sue's efforts to see Graduate Social Pedagogue Practitioner approved as a pathway had paid off. The momentum that had begun through those initial revalidation conversations between colleagues culminated in an international event with the SPAA network, which we hosted at The Hive Library in Worcester in 2023. This was repeated in November 2024, by which time our SPRiG membership had bloomed to just over fifty and Angela Hodgkins had been recruited as co-lead. This last event, based upon the transformative potential of storytelling, brought together colleagues from health, social care and education, from academia and external organisations and from nine locations across Europe, all connected via Zoom. Following the event, our SPRiG decided to follow up the event with a book on storytelling and its place in social care and education: twenty-seven abstracts were received.

The time for a Social Pedagogy Research Interest Group (SPRiG) is now. Build it, and they will come. They did, and they did. And now to this book.

The next chapter

An obvious next step for a research interest group is to broaden and sustain its interest in research, and to account for the impact of that research in addressing the tensions, conflicts and contradictions it studies. This work is already underway by authors in this book, in particular Alison Prowle's co-ordination of a range of collaborative research projects with a local authority in Wales and citizens supported by its services and in Shaun McInerney's relationship-based and people-focused work with education leaders. We might imagine a collection such as Cameron et al.'s (2023) recent assemblage of research projects as a model to emulate. To take that next step, though, it is worth considering the context from which the SPRiG began its work. This might help us anticipate the plot of the group's next chapter.

One of Carla Solvason's earlier roles was to lead a module on undergraduate dissertations. Students proposed diverse research topics and learned to design diverse research methodologies to help them undertake small-scale, ethical research that supported the best interests of children and families, as well as respecting the practitioners undertaking this work. To answer the kinds of research questions that many students posed, it became clear that practitioner action research was often a best fit, alongside the reflective activism mentioned earlier in this chapter. Research was not about changing others but developing oneself. Only after that had happened could we share our findings with others.

Consequently, those of us who supervised students' dissertations became familiar with the work of Jean McNiff. In particular, Carla would remind us of Jean McNiff's (2010) maxim that we should 'hold our knowledge lightly' when we approach any research, as what we think may not be what we find. To remember that the knowledge that we hold is provisional, it is not a foothold on the cliff face of Truth. The research module created a culture (or Bildung) in which research was expressed as an ethic of care. Building on Thompson and Pascal's (2012) concept of reflection for action, it could be said that the dissertations produced offered a glimpse into a transformed relationship between researcher and those researched, one that enabled positive growth for all involved.

Abma et al. (2020) suggest there are various dimensions to the care that might be expressed through research: caring about, caring for, caregiving, care receiving and caring with. These are helpful dimensions to consider when making sense of the kind of action research our students were undertaking in the context of Early Years education and care settings. As they dared to hold knowledge lightly, at the same time they were articulating different dimensions of care – for children, Early Years colleagues, carers and families – within small-scale research contexts. And it is from that context that the SPRiG first emerged. Immediately, it assumed the familiar concerns of a research community: measurement of impact; securing funding; how to scale up findings; decision-making and direction-finding as a group; but it did not lose sight of our own continuous learning and growth as researchers; we continue to hold our knowledge lightly.

One of my contributions to this SPRiG was to pitch initial ideas to its members round ways we might progress research as a group. Although momentum around social pedagogy had been built and progress was well underway (such as the creation of this book), it seemed to me a good idea to return to our original practice, of meeting in gaps between classes, to consider how our work could or did not reflect social pedagogical theory and practice, and to build from those points. Drawing on Daedlow et al.'s (2016) criteria for socially responsible research, I suggested the SPRiG might use the discipline of answering these questions in order to help us become more explicit in our research interest in social pedagogy approaches:

- How is the way I conduct research related to social pedagogy?
- Who should be included in research processes to fulfil social pedagogy requirements?

- For whom are we conducting our research and why?
- What can I contribute to research processes to ensure we are progressing social pedagogy?
- How does my position within a research process influence a reflection on social pedagogy processes?

Also, from where I stood, as a higher education professional, carefully weighing research in the balance alongside teaching, CPD and other scholarly activity, there were at least three routes we could take in our research work and collaborations: an *evaluative* route, an *analytical* route and an *ethical* route. The evaluative route was to research the impact of social pedagogy in action. The analytical route was to research practice where adopting a social pedagogy approach might make a positive difference. And the ethical route was to consider how we might research in a social pedagogical way. It seemed important to distinguish each of these routes from the others so that we might make best sense of the next chapter in the SPRiG's development and allow the group to grow distinct research practices and focuses without disconnecting from the overall focus on social pedagogy. The distinct routes might also help us decide which questions (from the list above) to emphasise as we reflect in, on and for our research practice.

Against-the-odds pedagogy

Whilst this chapter closes this book, it is also intended to be a signpost to the SPRiG's next chapter. I chose to do this by retracing the group's origins and its early momentum to the point where its members authored and co-authored the present book. I also pitched some routes for research that its members might now choose to follow.

But really, what I come back to is an observation Niki Stobbs shared with me in an exchange of messages. What Niki observed was that social pedagogy could frequently be considered 'against-the-odds pedagogy'. In other words, social pedagogy did not go with the flow; its approach was unlikely to satisfy calls for short-term efficiency, and it would be inconvenient to undertake it within current practices. Its chances of immediate success, based on existing structural arrangements and measures, were not good. So, our next chapter needs to tell a story of going against, and of beating, the odds.

It is no surprise to read Niki's call for disruptors in this book's opening chapter. That call can be understood in the context of against-the-odds pedagogy. Our experience of pursuing social pedagogy, initially through an undergraduate Early Childhood course's design and delivery, then through collaborations within our education faculty and with partnerships beyond our university, is that we underestimate the appetite for positive change. A practical problem is that the SPRiG's momentum, collaborations and best-laid plans are interrupted by the familiar churn of people, as retirement, new roles, and career changes occur. Perhaps we cannot avoid these interruptions. But the next chapter can tell the story of how we disrupted the odds to see the SPRiG continue its development. I cannot predict how that chapter will unfold. I can only imagine that it might tell a story of overcoming the paucity of time to undertake research, perhaps through the pooling of time. Or it might tell a story of succession planning, so that interruptions can be quickly overcome and momentum sustained. What I am sure of, however, is that the next chapter will tell a story of knowledge, however lightly held, being in the hands of those who can put it to best use.

References

Abma, T.A., Visse, M., Hanberger, A., Simons, H. and Greene, J.C. (2020) 'Enriching evaluation practice through care ethics', *Evaluation*, vol 26, no 2, 131–46.

Cameron, C., Koslowski, A., Lamont, A. and Moss, P. (2023) *Social Research for Our Times: Thomas Coram Research Unit, Past, Present and Future*, London: UCL Press.

Cliffe, J. (2024) '(Re)imagining the social pedagogy within early childhood education and care: a (re)exploration of the power and importance of relationships and connections', *International Journal of Social Pedagogy*, vol 13, no 1, 14. https://doi.org/10.14324/111.444.ijsp.2024.v13.x.014

Daedlow, K., Podhora, A., Winkelmann, M., Kopfmüller, J., Walz, R. and Helming, K. (2016) 'Socially responsible research processes for sustainability transformation: an integrated assessment framework', *Current Opinion in Environmental Sustainability*, vol 23, 1–11.

Gallagher, S. (2023) Early Childhood Studies in a Polarised Dystopia: Pedagogy as Ethical Leadership in Education. In: C. Solvason and G. Elliott (eds) *Ethics in Education*. UK: Ethics International Press Ltd.

Gallagher, S. and Stobbs, N. (2023) 'Creating hope in dystopia: Utopia as method as social pedagogy in early childhood studies', *International Journal of Social Pedagogy*, vol 12, no 1. https://journals.uclpress.co.uk/ijsp/article/pubid/IJSP-12-5/

Hanson, K. and Appleby, K. (2015) Reflective Practice. In: Reed, M. & Walker, R. (eds) *Early Childhood Studies: A Critical Reader*. London: Sage Publications. pp. 24–3.

McNiff, J. (2010) *Action Research for Professional Development: Concise Advice for New Action Researchers*. Dorset: September Books.

Solvason, C. and Elliot, G. (eds) (2023) *Ethics in Education*. Cambridge: Ethics International Press Ltd.

Stobbs, N. (2023) Social Pedagogy as a Lens for Re-focussing Ethics in Education. In: C. Solvason and G. Elliott (eds) *Ethics in Education*. UK: Ethics International Press Ltd.

Stobbs, N., Solvason, C., Gallagher, S. and Baylis, S. (2023) 'A human approach to restructuring the education system: why schools in England need social pedagogy', *International Journal of Social Pedagogy*, vol 12, no 1, 8.

Thompson, N. and Pascal, J. (2012) 'Developing critically reflective practice', *Reflective Practice*, vol 13, no. 2. https://doi.org/10.1080/14623943.2012.657795

Index

agency 15–16, 26, 37–9, 77, 91, 99, 107, 143, 145, 147, 148, 151
anthropocene 4, 24, 29–30
appreciative inquiry 147, 150
apprentice 4; apprenticeship 21, 23, 24, 30
art 41–9, 82
artistic 41–5, 47, 48, 74, 76
aspirations 5, 7, 46, 62, 107–9, 147
attachment 22, 35
authentic 3, 8, 15, 19, 30, 37, 46, 48, 56, 65, 77, 85, 86, 92, 122, 124, 143–6, 157, 162; authentically 6, 15, 58, 66, 82, 103, 151; authenticity 8, 14–15, 18, 35, 37, 57, 85, 86, 101, 113, 144, 147, 152, 158
autonomy 13, 26, 35, 38, 91, 104, 119, 125, 128, 142
awareness 19, 23–5, 28, 29, 37, 49, 52, 56–9, 65–7, 78, 86, 90–2, 140, 147–51, 160
awe 4, 21–30, 44, 155, 156

barriers /13, 15, 16, 23, 34, 41–9, 54, 55, 57, 63–5, 78, 88, 118, 119, 144, 155
bias 5, 7, 65, 107–15, 156–7, 160, 162
bioecological theory 22
Breath of Life 3, 6, 96–9
Bronfenbrenner, U. 13, 22
boundaries 5, 15, 25, 37, 38, 44–6, 56, 58, 77–8, 90, 91, 100, 130, 135, 144, 167

caring 4, 13, 21, 23–5, 30, 34–6, 150, 151, 168
changemaking 148, 151, 152; changemaking leadership 148
collaboration/s 45, 46, 48, 57, 76, 78, 79, 85, 98, 99, 101, 103, 120, 122, 124–5, 133, 134, 144–5, 165, 169
comfort-zone 132, 136, 137
Common Third 6, 7, 43–9, 54, 56, 69, 72–80, 96, 101–3, 121, 123–4, 133, 137, 138, 162, 166
companionship 22, 30
congruence 68, 86, 91, 92, 144

core conditions 86, 87
culture/s 4, 5, 13, 22, 24, 32, 34, 36, 41, 44–8, 54–7, 62–4, 66, 68–70, 72, 73, 77, 98, 103–4, 107, 122, 145, 146, 150, 152, 168; culturally accepted 54; culturally responsive 56, 135
curiosity 5, 6, 8, 21, 22, 27–30, 45, 74–6, 78–80

democratic 5–7, 72–4, 78, 80, 101, 113, 132, 137
diamond model 6, 12, 14, 17, 26, 27, 30, 38, 73–4, 76, 82, 89, 91, 92, 100, 119–20, 122–4, 127, 128, 148–9
disadvantage 63, 75, 95, 96, 107–10, 114

emotional intelligence 6, 84, 90
empathy 5, 8, 12, 13, 24, 34, 35, 38, 45, 46, 48, 59, 66, 68, 69, 74, 75, 80, 82–92, 100, 103, 114, 122–5, 145, 148, 150–2, 158, 162
empower/ment 2, 6, 12, 13, 15–16, 18, 26, 32, 36, 39, 43, 47, 55, 58, 75–6, 79, 82, 89, 112, 119, 124, 126–8, 137, 150
engagement 5, 26, 29, 35, 41–4, 47, 55, 63, 68–70, 103, 120, 125–7, 133, 135, 150
equal/s 29, 77–9, 97, 101, 109, 114, 121, 137, 138, 140, 150, 157; equality 32, 36, 132; inequalities 2, 5, 62–4, 108–11, 115, 166; unequal 95
ethics 114, 144, 167; ethical 13, 21, 79, 99, 104, 135, 141, 143, 147, 151, 152, 156, 160, 165–6, 168
expectations 7, 34, 37, 38, 68, 103, 104, 108–12, 114, 120, 123, 126, 143, 144, 156

family 4, 5, 8, 11, 16, 22–4, 27, 33, 41, 42, 45, 62–70, 73, 83, 92, 95, 119, 123, 142, 156–7, 161, 166, 168
flow 8, 26–7, 30, 42, 43, 85, 169
fulfilment 18, 32, 43, 75, 76, 89

Gypsy 5, 62–70

Haltung 6–8, 33–4, 66, 87, 91, 92, 96–8, 104, 114, 142–3, 152, 156–63, 166, 167
happiness 12, 13, 18, 26–7, 38, 39, 75, 89, 119, 122, 123, 127, 128
Head, Heart (and) Hands 5, 7, 8, 28, 35, 44, 48, 49, 69, 87, 92, 130–8, 149, 155, 159, 163
hierarchy/ies/hierarchical 7, 17, 19, 77, 78, 96, 97, 101–2, 104, 130, 132, 137, 141, 144, 160
history/ies/historical 3, 21, 45, 53, 54, 56, 57, 63–64, 66, 72, 98, 101–2, 104, 130, 135, 140–1, 156
holistic/ally 4–6, 8, 12–13, 15–17, 26, 33, 35, 39, 42–5, 47, 48, 52, 55, 58, 66, 74, 77, 82, 86, 89–92, 119, 120, 124, 125, 127, 128, 130, 131, 143–9, 151, 159
humanistic 6, 74, 147, 151
human-centred 142, 152

identity 4, 5, 11, 14, 15, 35, 45, 47, 49, 54, 57–9, 62, 80, 84, 96, 98, 144, 145, 148
imagination 6, 44, 74, 76–8, 80, 86, 165
inclusion 4–5, 34, 63, 68, 70, 75, 79, 82, 91, 97, 102, 108, 110, 115
independence 16, 39, 47, 87, 89, 92, 119, 131
interdependence 7, 39, 47, 86–9, 91, 92, 119, 122, 131, 152

leadership: authentic leadership 146; ethical leadership 143, 147; instructional leadership 142, 145; leadership development 145–51; relational leadership 147, 151; social pedagogical leadership 8, 140, 145–7, 150–2; transformational leadership 145
life-world orientation 12, 13, 35, 75, 96, 102, 104, 146–7, 158
literacy 24, 56, 63, 67, 69; eco-cultural literacy 24; musical literacy 56
love *see* professional love

marginalised/isation 5, 6, 23, 63–5, 70, 75, 97, 104
market 95, 96, 108, 109, 113, 160; labour market 95; market-driven 96
Maslow, A. 96–7
mentalising 86
mentee 7, 15, 74, 77, 130–8
mentor/ing 2, 4, 7, 74, 77, 83, 89, 130–8
mindfulness 86, 90
moral 13, 33, 36, 44, 72, 96, 114, 141, 151, 158; moral agent 36; moral compass 33, 44, 96, 114, 158
music/musicality 5, 32, 52–9, 77, 90

nature 23–6, 28, 35, 52, 57, 68, 75, 79, 120, 135, 141, 144
neo-liberal 22, 23, 29, 108, 142
neurodivergent 32
Noddings, N. 21, 23, 24, 36, 39, 86, 147
nomad/ic 25, 27, 29, 62

Ofsted 33, 41, 53, 63

policy 1–2, 4, 6, 14, 22, 23, 33, 35–7, 53, 63, 64, 66, 76–7, 95, 107–11, 113, 114, 142, 145, 151, 166
power-relations 113, 150
prejudice 5, 62–7, 70, 111, 114
professional boundaries 77–8, 144
professional curiosity 79
professional distance 87
professional identity 14, 144, 145
professional love 3, 6, 36–8, 83
professional standards 15

reflective 100–1, 132, 134–5, 137, 166, 168
reflexivity 147, 150
relationship-based practice 3, 5, 6, 35, 91–2
relationship-centred practice 85, 118, 120–1, 142
relational pedagogy 4, 21–3
relational universe 6, 85–6, 92
rhizome/rhizomatic 4, 25, 27, 29
risk 25, 45, 62, 74, 79, 80, 83
Rogers, C. 3, 6, 76, 86–7, 91, 113, 122, 147, 161
Roma 62–70, 84

safe/ty 2, 8, 15, 17, 38, 45, 47, 59, 64, 76, 86, 99, 100, 102, 122, 130, 134, 145, 146, 152
safeguard/ing 36, 46, 100
scaffold/ing 3, 6, 7, 78, 85, 124, 126, 132, 137
self-actualisation 82, 92, 96–7
self-awareness 49, 65–7, 78, 85, 151
self-care 90–1, 100, 123
self-determination 37–8
self-discipline 121–4, 126
self-identity 54, 98
SEND 4, 5, 32–40, 142
slow pedagogy 3, 4, 27–30
social capital 2, 27, 28, 98
social class 107–15
social-constructivist 131, 137
social justice 5–7, 18, 97–8, 108, 113, 132, 145, 148
social research 155–60, 163
stereotype/ing/ical 53, 58, 59, 111, 114
stigma 63, 64, 100, 109, 110
sustainability 24

Three Ps 6, 11, 13, 16, 37, 38, 66, 96, 100–1, 106
Togetherness Practice 148, 150, 151
transitions 68, 83–5, 91, 92, 110, 123, 142, 151
traveller 5, 62–70, 77
trust/ing 6, 8, 18, 35, 38, 39, 47, 52–3, 58, 59, 65–9, 78, 82, 87, 91, 100–4, 121, 122, 130, 133–5, 138, 146, 148, 150–2, 156, 160, 162

unconditional positive regard 3, 6, 8, 76, 86, 91, 92, 99, 100, 104, 113, 115, 122, 147, 161

vulnerable 1, 18, 57, 52–3, 83, 91, 137, 146, 167; vulnerabilities 85, 86, 133, 148

wholeness 18, 146
widening participation 95–7, 107–9
wonder 1, 4, 21–30, 42, 44, 57, 59, 74, 76, 122
working-class 7, 107–12, 114
wellbeing 5–8, 12, 13, 18, 22–7, 30, 37–9, 59, 60, 75, 76, 79, 82–92, 100, 103, 104, 119, 120, 122–4, 127, 128, 143, 147, 148, 150, 151, 161

Zone of Proximal Development 3, 7, 124, 131, 136, 137

For Product Safety Concerns and Information please contact our EU
representative GPSR@taylorandfrancis.com
Taylor & Francis Verlag GmbH, Kaufingerstraße 24, 80331 München, Germany